THE
BALOCH CONFLICT
WITH IRAN
AND PAKISTAN

Aspects of a National Liberation Struggle

NASEER DASHTI

Order this book online at www.trafford.com
or email orders@trafford.com

Most Trafford titles are also available at major online book retailers.

Print information available on the last page.

isbn: 978-1-4907-8091-7 (sc)
isbn: 978-1-4907-8093-1 (hc)
isbn: 978-1-4907-8092-4 (e)

Library of Congress Control Number: 2017902077

Trafford rev. 02/10/2017

www.trafford.com
North America & international
toll-free: 1 888 232 4444 (USA & Canada)
fax: 812 355 4082

FOREWORD

Many regions of Asia and Africa are engulfed in bloody conflicts between various national entities in multi-national states. This is because of mistaken and short-sighted policies of the colonial powers, which they adopted in the process of granting independence to their colonies after Second World War. In order to safeguard their vital economic and strategic interests, they drew artificial borders, created many artificial states, amalgamated different nations into newly independent countries. This not only caused misery to the nations incorporated into states against their will, but originated endless and protracted conflicts between various national entities.

The Baloch are among the victim of the mess created by the colonial powers in south central Asia. Their position is an extremely complex one. Their land, Balochistan, is divided into three different countries. They have been facing the might of two religious states and their future as a distinct national entity is in danger with the increased assimilation policies of Iran and Pakistan. The Baloch conflict with Iran and Pakistan is one of the bloodiest in the contemporary history of national liberation movements. It is certain that this conflict would be the cause of regional tension and destabilization in a strategically important but politically volatile region of the world.

This book is a logical continuation of Dr. Naseer Dashti's previous book 'The Baloch and Balochistan' published in 2012, which deals with history of the Baloch nation until the annexation of the Baloch state of Kalat by Pakistan in 1948. The present research work by Dr. Dashti would certainly remedy the lack of reliable and up-to-date information about the Baloch national question in both countries. This analytical work covers historical, political, social and economic aspects of the Baloch struggle for national sovereignty. The author approaches the relevant aspects of the issue in a wider theoretical perspective while furnishing original accounts of the events. I believe that this book will be an invaluable source of reference for those who are interested in the affairs of south central Asia.

This book is the labour of love of the author for his people and motherland and will be a reference for all those who want to change the future of Baloch nation by understanding and learning from the historical processes, strengths, weaknesses, and mistakes in the struggle of Baloch people that culminated to the present situation.

Dr. Lakhumal Luhana

Secretary General
World Sindhi Congress

London: 05/02/2017

ACKNOWLEDGEMENTS

Many people offered their exceptional cooperation in the completion of this book. I am thankful to Professor Hameed Baloch, Dr. Habibullah Malik, Waja Nasser Buledai, Mir Muhammad Khan Laashaari, Mir Muhammad Amin Laashaari, Waja Samad Baloch, Waja Hassan Hamdam, Waja Aziz Dadyar, Dr. Naguman Baloch, Waja Hammal Haider, Waja Jamshed Amiri, Waja Ismail Amiri, Waja Taj Buledai, Waja Mehrab Serjo, for sharing material, information and analysis regarding various topics of the book.

I would like to express my extreme indebtness to Dr. Beryl Magrath for the exceptional favour in the editing and proof reading of the manuscript, and for her overall support in my efforts for the completion of the book.

DEDICATION

No matter how many times a country has been conquered, subjugated and even destroyed by enemies, there is always a certain national core preserved in its character, and, before you are aware of it, a long-familiar popular phenomenon has emerged (Johan Wolfgang von Goethe).

The Baloch as a nation had not been able to overthrow the yoke of domination and subjugation but throughout history, their struggle for national sovereignty has emerged time and again. Their survival as a national entity against tremendous odds and their protracted struggle for acquiring a sovereign status is a unique socio-historical phenomenon. This work is dedicated to the extra-ordinary resilience of the Baloch which has manifested itself by rising again and again following heavy blows by powerful forces of history.

THE LIST OF ABBREVIATIONS

AI   Amnesty International

BLA   Baloch Liberation Army

BLF   Balochistan Liberation Front

BLM   Balochistan Liberation Movement

BLO   Baloch Liberation Organization

BNA   Balochistan National Alliance

BNDP   Balochistan National Democratic Party

BNM   Balochistan National Movement

BNP   Balochistan National Party

BNYM   Balochistan National Youth Movement

BPLF   Baloch People's Liberation Front

BRA   Baloch Republican Army

BRP   Baloch Republican Party

BRSO   Baloch Republican Students Organization

BSO   Baloch Students Organization

BSU   Balochistan States Union

FC   Frontier Corps

HRCP   Human Rights Commission of Pakistan

IB   Intelligence Bureau

ICG   International Crisis Group

ISI   Inter-Services Intelligence agency

JWP   Jamhoori Watan Party

KSNP   Kalat State National Party

LB   Lashkar e Balochistan

LFO   Legal Framework Order

MI   Military Intelligence

MMA   Muttahida Majlis e Amal

NAP   National Awami Party

NFC National Finance Commission
NP National Party
NWFP North West Frontier Province
OGDC Oil and Gas Development Corporation
PNP Pakistan National Party
PONM Pakistan Oppressed Nationalities Movement
PPL Pakistan Petroleum limited
PPP Pakistani People's Party
PRMI People's Resistance Movement of Iran
PYM Progressive Youth Movement
UBA United Baloch Army
UN United Nations Organization
UNPO Unrepresented Nations and Peoples Organization

Contents

CHAPTER 1

INTRODUCTION

The political scenario of the world has changed drastically during 20th century because of two great wars. Empires began to crumble and new power equations were developed. The status of Great Britain, Germany, France and Japan changed as the United States and Russia emerged as new great powers. This resulted in an increased momentum for national liberation among the colonised people. Because of devastating wars, the internal socio-economic and political dynamics of the imperial and colonial powers like Spain, Portugal, France and Great Britain also changed. This changing scenario forced them to draw up strategies for decolonization. However, the process of decolonization was not smooth and it was fairly unjust in the majority of cases. During long periods of occupation, colonial powers had developed vital economic and strategic interests in occupied regions and in order to safe guard these interests following withdrawal, they divided nations, and created artificial states by drawing arbitrary boundary lines. These lines drawn by colonial administrators ignored important cultural, historical and national aspects as well as the will of the people. As a result different national entities were forcefully amalgated in various post-colonial independent countries. In the majority of these artificially created countries, dominant nationalities-in the name of national integrity and state sovereignty-often oppress, exploit and treat unjustly those minority national entities who were made part of that state without

1

their consent. The mess created by the self-interested policies of colonial administrators in pursuit of short-term objectives created a situation in which several regions of Asia and Africa became zones of never ending conflicts and turmoil. The unjustly created post-colonial so-called international borders are still the cause of prolonged conflicts which continue to provoke atrocities, human right violations, hatred and bloodshed between various national and religious entities. In many cases, these conflicts not only destabilize a region but also endanger international peace and tranquillity.

The protracted conflict of the Baloch with the Iranian and Pakistani states is only one example of the complexities created by colonial powers in the process of implementing strategies to safeguard their political, economic and strategic interests in the Middle East, Central and South Asia. The Baloch are among many nations in the contemporary world who are still facing the curse of colonialism. They have faced the repression and subjugation of the religious and fanatical states of Iran and Pakistan for a long time. With the incorporation or occupation of their land in Iran and Pakistan, lives of countless millions of Baloch are characterized by oppression and exploitation in numerous ways. The violent confrontation between the Baloch resistance and the security forces of the two religious states has been accompanied by gross human rights violations and massive dislocation of the Baloch population. This has resulted in tremendous human suffering. Many actions of these states come within the definition of war crimes, genocide and crimes against humanity. By implication, the Baloch conflict with Iran and Pakistan is increasingly becoming one of the major threats to regional and international peace and security.

The Baloch are among the largest national entities (only second to Kurds) in the world without a state of their own. Originally, as part of great Aryan migrations 3000 years ago, the Baloch tribes after leaving their abode in Central Asia, settled in the North West Caspian region of Balashagan where they were known as Balaschik and their language which is a member of Indo-Iranic group of languages was known as Balaschuki. Circumstances forced this

2

group of tribes during the last decades of Sassanid rule in Iran to migrate *en masse* and settle in Kerman and Sistan; here they became known as the Baloch and their language became known as Balochi. During early medieval period, the majority of them were again forced to migrate and they settled in the region what is now called Balochistan. Balochistan (the land of the Baloch), the huge tract of a semi-desert land is stretches West-East from the Great Salt Lake (Dasht-e-Kavir) in north eastern Iran to the south west of Punjab; and North-South from Khorasan to the Indian Ocean. From 1666, Balochistan, was ruled by a loose confederacy of Baloch tribes under the Khanate of Kalat. In 1839, it was occupied by the British and finally divided and incorporated into Iran, Pakistan and Afghanistan. In this book, the part of Balochistan under the control of Iran has been referred to as Western Balochistan and the part controlled by Pakistan is referred to as Eastern Balochistan.

During the 18th and 19th centuries, certain events occurred in remote areas of the world, far away from Balochistan, which adversely affected the Baloch and their state-the Khanate of Kalat. They were caught up in the prolong conflict between the French, Russian and the British empires, all seeking imperial influence in Central Asia, the Middle East and India. A 'great game' of espionage and intrigues was initiated in Central Asia which resulted in the British invasions of Afghanistan in 19th century. As a consequence of the British wars with Afghans, Balochistan was occupied by the British in 1839. Later it was divided by granting half of Balochistan to Persians, and a small portion was incorporated into Afghanistan. The British withdrew from India in 1947 after partitioning it into Pakistan and India. The Khanate of Kalat declared its independence in the wake of the British withdrawal; however, the newly created religious state of Pakistan occupied the Baloch state on the first of April 1948.

The essential function of a national oppression is to maintain and perpetuate the domination of the occupying nation. This domination, as observed by Kendal (1980), is motivated by the economic, political or ideological interests of the occupier. The domination over the subjugated is exercised by means of two complex apparatus; an ideological machine whose task is to systematically destroy or negate the national identity of the subjugated nation and a powerful militant force, tasked to wipe out any resistance against the domination. Pakistan and Iran, historically pursued religious and mono-nationalist ideologies and implemented state policies of repressing the Baloch and other nationalities in their domains. The Baloch for a long time were the victim of dominating policies and strategies of states based on falsified ideologies and religious fundamentalism. They believe that since the occupation, they have been discriminated against as an ethnic entity, their language and cultural values have been suppressed, and they have been forced to live a life under economic exploitation. The cream of their society and a large part of the population have faced physical elimination as a consequence of acts of genocide by the occupying states. Both states have employed numerous socio-cultural, political and militant devices to eliminate everything that might suggest a separate Baloch national identity. In both countries, the Baloch have become the worst example of political, social and cultural exploitation.

The Iranian state uses a mixture of Persian nationalism and Shia fundamentalism as a tool in their endeavours to keep the Baloch and other national entities under the Iranian yoke. In official narratives, they consider the Baloch as a tribal people of larger Persian national identity and Balochi as a dialect of Farsi language. In Persian occupied Balochistan, the form of oppression practised is very brutal. The use of excessive military power has been the only response to the Baloch demands for national rights. As part of an assimilation policy, the Baloch are forced to adopt Persian language and Persian way of life. They are not only denied the right to read and write in Balochi language but also systematically being discouraged to speak in their mother tongue. The Baloch traditional or national dresses are ridiculed by officials and the most demeaning thing of all is that the Baloch have had to choose a name for their new born from an official list of Persian names. This has prevented them from taking traditional Balochi names for their sons and daughters. Thousand years old names of

Baloch townships are being replaced with manufactured Persian names. The Baloch in Iran have increasingly found that their own land is becoming alien to them.

The officially constructed national identity of Pakistan is based on the false perception of Muslims being one nation. Pakistan is an ethnically heterogeneous country comprised of Pashtuns, Punjabis, Seraiki, Sindhi and Baloch national entities; it has however, been the alliance of the Punjabi military and religious elite with Urdu speaking immigrants (*Muhajirs*) from India which has controlled and dominated the political, economic, and military landscape of Pakistan since its creation. Created by the British Empire and sustained and patronized by the United States and its Western allies, the religious state's emphasis has been on an 'Islamic Nation Ideology'. This ideology was manufactured and supported by the colonial administration in India. This was a part of their efforts to stop the Russian thrust towards India by exploiting the religious sentiments of Central Asian Muslims against Russian occupation. It later became a political tool in their strategies to divide India. The Islamic Nation Ideology is being used by Pakistan to justify the domination and subjugation of other national entities politically, socially and economically. To counter the Baloch resistance against subjugation, Pakistan used force with a Jihadist fervour. Economic exploitation is another aspect of subjugation measures. Balochistan provides the Pakistani state with its much needed energy resources. The Baloch wealth and resources drained away (or waiting to be drained away), to the advantage of the occupying state. The Baloch are considered to be the poorest people while their land is amongst the richest in the world.

The Baloch in Iran and Pakistan have been involved in a protracted resistance against the occupation of their land. Although, it has received minimal international attention, nevertheless, the Baloch conflict with Iranian and Pakistani states is amongst the bloodiest and persistent of the many post-colonial conflicts in Asia and Africa. The Baloch as a national entity, have found themselves marginalized, suppressed, and oppressed since the consolidation of the Persian state and the creation of a

5

fundamentalist religious state of Pakistan. They have reacted with political mobilization and armed resistance against the increased encroachments on their political, economic and social life. Their relations with Iran and Pakistan have been characterized by numerous uprisings against the occupation, subjugating measures, acts of repressions and gross human rights violations by the Iranian and Pakistani security establishment. Whilst, the Iranian and Pakistani states term the Baloch resistance as insurgency; for the Baloch, their national resistance against these states is to re-establish the Baloch sovereignty over Balochistan. Tortures of arrested activists, murders, extra-judicial killings of thousands of the Baloch political and social activists, the burning of the Baloch settlements and forceful dislocations of the population are the acts committed by the Iranian and Pakistani state authorities and the proxy organizations created by their secret services in the contemporary conflict.

The case of the Baloch in Afghanistan is quite different from that of Iran and Pakistan. In Afghanistan they are very much involved in the affairs of the state and there has been no voices against any form of discrimination, subjugation, or exploitation from the Baloch against the Afghan state. During 1978-79s, the Balochi along with Pashto, Dari, Uzbek, Turkmen and Nuristani languages, was granted the status of national languages in Afghanistan; a position the Baloch in Iran and Pakistan can only dream of.

A nation is a collection of individuals bound together by the territory, blood, culture and a common historical heritage. Nationalism is the deep commitment of a nation to its homeland and socio-cultural heritage while a national liberation struggle is the manifestation of this commitment. The Baloch are a specifically defined people with a language and culture, having their own historical traditions, and living in a well-defined geographical area. They have resisted the cultural assimilation which the dominant powers sought to impose upon them. In its essence, the Baloch national struggle is aiming to reunite Balochistan as an independent state; nevertheless, with the division of their territory mainly to Iran and Pakistan, which have differing historical, socio-political and cultural dimensions, their national struggle has faced different ways of engagement. Although, inspired by each other, the Baloch national struggle was waged by two different national resistances, corresponding to the two different contexts of Iran and Pakistan. The national resistance by the Baloch in Eastern Balochistan was led primarily by the politically conscious and left oriented tribal leaders while in Western Balochistan, it has been purely a tribal affair until the last decades of 20th century. During the 21st century, with drastic changes in the Baloch society, on both sides of the Goldsmid Line which divides Western and Eastern Balochistan, the character of the Baloch national struggle has also changed. The Baloch society is no more tribal; although, some of the tribal figures still enjoy widespread support from the Baloch masses because of their nationalistic credentials. With changing dynamics in the leadership, the participation of the resistance struggle has also been changed. Presently it is being dominated by a rising middle class leadership and activists.

The right of self-determination for colonized nations was declared as an inalienable right by the United Nation. In this context, the Baloch struggle for independence is a genuine exercise of the right sanctioned by international law. However, the international community has ignored the long standing Baloch national question in Pakistan and Iran, together with the narrow interests and short sighted policies of the major international powers which are stifling debates on the Baloch issue in international fora. Nevertheless, the protracted conflict between the Baloch and occupying states will inevitably cause of major destabilization in this strategically important region. This is a conflict in need of resolution sooner or later.

Writing the history of the Baloch national struggle presents a variety of challenges. The Baloch conflict with Iran and Pakistan is a complex one. Often, extreme versions of events were presented by opposing sides in the protracted conflict between the Baloch and the occupying powers. In many instances, reading between the lines has become an imperative in order to achieve a balanced opinion. This work employs a descriptive approach to explore and analyse various aspects of the Baloch struggle for national liberation. No significant effort was made to describe and analyse in detail the Baloch national resistance. Many works on the subject have been based on specific topics and failed to produce a comprehensive analysis and some have also failed to give a balanced picture of the issues. The book is an effort to present a thorough review of nearly all relevant aspects of the contemporary Baloch conflict with Iran and Pakistan in a context of historic relationship between the Baloch and both states. Although, this write up is an attempt to present the Baloch conflict with Iran and Pakistan from a Baloch perspective, every effort has been made to present known facts and figures, setting aside personal or national prejudice in describing and analysing events. It is hoped that the book would provide a useful background information on a long standing national question.

Chapter 2 is a contextual description of Baloch and Balochistan. It explores the Baloch journey as part of Indo-Iranic tribes from the Aryan migrations of ancient times, their primary abode in Balashagan, their dispersal and settlement in Kerman and Sistan during Sassanid period and their final migrations into present day Balochistan in medieval times. The chapter also discusses the root of Balochi language as belonging to the Iranian branch of the Indo-European family of languages and the development of Baloch social and cultural values in the long course of their wandering as agro-pastoralist nomadic tribes.

Although, the Persians and the Baloch share common linguistic roots and geographical boundaries; there is nevertheless a long history of conflict between them. The ancient history of the Baloch is a history of migration and persecution of an agro-pastoralist nomadic group of tribes by powerful dynasties that ruled the Iranian Plateau for centuries. The ever-present Baloch resistance against the mightier oppressor was rather a reaction against encroachments on their traditional way of living a life which was independent of any state or organized authority from dominant powers of the day. Chapter 3 is a narrative of long standing hostilities between the Baloch and Persian rulers from ancient times until the medieval period.

The combined events of the British occupation of Balochistan in 1839, Persian aggression and brutality in Western Balochistan together with the division of the Baloch land, brought long lasting adverse consequences for the Baloch. During the anarchic period in Persia, after the fall of Safavid dynasty, many Baloch chieftains and *Hakoms* of various regions in Western Balochistan tried to overthrow the Persian yoke. The Qajar family after establishing itself firmly on the Persian throne, began a process of subduing and subjugating various dissenting national entities into submission. The history of the Baloch conflict with Qajar Persia became one of the bloodiest in the Baloch memory. The Period of Qajar rule in Persia brought much misery to the Baloch and they faced such inhuman brutality that the word Qajar became a term of abuse and this abusive term became synonymous with all Persians for many of the Baloch until today. One of the major events during this period is the emergence of the first Baloch chiefdom under the rule of the Baraanzai (Barakzai) family. Chapter 4 is a narrative of the most eventful of the periods in the history of Western Balochistan.

The emergence of Reza Khan as the ruler of Persia after the anarchic situation during the last years of Qajar rule changed the dynamics of Baloch relations with the Persians. After occupying the Barakzai Chiefdom, and pacification of the Baloch tribes in Sarhad and Sistan regions, a vigorous state policy of assimilation of the Baloch into Persian national identity was initiated. Chapter 5 is the discussion and analysis of the Baloch resistance in Western Balochistan during the rule of Pahlavi dynasty in Iran. The chapter also analyses the resurgence and collapse of Baloch resistance in later decades of Pahlavi rule which was spearheaded by a clandestine organization; the Balochistan Liberation Front (BLF).

After the fall of Pahlavi regime, the Baloch exploited the anarchic situation prevailing in Iran. They began to mobilize politically and to set up armed resistance groups. However, the Baloch efforts for political mobilization and armed resistance were brutally crushed by the Ayatollahs using excessive state power and inhuman tactics. The Baloch sustained massive casualties and a total defeat against the religious forces of Iran. The Baloch nationalist leadership as well as religious elements fled to many countries as refugees. Chapter 6 explores and analyses events and developments regarding the Baloch mobilization and the collapse of their resistance in Western Balochistan after the fall of Pahlavi regime.

For last many decades, the Baloch in Iran have witnessed a reign of terror across various dimensions. A sense of social and political suffocation has prevailed in the life of every Baloch. In the face of mounting pressure from the religious state and with a state of endemic disunity among the Baloch leadership, the resistance has faced a retreat in Western Balochistan. Chapter 7 is a detailed discussion on the Baloch political endeavours inside and outside Balochistan since the exodus of the Baloch leadership from Iran during 1980s. The chapter discusses various aspects of the Baloch national struggle in 21st century Iran. It also deals with efforts of nationalist leaders in exile to highlight the Baloch issue in various international forums. It also explores the failure of the leadership in establishing unity among various Baloch groups and parties to create a platform for a united struggle against the Persian state. The chapter additionally analyses the situation inside Western Balochistan where the vacuum created by the absence of nationalist leadership is being filled by religious zealots. The chapter describes in detail the methodology adopted by the Iranian state in dealing with the Baloch national struggle.

The creation of the religious state of Pakistan from the division of India in 1947, was the continuation of the 'great game' which was the competition between the Russian and the British empires for colonial possessions in the Middle East and in Central and South Asia during 19th century. Sustaining and stabilizing Pakistan is believed to be the direct consequence of the cold war between the socialist bloc headed by the Soviet Union and Western alliance led by the United States of America following the Second World War. The creation of a religious state, and the use of political Islam as the doctrine for dividing India was a unique phenomenon in the political history of the world. It shows the brilliance of a colonial administration, at that time, in successfully carving out a client or subservient state to safeguard Western interests in the region after the British withdrawal from India. Chapter 8 is the description of contextual factors which led to the unique phenomenon of creating the state of Pakistan on purely religious grounds.

In the wake of the British withdrawal from India, the Baloch state of Kalat declared its independence on August 12, 1947. A constitution was promulgated by the Khan of the Baloch and elections were held for a bicameral legislative assembly. However, the Baloch were caught unaware by fast moving developments in international politics and their Khan was unable to comprehend the changing political and strategic situation in the region. The declared independence proved to be short lived, as the rulers of the newly created religious state began threatening the Khan into a merger of the Baloch state with Pakistan. In the face of stern opposition from both houses of the Baloch parliament, nationalist parties and tribal elite, for any merger or accession, Pakistan sent its forces, and compelled the Khan of the Baloch to sign the accession agreement and occupied Balochistan on April 1, 1948. Chapter 9 discusses the situation of Balochistan in the period preceding independence, developments after the declaration of independence by the Khan and the ultimate occupation of the Baloch state by Pakistan.

The Baloch reaction to the occupation of their land and loss of their sovereignty comprised of a short lived armed resistance led by Prince Abdul Karim, younger brother of the Khan. After the defeat of the armed resistance, the Baloch nationalists tried to regroup themselves in political parties and alliances in order to mobilize the Baloch masses. They also made alliances with or joined Pakistan based political parties which were championing the cause of national rights for constituent national entities in Pakistan. Baloch nationalist parties ultimately merged with the National Awami Party (NAP) which became the political front of the Baloch national struggle in Pakistan. The Khan of the Baloch after remaining politically inactive for many years, also became active in order to organize and mobilize different tribes of the Jhalawan and Sarawan regions. However, political activities and efforts to mobilize Baloch tribes by the Khan ended in 1958, when Martial Law was declared in Pakistan, and all political activities were banned. The Palace of the Khan in Kalat was bombed and the Khan was arrested on charges of conspiring with foreign countries to dismember Pakistan. This initiated an armed uprising against Pakistan when the tribes in Jhalawan rose in revolt. Chapter 10 is an account of events in the political history of Eastern Balochistan beginning with the occupation of the Baloch state in 1948 until 1958.

The arrest and humiliation of the Khan, persecution of Prince Abdul Karim and political activists belonging to NAP created a volatile situation in Balochistan. First, Zehri and then Mengal, Mari and Bugti tribes joined in an armed confrontation with Pakistani security forces while political workers under the banner of NAP began to mobilize the Baloch masses. The formation of the Baloch Students Organization (BSO) was an important political development of this period. The armed resistance by guerrilla units of Baloch tribes together with political agitation by nationalist activists, created a general state of unrest which prevailed throughout Balochistan. This ended when a new military dictator seized power in Pakistan in 1969. The new military government made an announcement of political reforms in Pakistan and also extended a reconciliatory gesture towards the Baloch by dismantling One Unit of West Pakistan and giving Balochistan a provincial status in the federation of Pakistan. Chapter 11 is the description of events in Balochistan during the military rule in Pakistan from 1958 to 1969.

By all accounts, the decade of 1970 was one of the most damaging in the history of the Baloch national struggle in Pakistan. As the Baloch nationalists won general elections held in 1970 under the banner of NAP, the state establishment of a truncated Pakistan, unwillingly agreed to transfer power to the people's representatives and the first Baloch nationalist government in Balochistan was formed in 1972. However, soon the establishment found excuses to dismiss the government, ban the NAP and arrest all Baloch leaders. The army was deployed in every corner of Balochistan and a bloody and ruthless campaign was initiated against the tribal and political supporters of the Baloch national struggle. The Baloch armed resistance was crushed after a few years and the political mobilization became ineffective following the banning of NAP. Major disagreements occurred between the Baloch leaders in 1972. A second division in Baloch leadership ranks occurred in 1976 concerning the strategy of the national struggle. This occurred while the Baloch leaders were in prison and caused much confusions among the Baloch nationalist cadre. These divisions trickled down and political activists and the BSO cadre were also divided on the issue of strategy. During this period, Pashtun and the Baloch nationalists also took separate political journeys. Chapter 12 describes and analyses events during 1970s, a period which became of fundamental importance in the history of the Baloch, in which far reaching changes occurred in Baloch politics in general and the Baloch national struggle of Eastern Balochistan in particular.

The last two decades of 20th century are important in the history of the Baloch national struggle in many ways. It was the period of regrouping for former political allies, formation and division of parties, and reflection on losses and gains of the national resistance during 1970s. After their release from prison, the two main leaders of the resistance, Nawab Khair Bakhsh Mari and Sardar Ataullah Mengal, went into exile for long periods. By returning from exile; participating in the political process and joining the two nationalist governments in Balochistan in 1988 and 1997, the Baloch leadership showed conciliatory gestures towards the Pakistani establishment for a peaceful resolution of the Baloch national question. Chapter 13 is an analysis of this turbulent period of Baloch political history. It discusses the political endeavours of Baloch leaders in exile and the intensive and heated political debates among nationalist circles regarding future strategy of the Baloch national struggle in Pakistan. The chapter also covers events leading to the unification and division of BSO and the phenomenon of youth movements in Eastern Balochistan.

The early years of 21ˢᵗ century witnessed the rising tension between Baloch nationalists and the state establishment of Pakistan. The military regime formulated and adopted various economic and strategic plans in Balochistan which included leasing out of Gwadar to Chinese and establishing several military bases in Balochistan. The Baloch nationalist parties and leadership perceived these plans as part of a grand design to exploit the natural resources of Balochistan for the benefit of ruling Punjab and bring about demographic changes in order to make the Baloch a minority in their own land. Ultimately, a situation of increased hostilities developed and in the ensuing armed conflict the Baloch suffered immense losses in men and material. Chapter 14 is a detailed account of the contemporary Baloch resistance against Pakistan. It analyses events leading to the assassination of one of the towering personalities of the Baloch national resistance, Nawab Akber Bugti. The chapter also discusses the role of Baloch nationalists in areas of political mobilization and armed resistance. The chapter also explores the human rights violation being perpetrated by the Pakistani military, the intelligence agencies and the 'proxy death squads'. It analyses the prevailing impasse in the conflict between Pakistan and the Baloch national resistance, besides identifying methods of the Pakistani state to counter the Baloch national resistance. These included creating divisions among the nationalist parties and personalities, infiltrating ranks of the resistance, bringing demographic changes and introducing religious fanaticism into the Baloch society.

An artificial national identity and superfluous state nationalism are common characteristics of countries occupying Balochistan. Iranian nationalism is based on a combination of Persian chauvinism and narrow Shiism which demands unqualified loyalty with family members of Prophet Muhammad as leaders of Muslims for all times. The identification of the state with the Persian hegemonic nationalism, has been the key objective of every ruler and dynasty in Iran. Pakistan is the first state created on the basis of religious faith, and has laboured to manufacture a state nationalism out of nothing. The Baloch national struggle which is the manifestation of their national aspirations for a sovereign and united Balochistan has faced the onslaught of artificially created nationalism in both Iran and Pakistan. Chapter 15 discusses how despite centuries of suffering, oppression and genocide, the Baloch have not accepted the occupation of their land and are hopeful for a bright future.

National liberation movements generally use the demand of right of self-determination as their political objective in line with the United Nation Charter, which emphasizes the granting of that right to all people. Chapter 16 is a theoretical discussion on the phenomenon of the national liberation struggle which began after First World War and the principle of the right of self-determination. The chapter also analyses the Baloch claim to self-determination and how its legal and humanitarian aspects can be used to end the protracted and bloody conflict between the Baloch and states occupying the Baloch land and how the principle of right of self-determination can be applied upon the completion of the incomplete agenda, the ending colonialism in a 21st century world.

Balochistan is situated in one of the most politically volatile regions of the world. With its huge unexplored energy resources and location at the mouth of Persian Gulf, it is becoming increasingly important for many regional and global powers both economically and strategically. The governments of Iran and Pakistan insist that the Baloch national struggle in their respective countries is being fuelled by many foreign powers. Pakistan has openly expressed concern over Indian and Afghan support for the Baloch. The US was also named by Iran as supporting the Baloch national resistance in Western Balochistan through Arab countries. Chapter 17 discusses the contextual factors of external involvements in the Baloch national struggle and the prospects of any assistance for the Baloch national struggle in the near future from regional or international powers.

Success and failure of a national liberation struggle depends on the strength of the resistance and weaknesses of the colonizing powers. On the one hand, the Baloch national struggle is facing structural and strategic problems and on the other

Introduction

hand, the countries occupying Baloch land are struggling with insurmountable economic, social and political problems internally together with growing isolation internationally resulting from their policies regarding terrorism and nuclear issues. The last chapter of the book analyses problems facing the Baloch national struggle and explores prospects for its success in achieving the goal of an independent Balochistan.

CHAPTER 2

THE BALOCH AND
BALOCHISTAN IN CONTEXT

The picture of distant past of the Baloch is quite obscure; however, there is strong evidence that they were part of a great Aryan migration some 3000 years ago. Leaving their abode in Central Asia, a group of Aryan tribes known as Balaschik, settled initially in Balashagan region of the North-Western Iranian plateau, speaking Balaschuki language. During the final decades of the Sassanid Empire, circumstances forced the agro-pastoralist Balaschik tribes to migrate *en masse* to Kerman and Sistan where their name changed from Balaschik to Baloch and their language became Balochi. During 12th and 13th century, the majority of the Baloch were again forced to migrate from Kerman and northern Sistan. They finally settled in present day Balochistan which is a huge landmass stretching from Khorasan to the Indian Ocean and from Dasht e Kavir to the Indus River.

THE BALOCH

Balochi language, legends, and customs strongly support observations of many researchers that the Baloch were part of ancient Aryan tribes, residing initially in the north-west of the Caspian Sea (Gangvosky, 1971; Naseer, 1979; Janmahmad, 1982).

17

A group of tribes known as Proto-Indo-Iranians, originated in the eastern European steppes in the third millennium BC moved eastward towards the region of southern Ural steppes and Volga, then further onto Central Asia. Kuzmina (2007), observed that at that stage, they appear to have already formed two groups: Proto-Iranians in the north, and Proto-Indo-Aryans in the south. After 2000 BC, the Indo-Aryans moved southeast via Afghanistan into the Indian subcontinent, as well as southwest via Iranian plateau into northern Mesopotamia (Ghirshman, 1954). According to Matthew (1999), the Iranian tribes may have been established throughout Iranian plateau by the beginning of the first millennium, except, perhaps, the southernmost parts. The migration of these tribes into the Iranian plateau took place through a succession of numerous groups of tribes, each tribe speaking its own variation of the Iranian language. Morris (1888) listed some of these migratory groups as Ossetes, Armenians, Kurds, the people of ancient Media and Persia, Afghans, Baloch, and Hindus of Indus and Ganges.

Reference to the Baloch, in ancient historical accounts, is very rare. This could be because the Baloch, as agro-pastoralist nomads, did not play significant roles in the political happenings of ancient Iran. On linguistic, cultural, and geographical grounds, it has been clearly established by works of imminent Iranologists that the Baloch origin can be traced within the northwest Iranian group of tribes. It is believed that the original homeland of the Baloch must have been in the area where other speakers of north-western Iranian languages were living. Rock inscriptions by different Iranian emperors such as Emperor Darius and Shahpur, mentioned a region called Balashagan or Balashakan under their rule and the Balaschik as their subject. This area was somewhere between the Caspian Sea and Lake Van. These emperors on these rock inscriptions claimed subjugation of many nations. Subjugation of the people of Balashagan was also mentioned alongside the account of victories over many other peoples. Von Voigtlander (1978), observed that Balashagan "the country of the Balas," was one of the lands (*Dahyus*) claimed by the Achaemenes Emperor Darius I

(Xerxes I 550-486 BC). The inscription of the Sassanid Emperor Shahpur I (AD 240-270) at *Naqsh-e-Rostam* describes the satrapy of Balashagan as "extending to the Caucasus mountains and the Gate of Albania (Gate of the Alans)." According to inscriptions; in the north, it bordered by the lower courses of the Kura and Aras (Araxes) rivers, and, in the south, it was bordered by Atropatene with the Caspian Sea to its east. Strabo in Book II of his geography quoted by Mackenzie (1998) gave one of the earliest accounts of the region and mentioned the kingdom of Atropatene that incorporated Balashagan. Strabo mentioned that the monarch of Balashagan also gained the title of king under Sassanid Emperor Ardashir, which, most probably, would indicate him being a vassal of Sassanid emperor.

Shahpur listed the provinces (*satrapy*) in the inscription of *Ka'be-ye Zardusht* as follows:

"And I [Shahpur I] possess the lands [provinces: Greek ethne]: Fars [Persis], Pahlav [Parthia], Huzestan [Khuzistan], Meshan [Maishan, Mesene], Asorestan [Mesopotamia], Nod-Ardakhshiragan [Adiabene], Arbayestan [Arabia], Adurbadagan [Atropatene], Armen [Armenia], Virozan [Iberia], Segan [Machelonia], Arran [Albania], Balasagan up to the Caucasus and to the 'gate of the Alans' and all of Padishkwar[gar] the entire Elburz chain = Tabaristan and Gelan, Mad [Media], Gurgan [Hyrcania], Marv [Margiana], Harey [Aria], and all of Abarshahr [all the upper (=eastern, Parthian) provinces], Kerman [Kerman], Sakastan, Turgistan, Makuran, Pardan [Paradene], Hind [Sind] and Kushanshahr all the way to Pashkibur [Peshavar?] And to the borders of Kashgaria, Sogdia and Chach [Tashken] and of the sea-coast Mazonshahr [Oman] (Schmitt, 2000 and Wiesehofer, 2006)."

The added list of Kerdir, the high priest of Emperor Shahpur I, at Naqsh-e Rostam comprised of Pars (Persis), Pahlav

(Parthia), Xuzestan (Susiane), Mesan (Mesene), Assrestan (Assyria), Nodsiragan (Adiabene), Adurbayagan (Atropatene), Spahan (Isfahan), Ray (Rhages), Kerman (Karmania), Sagestan (Sakastane), Gurgan (Hyrkania), Marw (Margiane), Harew (Areia), Abarsahr (Khorasan), Turestan (Turene), Makuran (Makuran), and Kusansahr ta fraz o Paskabur (the Kushans country up to Peshawar), May (Media), Hind (India), and "on that side of the sea" Mazunsahr (Oman), and others, namely Arman (Armenia), Wiruzan Iberia (Georgia), Alan (Albania), and Balashagan ta fraz o Kaf kof ud Alanan dar (Balashagan up to the Caucasus and the Gate of the Alans) (MacKenzie, 1961).

According to Shahpur's inscription, most of Transcaucasia was included in his empire, and in the inscription made by Kerdir (the high priest) at the same site, it is also proudly mentioned that— "the land of Armenia, Georgia, Albania and Balashagan, up to the Gate of the Albanians, Shahpur, the king of kings, with his horses and men pillaged, burned and devastated" (Frye, 1963). From the description of the Sassanid and Roman frontiers, it is obvious that Balashagan was in the same mountainous region where Greeks and Roman writers had listed several predatory mountainous ethnic groups. Strabo (2009), provided the names of some tribes that populated Caucasia and Albania, including regions of Artsakh and Utik, and incorporated Utians, Mycians, Caspians, Gargarians, Sakasenians, Gelians, Sodians, Lupenians, Balash [ak] anians, Parsians, and Parrasians. There is also the mention of a kingdom of Sanesanan, whose king during the reign of Armenian king Khusrow II, according to Thomas de Marga (1893), also ruled over other peoples, among whom figured the Balaschik. Having invaded Armenia, the army of this king was cut to pieces by the Armenians, and the survivors fell back toward the country of the Balaschik.

It appears that after the collapse of Sassanid Dynasty in the seventh century, the name Balashagan and the people mentioned as Balashchik began to disappear from historical accounts. However, a few mentions of Balashagan can be found in Arabic chronicles of that time. According to Baladhuri (1924), in the period of early Arab conquests, Balashagan spanned the plain extending across the lower course of the Aras (Araxes) river, from Barda through Baylaqan to Vartan, Bajarvan, and Barzand. It included the provinces of Arran and Mogan, though, as Minorsky (1958) noted, the name is common in Armenian sources but rare in Islamic ones. Baladhuri (1924) mentioned that in about AD 645, Caliph Othman sent Salman b. Rabi al Baheli to Arran. He summoned the Kurds of Balashagan to Islam and imposed the *jezya* (a tax that Muslim rulers demanded from their non-Muslim subjects) on some of them. Baladhuri further mentioned that when Hodayfa ibn Yaman made a peace treaty with the Marzban (governor) of Azerbaijan, one of the provisions was that the Arabs should not expose the local people to the depredations of the Kurds of Balashagan and the Shabalan mountains. Dashti (2012), observed that the mention of Kurds and absence of any reference to the presence of Balaschik in Balashagan by Arab writers was noteworthy. If it was not simply an inadvertent omission on their part, then it may have indicated that the Balaschik were removed from the area or could have migrated *en masse* from their original abode, from whence they derived their ethnic or national identity.

As discussed above, the region of Balashagan was part of the Achaemenes and Sassanid Empires but was sometimes claimed by the kings of Armenia, who were themselves subject to Achaemenes authority. The heart of Balashagan was the Dasht-e-Balashagan "Balashagan plain," which is virtually identical with the Mogan steppe. Adontz (1970), quoting references from Ebn Kordabeh, believed that this plain was located on the road from Barzand to Vartan (Vartanakert). In the Sassanid period, Balashagan extended as far as the Caucasus range and the Darband pass. During the Parthian supremacy of Iranian plateau beginning around 238 BC, Balashagan might also have become a dependency of the Ashkani (Arsacid) Dynasty, though there is no documentary evidence of that.

Among the Baloch, it is generally believed that the word "Baloch," if applied in the sense of cultural implications, manifests something magnificent, magnanimous, and powerful. However, the word Baloch is most probably a rather small modification or transformation of the term Balaschik, after their expulsion or migration from Balashagan (Dashti, 2012). There is not much difference in the pronunciation of Balaschik, Balashchik, Baloachik, or Baloch. It is most probable that the group of tribes who were living in Balashagan was named after the region, or the region itself was named after its inhabitants, the Balaschik.

The Balaschik were not alone in Balashagan but were with other tribes in the area between the Caspian Sea, Lake Van and the Alborz Mountain like Cyrtii (Kurds), Cadusii, Caspians, and Mardis. Descriptions of some predatory tribes in the region can be found in the works of writers dealing with ancient history of Iran. Arrian (1958) mentioned many mountain-dwelling and predatory tribes living in the region in or around Balashagan. Strabo mentioned the Cossaei and the Paraetaceni, who bordered on Assyria and Media, respectively. The Cossaei were possibly the remnants of the ancient Kassites, and the Paraetaceni occupied mountains of northern Persia. Strabo (2009) mentioned four predatory peoples who were not the subject of the Persian Empire and receiving "tributes" from the king, in consideration for road passage. This may be tantamount to modern day "protection money." These were semi-independent or "not subject" nations, meaning, they were not in direct control of the empires of the day. Arrian (1958) pointed out that the two sides, that is, the emperor and tribes of that region, presumably, tried to maintain a standing agreement on this. They lived their independent lives, providing they protected the trade routes running through Persia and Armenia or Greece.

There is historical evidence that the Baloch were part of the military forces of Emperor Cyrus, Xerxes, and Cambyses of the Achaemenes dynasty. Firdausi in his 'Book of Kings' (*Shahnama*) described the Baloch as part of the army of Cambyses (Siahwash) son of Kai Kaous of the Achaemenes dynasty. The second mention of the Baloch in the 'Book of Kings' is during the rule of Khusro I (Anosharvan) from 531 AD to 579 AD of Sassanid dynasty. From the time of Kai Kaous to Anosharvan, nothing can be found in historical documents about the Baloch, for a period that spans up to a thousand years. It is not clear what happened to this ethnic group during this period-a people whose inclusion in the armies of different Achaemenes emperors was mentioned graphically by Iranian historians in medieval times.

The Balaschik of Balashagan, although unreported in the historical accounts of ancient Iran; nevertheless, continued their journey into history as the Baloch of the contemporary world. They appeared as Baloch in Kerman and Sistan during the last decades of the Sassanid Empire, and before the Arab invasion of Iran. Starting from the invasion of Iran by Arab tribes during 7th century, the history of the Baloch is a history of persecution, deportation, and migration. Although some of the Baloch tribes initially sided with the invading Arabs; soon the Arab conquerors began to persecute the Baloch on various pretexts. After the weakening of Arab power during 9th century, Iran was ruled by powerful local dynasties for many centuries. The Baloch also faced some of the worst treatments during this period. Saffarids, Buyids, Samanids, Ghaznavids, Seljuqs, Mongols and Timurids were among major political powers and dynasties who committed their share of atrocities on the Baloch. These atrocities included genocide acts of high magnitude that this finally pushed the Baloch from Kerman and the northern regions of Sistan further east towards southern Sistan, Makuran, and Turan. With this huge influx of Baloch tribes, the socio-political picture of the region changed drastically and the area began to take on the character of the Baloch people. The language of the migrating Baloch tribes 'Balochi' became the *lingua franca* of the area and the whole region came to be known as Balochistan. During Seljuq period, it was officially named as a province of their empire.

The majority of the Baloch in modern times live in the Pakistani province of Balochistan and the Iranian province of Sistan-wa-Balochistan. In Afghanistan the Baloch are concentrated in the southwestern regions of Nemroz, Farah and western Helmand. A large number of the Baloch are also living in the Pakistani provinces of Punjab and Sindh. A considerable number of them have also settled in the Persian Gulf states and a small number in different European countries as refugees. It is estimated that the present population of the Baloch, is more than 20 million. Harrison (1981) observed that ethnically, the Baloch are no longer homogeneous, since the original nucleus that migrated from the Caspian has absorbed a variety of disparate groups along the way. Nevertheless, in cultural terms, the Baloch have been remarkably successful in preserving a distinct identity in the face of continuous pressure from the strong cultures of neighbouring areas. Despite the isolation of pastoral communities in Balochistan, the Balochi language and a relatively uniform Baloch folklore tradition and value system have provided a common denominator for diverse Baloch tribal groupings scattered over the vast area from the Indus River in the east to Kerman in the west.

BALOCHI

Balochi, the language of the Baloch is a member of the north-western group of Iranian languages, along with Zazaki, Kurdish, Gilaki, Mazandarani, and Talyshi (Jahani, 2003; Axenov, 2006). Korn (2003) places Balochi among transitional Western Iranian languages, categorizing it as a group in the sense of being a third member in-between north-and southwestern Iranian languages. Of ancient languages, Balochi bears affinities to both Middle Persian (Pahlavi) and Parthian. However, it has also been identified that Balochi has a marked individuality of its own and differs from both of these languages in important respects. Tedesco (1921) and Mackenzie (1961) developed the hypothesis, which has not been contested by other researchers on Iran and Iranian languages that Persian, Balochi, and Kurdish share common phonetic isoglosses. MacKenzie (1961) observed that the speakers of these three languages might once have been in closer contact geographically and ethnically. MacKenzie believed that the people who later became Persians occupied the province of Fars in the southwest Iran, whereas ancestors of the Baloch inhabited central areas of western Iran, and the people who later became known as Kurds lived either in north-western Luristan or in the province of Isfahan. Tedesco (1921) and Windfuhr (1975) saw various connections

24

between Persian, Kurdish, and Balochi and in their works corroborated the close relationship between these languages.

BALOCH SOCIO-CULTURAL VALUES

It can be presumed that contemporary Baloch cultural values developed during their long journey from Balashagan to Balochistan and from the transformation of being Balaschik to be Baloch. Their socio-cultural traditions were influenced by the history of their migration from Central Asia and many other historical happenings. While living in Balashagan, the Baloch were a well-established ethnic entity, having their own territorial region while living in alliance with other ethnic groups on regional, linguistic or cultural grounds and, most probably, sharing some of the cultural and linguistic features with their neighbours and allies. Due to scanty evidence of their migrations to the north-western Caspian region, and their settlements in Balashagan, it is hard to visualize a clear picture of the Baloch sociocultural life at that time; however, bearing in mind the general milieu of the era, it can be suggested that they were pastoralist nomads, herding sheep and goats and living in tribal communities. The structure, behaviour and social set-up of contemporary Baloch society in its essence is influenced by nomadism and tribalism.

The family system among the Baloch, and particularly the extended family is a kind of communal arrangement headed by a patriarch. Because of such a structure, Baloch society is hierarchical, and the dominance of male over female and older over younger is observed. The family is the basic unit and many families make a sub-clan. Several sub-clans are grouped together to form a clan or *bolak* and several cognate *bolaks* form a tribe with its administration centralized at the top level in the respective leading personality or tribal chief (*Sardar, Tumandar*) (Baloch, 1958; Janmahmad, 1989).

The tribal structure of the Baloch society is no longer functional in 21st century Balochistan. A typical Baloch tribe can be categorized as consisting of the following segments:

- The tribal leader (*Sardar/tumandar*)
- The tribal elders (*Wadera, takri*)
- All the remaining members of the tribe, which may include agro-pastoralists, traders, artisans and musicians (*Ludis and domes*)
- The indigenous inhabitant of Balochistan and people of African origin, incorporated into Baloch society.

Contemporary Baloch society generally contains nomadic, semi-nomadic and sedentary segments. Salzman (1971) described the present social organization of the Baloch as:

"Among the Baloch the tribal socio-political organization is a highly diverse phenomenon and it ranges from tribally organized nomadic pastoralists to peasants living under feudal like structures" (1971:432).

From the beginning of 20th century, the tribal structure in Balochistan witnessed significant weakening and in some areas, a total break-up of the old system. With this breakup some observable changes also occurred in Baloch social traditions. Redaelli (2003) observed that:

"A few decades before, shop keeping or trade were something, which did not suit an 'honourable Baloch'. However, in recent decades especially from the mid-20th century a flourishing class of small traders and entrepreneurs is emerging in Baloch townships" (2003:24).

The vast majority of contemporary Baloch live in villages and small townships, which are scattered in the sparsely populated Balochistan. This segment of the Baloch society consists of a symbolic tribal leadership class, traders, artisans and an urban marginalized class. The recent development of an agricultural infrastructure in several parts of Balochistan has produced a class of farmers and small entrepreneurs in townships overlapping the old tribal structure of Baloch society. The town-dweller segment of the society is increasingly absorbing the nomadic and semi-nomadic segments of Baloch society as due to political and ecological happenings their mode of survival is becoming increasingly untenable. Since the start of 21st century, nomadism has practically not existed in Balochistan and only a few families from *Ludis* are living a nomadic life.

The Baloch focus on their peculiar ethnic identity is very strong. The difficult terrain and scattered population allowed the Baloch to maintain their distinct socio-cultural identity. Compare to other nationalities in the neighbourhood of the Baloch, the linguistic and cultural transformation of the Baloch is surprisingly slow and without any mark or drastic impact on their general cultural outlook (Naseer, 1979; Janmahmad, 1982; Baloch, 1987). Special personal qualities are thought to be embodied by the Baloch and inherited as part of their start in life. Over a lifetime, a Baloch is expected to build on privileged inherited characteristics and to do so according to standards of what is called the "Balochi Way". These are demanding measures but, clearly, this does not mean that every Baloch meets the standards; nevertheless, inattention to these standards may threaten everybody. These standards or codes of cultural ethics guide every Baloch in his religious, economic, and socio-political affairs. The term 'Baloch', in individual and collective sense, characterizes a person who is acting in accordance with the code of conduct prescribed by the society. "He is not a Baloch" emphatically denotes a person not acting in accordance with traditional mores in his or her individual life, or even referring to a person without a living soul, observed Janmahmad (1989).

As a community, the Baloch have developed a fierce sense of independence, a life without hegemony or domination by others whether it is an individual, another nation or a state power. As a national entity they have never accepted any form of alien domination. Developed from an agro-pastoralist background, in the Baloch social code, once an enmity is developed with others or a perception of any unjustified action against a Baloch is involved, then it would be very hard for a Baloch to overlook. Any peace with a presumed enemy would be near impossible until the wrong has been undone either by the perpetrator or by taking vengeance by the affected. Fighting for a just cause has become synonymous with dignity, honour and nobility in the Baloch social and cultural code.

Historically, there is no documented evidence of religious practices of the Baloch in ancient times. Many among the Baloch writers (Janmahmad, 1982; Mari, 1974; Naseer, 1979) observed that persecutions of the Baloch by Sassanid emperors Shahpur and Khusrow 1 had a strong religious or sectarian element. They believed that there were strong indications of the Baloch being the followers of Mazdakian and Manichean sects of Zoroastrian religion at the time of their fatal encounters with Sassanid forces. Persecution by the strong and organized religions for the last 2000 years has shaped the secular attitude of the Baloch about religion in their social and community affairs. Medieval Persian and Arab writers portrayed them as least enthusiastic about their religious obligations be it Zoroastrianism or Islam. The long adopted secular mind-set is still observable today in Baloch social behaviours and practices. At the present time, the Baloch enjoy an identity regarding their religious beliefs, which is significantly different from their neighbouring Persian, Afghan, and Pakistani fundamentalist religious mind-set. The Baloch are distinct in their attitude toward religious tolerance, having a liberal or secular attitude compared to other neighbouring nations. Redaelli (2003, p. 21) put it thus:

> *"It is not by chance that the Baloch enjoy the unenviable reputation of being 'bad Muslims.'"*

The orthodox religious institutions in Iran and Pakistan have used the term "bad Muslim" for the Baloch in order to exploit the Baloch indifference in following the strict or fundamentalist Muslim tenets in their social affairs. In fact, unlike other Muslim people of the area, they have never politicized their own religious faith, which has remained linked to the personal sphere and to tradition, without becoming a real socio-political discriminating factor. Another factor in calling the Baloch bad Muslims by Iranian and Pakistani religious elements is that a section of the Baloch population belongs to a religious sect *Zigri (Zikri)*, which the orthodox Muslim religious leaders consider non-Islamic. As observed by Janmahmad (1989), the Baloch are neither irreligious nor atheists. The majority considered themselves as Muslims; nevertheless, the Baloch had never accepted the dominance of religious beliefs over their cherished sociocultural values and ethos.

BALOCHISTAN

The huge land mass stretching from south-eastern Iran to the east bank of River Sindh in Punjab, and from the lower reaches of Helmand in Afghanistan to the Indian Ocean is called Balochistan. The region was named Balochistan and became a province of Seljuq Empire in 12th century after it was dominated socially and culturally by migrating Baloch tribes. Spooner (1983) defined Balochistan as a semi-circle of historically important towns and agricultural areas that stretches from Bandar Abbas on the Persian Gulf, through Kerman, the Delta of the Helmand River in Sistan, Kandahar, and Sindh. It is a borderland between India and Iran and a bridge between the Iranian plateau and the Arabian Peninsula. Geographically, in the west, Dasht-e-Lut, Dasht-e-Kavir, and Kerman Mountains separate it from Persia Proper and the Persian speaking regions of Kerman, in the south east, the Hub River, and the Kirther range of Mountains separate it from Sindh. In the north east, the right bank of Indus separates it from Pashtunistan and Punjab. In the North, Balochistan is naturally separated from Afghanistan by the natural boundaries of Helmand and the Mountain range north of Quetta. In the South, the Indian Ocean separates Balochistan from Sultanate of Oman.

Balochistan is situated at the convergence of Central Asia, South Asia and the Middle East. Historically, it has been a meeting place of various civilizations of Asia geographically and politically (Fairservis, 1961; Cardi, 1966; Scholz, 2002). From archaeological excavations, it was discovered that Balochistan had a bridging function between various cultures in Mesopotamia and the Iranian highland on the one hand, and those in the Indus lowland, on the other. There is archaeological evidence of overland connections between early civilizations of the Indus valley and Mesopotamia through Balochistan. From the mid-1ˢᵗ millennium, the area was divided into many provinces of Achaemenes Empire such as Maka (Makuran) and Zaranka (Sistan). The Greeks during campaigns of Alexander the Great, named the southern regions of Balochistan as Gedrosia. From 4ᵗʰ to 7ᵗʰ century, it changed hands frequently between great empires of the ancient epochs (Fairservis, 1961; Cardi, 1966; Baloch, 1974; Farzanfar, 1992; Hosseinbor, 2000; Scholz, 2002). During the Sassanid period, the regions which comprised present day Balochistan were called Turan (corresponding to present day Sarhad, Sarawan and Jhalawan regions), Pradhan (probably modern day Kharan and Chagai), Makuran, and Sakastan (modern day Sistan).

Contemporary Baloch nationalists recognize boundaries of Balochistan at the time of Mir Naseer Khan I as the Baloch homeland. The Khanate of Kalat under Mir Naseer Khan I extended to Hasanabad (Sistan) and the Helmand River near Rudbar in Afghanistan. The areas in the control of the Khan of the Baloch included Nemroz, south of Helmand and southwest of Farah of modern Afghanistan. Western Makuran up to the Baloch regions of Kerman and Sarhad (southern Sistan) up to the great salt desert (*Dasht e Kavir*) formed western boundaries of the Baloch state. In the east, included in Balochistan were Dera Ismael Khan and Dera Ghazi Khan Regions as Arund and Dajal provinces of the Khanate, in the south Balochistan bordered with Sindh under Kalhoda dynasty while the Persian Gulf separated it from Sultanate of Muscat. In the contemporary world, Balochistan is divided between Iran, Pakistan and Afghanistan.

THE HISTORICAL JOURNEY OF THE BALOCH

The history of the Baloch from Central Asia to present-day Balochistan has been tortuous. Dashti (2012) divided the historical journey of the Baloch into five different periods. The first period encompasses their migration along with other Indo-Iranic tribes into Iranian plateau and settlement into Balashakan/Balashagan. It was the period in which the Baloch distinguished themselves as a separate ethnic entity among other pastoralist nomadic tribes in north-western region of Caspian Sea. In this phase, they were called Balaschik. Probably the Balochi language began to shape its distinguishing features from other Iranian languages at that time. During this period they were reported to be parts of armies of many Iranian emperors. It was at this same time when the persecution of the Baloch began on various pretexts and they migrated en masse or were deported to other parts of Iranian plateau. At the end of this era, the Balaschik and Balashagan vanished from historical accounts. In the second period of the Baloch history, the Balaschik of Balashagan made their presence noted in Kerman, Sistan, Makuran, and Turan as wandering pastoralist nomads having a new identity as the Baloch. The Baloch, mostly based in Kerman and Sistan, became engaged in constant conflict with various regional powers, who were trying to exert their authority over Iran, after the authority of the Arab Caliphate in Baghdad eclipsed at the beginning of 10th century. This period is also characterized by mass movements of the Baloch from Kerman and northern parts of Sistan. Perhaps, also at this time there was an almost total evacuation of the Brahui (Barezui) group of Baloch tribes occurred from eastern Kerman and their settlement in Turan begun. During the third period of their history, with increased diffusion into Makuran, southern Sistan, Turan, and Kachchi, the Baloch began to exert their influence culturally, politically and militarily in these areas. Their culture began to dominate the region, Balochi became the *lingua franca* of the region, and different indigenous tribes began to merge into identities of various Baloch tribes or they became allied to various Baloch tribal confederacies. The whole region was entitled Balochistan in this period. The next period (The golden age of the Baloch) was the emergence of the Baloch state in Kalat during 17th century. The Baloch State of Kalat was the first and the last symbol of Baloch political power in the region. This period ended in 1839 AD when the British, who were consolidating their position in Central Asia against a threatening Russian advance towards their precious Indian colonies, invaded and occupied the Baloch State. Balochistan witnessed its division and gradual strangulation by the emerging Persian dynasties, and the newly established buffer state of Afghanistan. Major changes occurred in the tribal and social structure of the Baloch as a result of various administrative measures taken by the government of British India in the region. With the British withdrawal from India in 1947, there was a short-lived independence for Balochistan and subsequent occupation by Pakistan in 1948. The contemporary history of the Baloch is a tale of the Baloch resistance against the Persian and Pakistani states.

The Baloch are among those national entities in south Central Asia whose tracks of origin had been obscured by the dust of history. However, from the limited available resources and by tracing their linguistic and cultural affiliations, a somewhat definite historical picture of the Baloch can be visualized. Now it has been well established that the Baloch were part of ancient tribes of Indo-Iranic group who migrated from Central Asia 3000 thousand years ago. Initially they settled in the north-western Caspian region of Balashagan where they were known as Balaschik. Here, their language Balaschuki distinguished itself from other north-western Iranian languages. They were uprooted from Balashagan and settled in Kerman and Sistan during Sassanid Era. At this time, they became known as the Baloch and their language became known as Balochi. In the medieval period, they were again forced to migrate from these regions and the majority of them ultimately settled in present-day Balochistan which they have been dominating, linguistically, culturally and politically since.

An overlapping of pastoral ecology and tribal structure has shaped Baloch cultural values. The contemporary Baloch cultural values bear the imprint of the long suffering inflicted by mighty state powers and organized religions on an agro-pastoral nomadic people established in tribal groupings. Their resistance to the assimilation attempts of various occupiers, their secular attitude in social or community affairs, together with an independent and stubborn streak consistent with their nomadic or agro-pastoral past are the distinctive features of Baloch cultural identity. The Baloch developed a strong sense of national identity in medieval times because of aggression from various ruling dynasties of Iran and continued persecution by them. Socio-cultural values of the Baloch have been influenced heavily by their agro-pastoralist and nomadic background.

CHAPTER 3

PERSO-BALOCH RELATIONS
IN CONTEXT

The Baloch and Persians not only share common linguistic roots and geographical boundaries but there is a long history of conflict between the Baloch and various Persian dynasties. In ancient times, the Baloch have been reported to be part of armies of various Persian empires and at the same time it has also received mention in Persian chronicles of the total annihilation of the Baloch on orders of Persian emperors. In medieval times, the Baloch faced massacre, genocide and forced migration from various dynastic rulers in Iran. The hallmark of Perso-Baloch relations had been a fierce struggle by the Baloch to maintain their national identity and to overthrow the Persian yoke and the ruthless and brutal retaliation from the Persians to suppress the Baloch national aspirations.

PERSO-BALOCH RELATION IN ANCIENT IRAN

Around 550 BC, the Persians dominated the Iranian Plateau and they spread their language and culture to the east and west. The powerful empires of Achaemenes (550–330 BC) and Sassanid (AD 226–651) were supposed to be the Persian-dominated powers in Iranian history and were multi-lingual, multi-cultural and multi-religious states (Herzfeld, 1968). However, during Sassanid period, Zoroastrianism was proclaimed as the official religion of the empire. The Baloch came into confrontation with the ancient empires of Iran, the actual cause of this confrontation is still a matter of conjecture, but it is most likely that a sectarian element was responsible for the suffering of the Baloch.

The "love-hate" relationship between the Baloch and ancient Iranian empires can be observed in the pages of Firdausi's famous book of kings (*Shahnama*). Cordial relations between the Baloch and Achaemenes and Sassanid empires were identified by Firdausi and other Persian writers. They narrated that the Baloch, on many occasions, were part of Persian armies (Firdausi, 1915; Shustheri, 1925). However, the friendship appears not to be on permanent basis. Intermittent hostilities broke out between the Baloch and Persians, which led to massacres of the Baloch on many occasions. In narrating the story of how the Baloch were annihilated by the 'Just and Brave' Sassanid Emperor Khusrow I (Anosharvan), Firdausi mentioned that exemplary peace prevailed in Iran after the Baloch were subdued.

> "…..*The Shah marched thence to Hindustan and sojourned there.*
> *At his commandment all folk came to him,*
> *Came seeking to ingratiate themselves,*
> *And for two miles beside the Indus-bank,*
> *Where horses, elephants, brocades and coin.*
> *The great men all with honesty of heart*
> *And loyalty appeared before the Shah,*
> *Who questioned them in accordance to their rank?*
> *With jocund heart the Shah departed thence:*
> *Troops, steeds, and elephants fulfilled the world.*
> *He went his way, and tidings came to him:—*
> *'The world is wasted by the Baluchis,*
> *Till from exceeding slaughter, pillaging*
> *And harrying, the earth is overwhelmed,*
> *But greater ruin cometh from Gilan,*
> *And curses banish blessings.'*

Then the heart of Anosharvan, the Shah, was sorrowful,
And grief commingled with his joy. He said
To the Iranians: "The Alans and Hind
Were, in the terror of our scimitars, like silk.
Now our own realm is turned against us:
Shall we hunt lions and forego the sheep?"
One said to him: "The garden hath no rose
Without a thorn, O King! So too these marches,
Are ever troublesome and treasure-wasting.
As for Baloch the glorious Ardashir
Tried it with all his veteran officers,
But all his stratagems and artifices,
His feints, his labors, arms, and fighting failed.
And though the enterprise succeeded ill,
He cloaked the failure even to himself."
This story of the thane enraged the Shah,
Who went upon his way toward Baluch?
Now when he drew near those lofty mountains,
He went around them with his retinue,
And his entire host encircled them about,
And barred the passage e'en to wind and ant.
The troops, like ants and locusts, occupied
The mountain-outskirts to the sandy desert.
A herald went his rounds about the host,
Proclaiming from the mountains, caves, and plains:—
"Whenever the Baluchis are seeking food,
If they be warriors and carrying arms,
However many or however few,
Let not a single one of them escape."
The troops, aware of the anger of the Shah,
Stopped every outlet with their horse and foot;
Few of the Baluchis or none survived.
No women, children, warriors were left.
All of them perished by the scimitar,
And all their evil doings had an end,
The world had quiet from their ravaging:

No Baluchi, seen or unseen, remained,
While on their mountains, so it came to pass,
The herds thenceforward strayed without a guard;
Alike on waste and lofty mountain-top,
The sheep required no shepherd. All the folk
Around thought nothing of past sufferings,
And looked on vale and mountain as their home" (Firdausi
(1915, pp. 241–243).

But as became apparent, the Persians were unable to totally wipe out the Baloch from the face of earth and some of the Baloch managed to flee and scattered in various directions settling in different regions of the empire out of sight and away from main administrative centres. Another possibility is that the surviving Baloch might have been forced to leave their abode in Balashagan or they resettled in the remotest corners of the empire. This was the norm of the Sassanid Empire in dealing with hostile elements. Perhaps, it took many hundreds of years for the Baloch to reappear on the socio-political scene of ancient Iran and this can explain why for a long period, there is no mention of the Baloch in historical chronicles (Dashti, 2012).

One cannot be ascertain with certainty why the Persians went to such length to wipe out a whole segment of their population. Atrocities, the Baloch faced from ancient Persian emperors were unlikely to result merely from their involvement in acts of robbery or disturbing caravan routes as documented by Persian writers. Janmahmad (1982), observed that in the bloody conflict of Sassanid with the Baloch, which culminated in the slaughter of the Baloch, religious or sectarian aspects of the conflict cannot be ruled out. It is an established historical fact that in the ancient Iran, religious zeal of some Sassanid emperors fuelled upheaval and ethnoreligious disputes in the empire causing genocide and deportation of many tribes and ethnic groups. Perhaps the Baloch became the prime target for being the followers of one of the non-official or renegade sects of Zoroastrianism. It would have been quite natural of agro-pastoralist nomads like the Baloch to have been influenced by the

Mazdakian doctrine of equality and equal distribution of wealth. On the other hand, Sassanid emperors, Shahpur and Khusrow I, were known religious fanatics and for them annihilation of so-called heretic Baloch became the prime objective and a divine obligation. After these acts of genocide, there developed among the Baloch a sense of deep hatred and disgust against the Persians. Perhaps, this inherent distrust between the Baloch and the Persians was one of the reasons for the defection of some of the Baloch tribes to invading Arabs during last years of the Sassanid Empire.

PERSO-BALOCH RELATIONS AFTER THE ARAB OCCUPATION

During 7th century, the face of Persian history changed with the occupation of Iran by Bedouin Arabs and the replacement of the powerful Persian God 'Ahura Mazda' with that of Arabian God 'Allah'. During this period of constant upheavals on the Iranian Plateau, the Baloch and Persians were both subjugated by Arabs. Some of the Baloch and Persians sided with invading Arabs and others fiercely resisted the Arab onslaught. With the final defeat of Iranian resistance, Arabs remained in total control of Iran for nearly 150 years. At the beginning of the 9th century, as a result of decades of civil war between various Islamic religious sects and outbreaks of unresolvable regional conflicts among the ruling Arab tribes, various Persian dynasties emerged on the Iranian scene and they became virtually independent rulers. The Caliph in Baghdad becoming only a titular Monarch.

First to emerge as powerful Persian dynasties after the collapse of Arab rule in Iran, were the Tahirids and the Saffarids. They ruled eastern Iran independently from AD 821 to AD 1003 (Bosworth, 1977). There is no precise and detailed account of any major encounter of the Baloch tribes with Saffarids rulers; however, according to *Tarikh-e-Sistan* (Gold, 1976), the Baloch, living in Barez Mountain in Kerman, fought against Saffarid ruler Yaqub bin Laith at least once. In AD 863, Yaqub attacked and captured

Bam and advanced toward Kerman. Some of the writers mentioned Ali Barezui as the chief of the Baloch tribes living in the Barez Mountains. The governor of Kerman Ali ibn Husain (also called Kursh) assembled an army with the help of the Baloch and their allied tribes. The army was called the "Army of Kursh" and the fighters were known as Kurshi. The Army of Kursh was defeated and Ali ibn Husain was taken prisoner, taken to Bam where he was executed (Istakhri, 1800). A number of Baloch families were also deported into various regions in Persia. Some of the Baloch tribes fled the area and settled in Makuran and Turan during this period. With the pacification of the Baloch, the Saffarids introduced Islam in Kerman, which, until then, had been a bastion of Zoroastrianism.

During 11ᵗʰ century, the Baloch were mainly concentrated in Kerman and surrounding regions. According to Istakhri (1961), the country of the Baloch in Kerman lay between Barez Mountain and Gulf of Oman. Minorsky (1937) suggested that a number of the Baloch tribes were in a dominant position in an area bounded by the sea in the south, Hormuz and Manujan in the west, the districts of Rudbar and the hill region called Kohistan-e-Abu Ghanim in the north, and Khwash and the desert in the east. Hudud al Alam described the Kuh-e-Kufij as a chain of seven mountains running from Jiruft to the sea, with seven tribes, each with its own chief and living as "professional looters" (Minorsky, 1937). However, looking at later events, it became obvious that either these mentioned entities were in fact different Baloch tribes, or they were under a tribal confederacy led by the Baloch.

Based in northern Persia, the Deylamite Ziyarids and the Buyids ruled major parts of north and west of Iran between AD 928 and AD 1055 (Bosworth, 1994). The conflict between the Baloch and the Buyids was well documented by Persian writers. Events developed in such a way that the Baloch became engaged in a protracted and bloody conflict with Buyids, resulting in immense sufferings for the Baloch. Bosworth (1994) observed that eastern Kerman and southwestern Makuran were under the effective control of Koch o Baloch tribes in AD 971 (the Baloch tribes were documented by medieval Persian and Arab writers as Koch o Baloch), when Buyids General Abid ibn Ali captured Tiz and the surrounding territory and converted the population to Islam. In the process of subduing the Baloch, Buyids chiefs Mu'izz ad-Daula and Adud ad-Daula took draconian measures against the Koch o Baloch in Kerman. Maqaddesi was very proud of the actions of Adud ad-Daula by stating that he destroyed them and wrought damage among the Koch and Baloch. In AD 933, Ali Buya, also known as Imad al-Daulah, recruited an army of 1,600 Deylamites and 500 Turks to subjugate the Baloch. He made his younger brother Ahmad Buya, known also as Mu'izz al-Daulah as the commander of the force. According to Tabari (2007), first, Ahmad Buya took Bam and approaching Jiruft, he was received by a delegation of the Baloch sent by Ali ibn Kulwaihi (Ali Guluya), the chief of the Baloch, and other tribes in the area allied with the Baloch. The Baloch agreed to evacuate the city of Jiruft; however, the Buyids violated the agreement and set out to attack the Baloch off guard. A bloody conflict ensued at the mountainous pass of Dar-e-Farid or Dilfiirid in which the Baloch had the upper hand and only few of the Buyids forces could escape (Bosworth, 1977). Another agreement was reached between the Buyid ruler and the Baloch after this debacle; however, despite the agreement of his brother, Ahmad Buya launched a reprisal attack from Sirjan to avenge his defeat. The Baloch were defeated massively this time. According to Meskawiah (1915), after a decade or so, the Buyids again turned their attention toward Kerman. The Buyids chief of Fars and Khuzestan, Adud ad-Daula, launched many punitive expeditions against the Koch and Baloch. The court poet of Adud ad-Daula, Mutanabbi, in AD 965, mentioned in a verse that his patron was the one who offered cups of death to his foes on the one hand and cups of wine to his intimates on the other hand, when he made the Baloch like the previous day that had passed away totally (Bosworth, 1977). However, it appeared that despite this boast, the resistance against the Buyids from the Baloch continued and Istakhri (1961) observed that this resistance, whose leaders included Abu Saeed Baloch and his sons, compelled Adud ad-Daula to take as severe drastic measures as possible against this running sore of the Koch o Baloch. In AD 970 and AD 972, two campaigns were launched against them, and, as a result, the Buyids authority was extended as far eastward as Makuran. According to Istakhri (1961), in the first campaign, the Buyids generals Kurkir ibn Jastin and Abid ibn Ali marched southward from Jiruft, defeating an army of the Baloch and the Manujaniyans in the south of Jiruft in December AD 970. The Baloch force was routed, with five thousand of their numbers killed, including two sons of their chief, Abu Saeed. The Buyids forces then turned eastward to Tiz. In the second campaign, the Buyid army penetrated into Barez Mountain, defeating the Baloch under the leadership of Ali Barezui, slaughtering their males, and enslaving the women and children in AD 972 (Bosworth, 1977). The remnants of the Baloch were deported from the Barez Mountain, and peasants and cultivators from other parts of his domain were settled in their place. Maqaddesi (1906) observed that after repeated aggressive and extensive campaigns, the Buyids ruler had scattered the Baloch and laid waste to their lands, taking some into slavery and settling others elsewhere. Later events in Baloch history showed that the annihilation of the Baloch was not total. The Baloch were still in Kerman after the victorious campaigns of the Buyids. However, defeats and genocide acts by the Buyids rulers forced an *en masse* migration of the surviving Baloch tribes towards the east into Makuran, southern Sistan, and Turan. In many ways, this was one of the major exoduses of the Baloch from west to east, toward the lands that later formed the present-day Balochistan.

The Baloch relations with the Persianized Turk dynasties of Ghaznavids and Seljuqs were never been peaceful. The Baloch were engaged in various encounters with the Ghaznavids rulers. Turan and Makuran came under the Ghaznavids founder Sebuktegin's suzerainty as early as AD 976–977 (Bosworth, 1963). At that time, some of the migrating Baloch tribes were already settled in Turan. The Baloch tribes fought against Sebuktegin when he attacked Khuzdar in AD 994. The Baloch in the army of Amir Khalaf of the Saffarids fought against Mahmud Ghaznavi, when the Ghaznavids

41

forces invaded Sistan in AD 1013 (Muir, 1924). The Baloch resisted the occupation of Kerman by Ghaznavids as an ally of local ruler. In order to settle the score with the Baloch, the Ghaznavids launched a bloody campaign against them under the leadership of Mahmud's son Masud Ghaznavi (Dames, 1904). The Baloch in Sistan engaged the Ghaznavid forces three times, and in one of the encounters, they were able to defeat the Ghaznavids contingent but were then defeated in the following two. Many were killed and captured, and their settlements were looted. Masud Ghaznavi returned home with immense booty (Nizam al-Mulk, 1960). There were other skirmishes between the Baloch and Ghaznavids in Turan and Makuran when the Ghaznavids tried to expand their empire in the south towards Persian Gulf regions. The migrating Baloch tribes there became part of the conflict as they were part of local armies resisting Ghaznavid plunderers.

PERSO-BALOCH RELATIONS IN MEDIEVAL TIMES

Medieval Iran witnessed the rule of many Turk, Mongol and Persian rulers. The long rule of Seljuqs which spans many hundreds of years was followed by the invasion of the Mongol hordes under the leadership of Changiz Khan. After 150 years of Mongol rule and a long period of anarchy, Safavids created a strong dynastic empire. Their empire lasted for many centuries before crumbling in 17th century. The Baloch faced persecution from all ruling dynasties of medieval Iran.

As observed by Morgan (1988) and Lange, 2011), around AD 1059, the Seljuqs rule was established throughout Persia and Iraq as far as the frontiers of Syria and the Byzantine Empire in Anatolia. During early Seljuqs period, the bulk of the Baloch tribes were living in Kerman and Sistan, but some of them were also settled in Makuran and Turan in relative peace. However, hostilities soon developed between the Seljuqs and the Baloch. Most probably, it was because of the increasing encroachment of the Guzz pastoralist Turks on the traditional Baloch grazing fields in Sistan and Kerman. The Seljuqs unleashed their state power against the Baloch in support of their kins-the Guzz nomads. According to Tabari (2007), Seljuq rulers Chaghri Beg and Qawurd made their hostile advances against the Baloch during mid-eleventh century on the pretext of maintaining law and order as the Baloch continued to prey upon travellers through the Great Desert, so the Seljuqs reduced their activities to more tolerable proportions by unleashing a reign of terror on the Baloch in Kerman around AD 1074. The historian of the Seljuqs of Kerman—Muhammad ibn Ibrahim (as quoted by Bosworth, 1977 and Lange, 2011)—relates how Qawurd prepared an army to overrun the Garmsir region of Kerman, which was a major source of the province's revenues but since the time of Adud ad-Daula, had relapsed into anarchy. The seat of the Baloch power was in the Barez Mountains (Jebel Barez), and Qawurd's spies informed him about a grand gathering of tribal chiefs in a traditional festival at a certain time and place. The place was considered by leaders of Baloch tribes as almost inaccessible to any outside force. However, using his espionage network successdully, Qawurd marched out of Jiruft with a massive army, swept down on the Baloch chiefs at their meeting place, and massacred them to a man.

The hostilities between the encroaching Guzz Turks on the grazing fields of the Baloch in Kerman and Sistan intensified, and the resulting attack on the Baloch by the Seljuqs forces was the final act which compelled the migration of almost all the Baloch tribes from Kerman and many parts of northern Sistan. It is obvious that the second and, perhaps, the last wholesale migration of Baloch tribes during the Seljuqs era was mainly due to atrocities of Seljuqs rulers prompted by the rivalries of the Baloch with encroaching Guzz pastoralist nomadic tribes.

The mass exodus of the Baloch nearly put an end to the political influence of the Baloch in Kerman. The migrating tribes entered Sistan and then into Makuran and Turan. Later, these tribes organized themselves into tribal confederacies, which shaped the present Baloch national entity. One of these tribal confederacies was able to establish the first Baloch state, The Khanate of Kalat, in the confinement of present-day Balochistan. Two other tribal confederacies due to various reasons were compelled to march further eastward into Punjab and Sindh of present-day Pakistan. With the intensification of the Baloch migrations into Makuran and Turan, the area began to take on the character of modern-day Balochistan. The migrating Baloch tribes became dominant in every aspect of the region, Balochi started to become the *lingua franca*, and many indigenous tribes and populace began to merge in the emergent and newly dominant Baloch national identity. In this perspective of the Baloch domination of the region when various administrative changes were brought by Seljuq Prime Minister Nizam ul Mulk, the region was named Balochistan and became an Ostan (province) of the Seljuq Empire.

After the collapse of Seljuq Empire, Iran faced the onslaught of Mongols and Timurid hordes. An anarchic situation prevailed for many centuries until the establishment of the Safavid rule in 16th century. The Safavid established Persian control in Makuran, mainly from Bampur, Dezzak, and Sistan. In the face of growing resistance from the Baloch, Shah Esmail Safavi, in 1515, was forced to seek Portuguese assistance in suppressing the revolt in Makuran. During the reign of Shah Abbas, under the command of Ganj Ali Khan, a strong Persian force attacked Bampur. The Baloch forces under the command of Malik Shamsuddin, were defeated, and Malik Shamsuddin was arrested and taken to the Safavid capital of Isfahan along with several Baloch chiefs of Dezzak, Panouch, and Kasarkand. Later, as part of a reconciliatory process with the Baloch, Malik Mirza, son of Malik Shamsuddin, was recognised as the ruler of Bampur by the Safavid king.

During the reign of Shah Hussain Safavi, various Baloch chiefs ruled different regions of Western Balochistan in a semi-autonomous relationship with the Persian Government. Around 1620, Kech was taken over by Buledai tribe, who dominated the whole of Makuran up to Jask until 1740 (Naseer, 1979). Malik Dinar was the ruler of Bampur, Purdil Khan was the ruler of Jalk, and Khusrow Bozorgzada was the ruler of Shustun while

Shah Salim Nosherwani ruled the Kharan region. The Baloch fought intermittent battles against Persian forces concentrated in Kerman, which were increasingly interfering with affairs in the Baloch regions. During 1691, a huge Baloch army under the joint command of Shah Salim Nosherwani and Khusrow Bozorgzada invaded Kerman, devastating many surrounding settlements of Kerman before retreating. In 1700, Shah Salim Nosherwani and Sardar Purdil Khan renewed their attacks on Kerman, and this time, they occupied Bam and retained it for many months. Shah Salim Nosherwani, attacked the Rudbar region in 1701. The Persian Army, under the command of Alexander, the nephew of Gurgin Khan, the governor of Kandahar attacked Sarhad, devastating this vast area, killing hundreds of the Baloch and burning their settlements. Shah Salim Nosherwani hastily returned from Rudbar after hearing about the Persian attack on Sarhad but was captured in an ambush set by Persian forces along with several of his chiefs and fighters. The captured Baloch were executed, and Alexander sent the heads of sixty-six Baloch chiefs to Isfahan, including the head of Shah Salim Nosherwani. After a year, to avenge the murder of his uncle and other Baloch chiefs, the nephew of Shah Salim Nosherwani, Mir Shahdad Nosherwani attacked and occupied Kerman for a while. The Baloch in Sistan had an opportunity for revenge against the Safavids, when they became part of the invading army of Afghans. The Safavids were defeated and major areas of Persia came under the occupation of the Afghans for the next twenty-five years during the first quarter of the eighteenth century. The Baloch leader Muhammad Khan Baloch acted as foreign minister of the Afghan occupation forces (Lockhart, 1938). However, after the end of Afghan occupation of Iran, the Baloch reconciled with the Persians for a brief period when Muhammad Khan Baloch was made the governor of Kuhgilu in 1729 by Shah Tahmasp Safavi. After Nader Shah Afshar ultimately overthrew the Safavid dynasty, the Baloch came into conflict with Afshar forces. In 1733, Muhammad Khan Baloch collected a large force, which was also joined by the sympathizers of the Safavid king and Arab tribes of Ahwaz to counter advances of

Nader Shah Afshar. In a bloody battle in the Shulistan defile near Fahliyan between forces of Nader Shah Afshar and Muhammad Khan Baloch, the Baloch were heavily defeated with the loss of three thousand fighters. Muhammad Khan Baloch escaped to Shiraz, and from there, he made his way to the island of Qais. He was arrested in Qais and brought to Shiraz where he was blinded on the orders of Nader Shah Afshar and died in prison (Lockhart, 1938). Nader Shah Afshar tried to consolidate Persian power in Balochistan by sending many expeditionary forces. In 1737, a Persian contingent, under the command of Pir Muhammad, governor of Herat, marched toward Sarhad and western Makuran (Sykes, 1902). The Persian Army captured Bampur, Pahraj, Laashaar, and Tiz after bloody conflicts with Malik rulers of Makuran. Another force was sent to Sarhad region, and the Baloch tribes of Sanjarani and Narui were heavily defeated by Persian forces in the region of Kharan. Kech and other places in Makuran were also occupied by an expeditionary force sent from Fars. In 1739, a Persian expeditionary force under the command of Admiral Taqi Khan, invaded Gwadar on his way to Sindh. However, in Kech, this force was heavily defeated by the Baloch under the leadership of Malik Dinar, and the Persians were forced to withdraw from Gwadar (Lockhart, 1938).

The Baloch opposition to Safavid excesses was not unified and they resisted in various regions against overwhelming Persian advances as individual rulers and various tribes failed to unify in order to face the Persians with a joint strategy. The disunity was the main factor in the defeats and sufferings during Safavid and Nader Shah Afshar periods. Dashti (2012) observed that various regional powers in Persia dealt heavy blows to the Baloch in ancient and medieval Iran, sometimes adopting inhuman tactics; the effects of these conflicts were so devastating that it took many centuries for the Baloch to assert themselves as a significant political or social entity in the regions which, today, form the landmass of Balochistan.

From ancient times, there has been a love-hate relation between the Baloch and the Persians. The Baloch were part of armies of several Persian dynasties and at the same time faced genocide and deportation on the orders of the Persian emperors. They were uprooted from their original abode in Balashagan and for a while they were mainly concentrated in the Kerman and Sistan regions of the Eastern and Southern Iranian Plateau. After the collapse of the Arab rule in Iran, the Baloch came into confrontation with Persian and Persianized Turkic regional powers of Iran. Massacre, genocide and forced deportation of the Baloch continued during the reign of almost all rulers. However, despite taking heavy blows from the powerful forces, the Baloch never gave up their quest for a sovereign and dignified status. The confrontation with the mighty Seljuqs caused the Baloch to abandon their abode in Kerman and Sistan and they dispersed in Makuran, Turan, and further east into Sindh and Punjab.

In medieval Balochistan, many tribes and ethnic groups began to think of themselves as part of the greater Baloch identity and, ultimately, were very much absorbed into the Baloch national identity. The spreading and expanding of the Baloch tribal confederacies led to the incorporation of new human and material resources for confederating Baloch tribes, enhancing their power of resistance. With the consolidation of power in Kalat, one of the Baloch confederacies was successful in establishing the first and the last Baloch state.

The ancient and medieval history of the Baloch is an account of migration and persecution of an agro-pastoral nomadic group of tribes by powerful dynasties of the region. It might be puzzling for many why the Baloch were at loggerhead with every emerging power in the region. The answer to the question lies in the strong sense of national identity among the Baloch. It is not that the Baloch were fond of confronting the powerful but the ever present Baloch resistance was rather a reaction from them against encroachments on their traditional way of living a life independent of any state or organized authority. Distrust and disgust became the fundamental elements of the Perso-Baloch relations because of the long history of conflict and blood shed during ancient and medieval times.

CHAPTER 4

THE BALOCH RESISTANCE AGAINST QAJAR DYNASTY

Persia was ruled by the Qajar, a Persianized Turkish tribe after a prolonged period of widespread anarchy, which resulted from the murder of Nader Shah Afshar in 1747. During the anarchic period in Persia, many Baloch chieftains and *Hakoms* (rulers) of various regions in Western Balochistan tried to overthrow the Persian yoke. Some of the regions in the south came under the direct suzerainty of the Baloch State of Kalat while others in Sarhad and Sistan took inspiration from the establishment of the Khanate of Kalat as an independent Baloch state. One way or the other they became affiliated with the Khanate. However, in 1794, after the collapse of Zand rule, the Qajar established themselves firmly on the Persian throne and in the fulfilment of their ambition to establish a united Persian empire, the Qajar began a process of subduing and subjugating various national entities into submission. From the perspective of the 'great game' between Russia and Great Britain in Central Asia, Balochistan became a victim by default. The Baloch destiny underwent a drastic change when the British invaded Balochistan and occupied Kalat in 1839. It was divided and ultimately the whole of Western Balochistan came under the occupation of Persia.

THE ESSENCE OF BALOCH CONFLICT WITH QAJAR

After the British occupation of Kalat, Qajar rulers of Persia made sustained efforts to strengthen their grip on Western Balochistan. The Baloch for a while became involved in the rivalry of the Ismaili spiritual leader Agha Khan and his brother with the Qajar for the throne of Iran. Under the leadership of Mir Muhammad Ali (the ruler of Sib), the Baloch decided to support Agha Khan and his brother in their endeavours to overthrow Qajar from power. For many Baloch analysts, this support was the essence of Qajar hatred towards the Baloch. To confront the Ismaili challenge, a formidable contingent of the Qajar army was permanently stationed at Kerman. This army in 1843 moved eastward and occupied Bampur, the main fortress in Western Balochistan (Watson, 1866). From their base in Bampur, military expeditions were periodically mounted into the surrounding regions in order to chase or disperse the Baloch tribes allied with the Agha Khan.

In one of the tragic events of the Baloch–Persian conflict of that time, foreseeing an imminent defeat from the Persians under the command of Habibullah Shahsevan, the Baloch killed their women before charging toward the Persian artillery positions. This was to prevent their women folk coming into hands of Persian soldiers. In the subsequent hand to hand battle, hundreds of the Baloch and Persians were killed (Watson, 1866). Later, the Persians arrested 3,700 Baloch from the surrounding regions of Bampur and sold them into slavery.

The Baloch were fighting the might of Persians in a very disorganized and divided way, while Persian officials were steadily working on a strategy of playing local rulers one against another, with the aim of reducing the authority of those leaders and establishing their own as far as possible. Sykes (1902) observed that Persian officials effectively exploited the differences between various Baloch chiefs of the Makuran and Sarhad regions. They successfully pursued a policy of encouraging the local *Hakoms* (rulers) to compete for formal titles in return for the obligation to levy and remit annual taxes. One by one, Baloch chiefs of Dezzak, Sarbaz, Geh, and Kasarkand acknowledged the obligation to pay taxes to the Persian governor. The resistance from the ruler of Sib Mir Muhammad Ali was overcome by a strong Persian contingent sent from Kerman in 1856 and the relatively solid Fort at Sib was occupied after a fierce battle (Sykes, 1902). The Persians successfully exploited differences between Mir Abdullah Khan Buladai of Geh who controlled the coast from Jask to Chahbar, and Mir Din Muhammad Sardarzai in Bahau who, besides Dashtyari, controlled the coast from Chahbar to Gwadar. In southern Sistan, the Persians occupied the Sarhad region by defeating Sardar Said Khan Kurd, who was the chief of Baloch tribes in Sarhad and was based in Khwash (Sykes, 1902). During 1888, a Persian force crushed the resistance of Yarahmadzai tribe in Sarhad. Persian officials continued their harassment and humiliation of the Baloch, and in 1891, several Baloch leaders of Sarhad were treacherously seized and detained for several years (Sykes, 1902).

DIVISION OF BALOCHISTAN

Beginning in the 18th century and continuing into the 19th century, a high-profile diplomatic and espionage game was played out in Central Asia between Russia and Britain. This was in order to protect their colonial interests in Central Asia and the Middle East. It brought negative consequences for many small states and nationalities in the region. The occupation and subsequent division of Balochistan was one such consequence. During the second half of 19th century, the Baloch land was formally divided, with the signing of various agreements between the British, Persians and Afghans. Ironically, the Baloch State of Kalat which was a protectorate of the United Kingdom after its occupation in 1839, was not consulted, nor were its views ever considered in the process of the demarcation of its new boundaries.

Afghanistan and Iran were viewed by the British as the vulnerable spots from where any Russian advance could proceed towards the warm waters of the Indian Ocean, posing a direct threat to the precious British possession of India. The Russo-French Agreement of Tilsit signed in 1808, prompted the British authorities to increase their efforts in securing an alliance with the Persians. This was in order to dissuade them from joining hostile alliances against the British interests in Middle East and Central Asia (Janmahmad, 1989). A stick and carrot approach was adopted in dealing with the Persians to gain their allegiance, so that the Persian border became the final defensive line against any further Russian advance (Dickson, 1924). On the one hand, the British forces in the Gulf were used to frighten Qajar rulers and on the other hand, the British extended financial and diplomatic support to a politically weak and financially bankrupt dynasty. The stabilization of Afghanistan was also an important component of the British policy in stopping Russian advances towards warm waters of the Indian Ocean. As a part of strategies to make Afghanistan a viable state, the Persian Government was pressurized to cede control of Herat and Sistan to Afghanistan. With these territories, Afghanistan would have been in a geographical position to serve as a buffer between the British India and Russia. In the grinding actions of the two most powerful imperialist states of 19th century in their 'great game' in Central Asia, Balochistan became finely minced as it lost its independence and was divided into many parts.

The Russian encroachments on Persian territory began in the time of Czar Peter the Great when their forces occupied Gilan in 1724. A series of wars beginning in 1796 and lasting until 1828, with the signing of two treaties, the Treaty of Gulistan in 1813 and the Treaty of Turkomanchai. This resulted in the loss of Persian territories of Mingrelia, Karabagh, Shirvan, Derbent, Baku, Erivan, and Nakhichivan to Russia. Lenczowski (1949), observed that with conclusions of these treaties, the Qajar dynasty accepted the Russian supremacy and the Russians assumed the role of protector of the dynasty. This was totally unacceptable to the British. Lord Daniel Nathalie Curzon who was a viceroy of India and also served as Foreign Minister of the Great Britain described 19th century Persia as pieces on a chessboard upon which is being played out a game for the domination of the world. Thus maintenance of Persia as a buffer state became one of Britain's basic objectives in the Middle East during 19th and 20th centuries. The British influence was much increased in Persia with the employment of an effective policy of stick and carrot towards weak Qajar rulers. In 1872, Persia granted a British subject Baron Julius de Reuter the right to build railways, found a bank and collect revenue for twenty years. Curzon jubilantly described the event as total surrender of the entire industrial resources of a kingdom into foreign hands. With British manipulation, Qajar Persia virtually became a buffer between Russia and the Great Britain. The British took it upon themselves to compensate for the territories which Persia ceded to Russia, Afghanistan and Turkey. They selected the western regions of Balochistan for handing over to Persia. The architect of the division of Balochistan, Major General Goldsmid, supporting Persian claims on the Baloch land on the grounds that Persia had been losing territory to Russia in the north, to the Ottomans in the west, and to Afghanistan in the east, thus the only avenue left for her was to expand in the southeast. He identified Western Balochistan, where the constant feud between the Baloch tribal chiefs had made that land as an easy prey to the Persian designs of expansion (Goldsmid, 1873).

The ultimate loser in the 'great game,' from a Baloch point of view was the Baloch state of Khanate of Kalat, which was not only occupied but divided into different parts. Some of the Baloch territories were ceded to Afghanistan and nearly half of the Baloch land was awarded to Persia. During 1871, the British agreed to the Persian proposal for the division of Balochistan by officially demarcating a boundary line separating the British and Persian areas of influence in Balochistan (Goldsmid, 1873). The border between the Khanate of Kalat and Persia was demarcated under Makran Boundary Commission (1870–1871) and Perso-Baloch Boundary Commission (1896). The Baloch areas of Sistan were allocated to Persia and Afghanistan under the two Sistan Arbitration Commissions of 1872 and 1903. The final demarcation of Sistan occurred in 1904 by the British Commissioner, Sir Henry McMahon. The line approved by Sir Henry McMahon was the extension of Durand Line, and it demarcated the Baloch–Afghan border. The McMahon Line covers an area from Chaman in the east to the Perso–Baloch border in the west near Taftan.

Major General Goldsmid was appointed as the chief commissioner of the Makran Boundary Commission which was formed in 1870 in order to divide Southern Balochistan. The boundary between Persia and the Khanate of Kalat which was subsequently drawn on the recommendations of the commission, became known as the Goldsmid Line. Delimitation of the boundary began from a point east of Guattar up to Kuhak (Mojtahed-Zadeh, 1995). On September 1, 1871, the British minister at Tehran conveyed the details of the Perso–Baloch boundaries to the Persian authorities for acceptance in a memorandum, which partly read that:

> *"The undersigned, Her Britannic Majesty's Envoy Extraordinary and Minister Plenipotentiary at the Court of Persia, acting on the part of his Government, has the honour to submit, for the approval of His Majesty the Shah, a map in which the boundary line between the territories possessed in Belochistan by Persia, and the territories forming the exclusive property of the independent State of Khelat, is delineated."*

> *"This line may be thus described: Commencing from the northernmost point, or that which is furthest from the sea, the territory of Khelat is bounded to the west by the large Persian District of Dizzuk, which is composed of many Dehs or minor Districts, those on the frontier being Jalk and Kallegan. Below these two last-named is the small District of Kohuk, which, together with Punjgur, comprising Parum and other dependencies, is on the Khelat side of the frontier, while on the Persian side is Bampusht."*

> *"Below Punjgur, the frontier, possessions of Khelat to the sea are Boleida, including Zamiran and other dependencies, Mund and Dusht. Withing the Persian line of frontier are the*

villages or tracts belonging to Sirbaz and Bahu Dustyari. The boundary of Dusht is marked by a long line drawn through the Drabol hill situated between the Rivers Bahu and Dusht, to the sea in the Bay of Gwuttur."

"to summarise: Punjgur and Parum and other dependencies with Kohuk; Boleida, including Zamiran and other dependencies; Mund, including Tump, Nasserabad, Kedj, and all Districts, dehs and dependencies to the eastward; Dusht with its dependencies as far as the sea: these names exhibit the line of actual possession of Khelat, that is to say, all tracts to the east of the frontier of actual Persian possession, which frontier comprises Dizzuk and Bampusht, Sirbaz, Pishin, Bahu and Dustyari" (Mojtahed-Zadeh, 1995, p. 78).

The Goldsmid line was accepted by Persia while the helpless Baloch state of Kalat mutely protested about the division of its land. Another boundary commission in the name of the Perso-Baloch Frontier Delimitation Commission was formed in 1895 with Sir Thomas Holdich as the chief commissioner. This commission in 1896 formally awarded Kuhak, Kenarbasteh, Esfandak, and areas to the west of Mashkhel River to the Persians (Baloch, 1987). The Sistan Arbitration Commission (1872) with Major General Goldsmid being the chief commissioner produced boundary lines dividing Sistan into outer and proper Sistan. Outer Sistan was awarded to Afghanistan while Sistan proper was given to Persia (Goldsmid, 1873), while "Baloch-Afghan Boundary Commission," instituted in 1895 with Sir Henry McMahon as the commissioner finalized the Baloch–Afghan border in 1896 (Baloch, 1987).

Arbitrarily drawn boundary lines completed the division of Balochistan into Persian and Afghan parts and a truncated Khanate of Kalat as a British protectorate. Under the boundary commissions, Khanate lost almost all its territories in Sistan to Afghanistan and Persia. Western Makuran and many parts of Sarhad and Sistan proper became parts of Iran. The Baloch areas of Nemroz, Outer Sistan and Registan were incorporated into Afghanistan.

TELEGRAPH LINE BECAME THE LINE OF DEATH

The Baloch also faced the anger of the British and Qajar's because of a telegraph line which was to link British India with Europe through Balochistan and Persia. Disturbances created by the Baloch on the construction of the line and the security of the telegraph line from Karachi to Basra passing through Southern Balochistan was another important factor for the division of Balochistan.

The Baloch resistance against the Persians and the British manifested itself in sporadic raids on camps of surveyors and other instalments of the Telegraph line. On several occasions, British officials were attacked and killed by groups of the Baloch, with the tacit endorsement of their chiefs. The British retaliation on the other hand was out of proportions. In November 1897, Mr. Graves, an intelligence officer attached with Indo-European Telegraph project was killed in Karawan region. In 1898, as a consequence of his murder, a massive invasion of southern Balochistan was launched by the British. Forces were sent from India, and stationed at Chahbar and Jask (Spooner, 1988). This British attack was with implicit approval of Persian authorities. A ruthless and bloody campaign was launched, and hundreds of the Baloch were killed and many of their settlements burnt during 1898 (Curzon, 1966). Another campaign in Magas and Erafshan areas caused huge destruction and casualties among the Baloch (Saldanha, 1905). Wynn (2003), mentioned that the expeditionary force also burnt several villages in Karawan region. The leader of the expedition Percy Sykes threatened the Baloch elders of Minaab, Panouch and Bashkard that he would make a tower with their heads if they did not surrender unconditionally and hand over persons wanted by the British.

In the absence of any central leadership to lead the Baloch in Western Balochistan, the Baloch resistance turned into a general uprising against Persians and the British. In 1897, Sardar Hussain Khan attacked Fahraj (Sykes, 1902) and led a general rebellion against the Persian Government in Sarhad, Sarawan, and Bampur. Several Baloch groups joined the revolt. It spread to Sarbaz, Dezzak, Laashaar, and Bamposhth. Sardar Hussain Khan occupied Bampur, Fahraj, and Bazman and other places, which had small Iranian garrisons, and controlled most of the northern part of the province. The Baloch forces defeated a large Persian army sent from Kerman to re-establish the Persian order in 1897 (Sykes, 1902).

THE EMERGENCE OF THE BARAKZAI CHIEFDOM

The general uprising in Western Balochistan during last years of the 19th century ended with the agreement that recognized Sardar Hussain Khan as the ruler of Baloch areas in southern Balochistan under the Persian sovereignty. In return, the Baloch leader acknowledged the claim made by Persians on Baloch territories. This was the beginning of a semi-sovereign Baloch chiefdom in Western Balochistan.

On the death of Sardar Hussain Khan in 1907, his son Sardar Sayyad Khan and the Barakzai chief Mir Bahram Khan tried to consolidate their power in Western Balochistan by asserting control on Geh, Benth, Kasarkand, Sarbaz, Bampur, and Fahraj (Sykes, 1902). However, under increased military pressure from Persians, Sardar Sayyad Khan later submitted to Persian authorities by accepting the title of *Sardar-e-Nizam*. The Persians recognized him as the nominal ruler of the region. While Mir Bahram Khan refused to submit, he rallied Baloch tribal chiefs, and became the actual authority in Western Balochistan. An army was sent from Kerman against the rising power of Mir Bahram Khan in 1910 (Spooner, 1988). The Persians, however, failed to overcome the Baloch resistance and retreated without achieving any objective. This event improved the credentials of Mir Bahram Khan among the Baloch and paved the way for the establishment of a short-lived Barakzai chiefdom in Western Balochistan.

Based in Bampur, the Barakzai family ruled the first Baloch chiefdom in Western Balochistan with the semblance of a semi-autonomous state for nearly three decades. Mir Bahram Khan in his efforts to confront the alliance of Persians and the British sought the help of a religious leader Khalifa Khair Muhammad of Karawan. Several of the Baloch fighters impressed by speeches of Khalifa, organized themselves into groups of *Mureeds* (followers). They frequently harassed the Persian security forces and the staff of the British Indo-European Telegraph Line. Mir Bahram Khan also raided the British-controlled Kech valley of eastern Makuran. In order to safeguard its growing interests in the region and to neutralize the emerging threat of Mir Bahram Khan, the British recognized the authority of Mir Bahram Khan over the Baloch territories in Western Balochistan by signing a treaty with him. It was mainly for the security of the Indo-European Telegraph Line. The British political agent Colonel Dew signed this agreement in 1916 (Sykes, 1902).

The history of the Baloch and Qajar is one of the bloodiest in the Baloch memory. The Baloch resistance against advances of Qajar was not successful despite the sacrifices of thousands of ordinary Baloch and the tribal chiefs and *Hakoms* from different regions in Western Balochistan. It was sporadic, disorganized, and without a central leadership. In the absence of any united and organized resistance, tribal chiefs, *Hakoms* and regions fought against the Qajar on their own. Another reason for the failure of the resistance was because during this period, the mighty power of the British Empire, was directly and indirectly with Qajar rulers of Iran. With the advent of the British on the Baloch scene in the second half of 19th century, the pressure on the Baloch tribes of Western Balochistan increased as combined Qajar and British forces tried to subdue the Baloch resistance. The Khanate of Kalat was facing a period of degeneration under British domination. The Khan acting on behalf of the British, serving only the British interests in the region. Such was the ineptitude of the Khanate that even the Baloch delegation was not allowed to participate in deliberation for the demarcation of a boundary between the Baloch state and Persia.

The division of Balochistan during the final decades of 19ᵗʰ century brought far reaching consequences for the Baloch. The British policy of appeasement toward Persia against Russian advances, their obsession for establishing Afghanistan and Persia as viable buffer states, together with the protection of Indo-European Telegraph Line were immediate causative factors in the division of Balochistan. This division caused tremendous geographical, political, cultural, social and psychological consequences for the Baloch. For many Baloch nationalists, the permanent division of their land is one of the causes of the Baloch national resistance being so ineffective against Persia and Pakistan in modern times.

The Qajar era in Persia was one of the most eventful for the Baloch in Western Balochistan. Thousands of them were killed, many of their settlements were destroyed, thousands were sold into slavery and many were forcibly displaced. However, in the context of the Baloch national struggle, the division of Balochistan and the beginning of the formation of semi-autonomous Barakzai chiefdom were the most important developments in the history of Western Balochistan. With a long history of bloodshed, antipathy between the Persians and the Baloch is clearly evident even to this day. The word Qajar became a term of abuse and the abusive term Qajar became synonymous with all Persians in Baloch vocabulary. It is believed that Qajar are responsible for the development of enduring political, social and cultural animosity between the Baloch and the Persians after the bitterness developed during Sassanid Era. The Baloch detest Persians almost as strongly as they are detested by them.

CHAPTER 5

THE BALOCH NATIONAL STRUGGLE AGAINST PAHLAVI REGIME

During the turmoil preceding the fall of Qajar dynasty in Iran, the confrontation between the Baloch and the joint forces of Britain and Persia continued into 20th century. During the anarchic period from early 19th century, with the agitation against the Qajar rule in Persia, the Baloch chiefdom headed by the Barakzai clan in Bampur was gaining ground and asserting its authority on the surrounding regions of Western Balochistan. While Baloch were basking in the glow of their newly acquired independence after the dark period of Qajar domination, things changed following the advent of the Pahlavi regime. The installation of Reza Khan as the new ruler of Persia changed dynamics of the Baloch-Persian relations. Persia soon invaded Balochistan, suppressed the resistance in Sarhad and occupied the Barakzai chiefdom in Bampur. A vigorous state policy of assimilation of the Baloch into the Persian national identity was initiated. After the collapse of Barakzai chiefdom, nature of the Baloch resistance in Iran also changed, and a kind of national liberation struggle was initiated by the Baloch under the banner of the Balochistan Liberation Front. At the time of the collapse of Pahlavi regime, Baloch masses in Western Balochistan were by and large mobilized in a way which was unprecedented in the history of the Baloch resistance in Iran.

THE FALL OF BARAKZAI CHIEFDOM

During years preceding the fall of Qajar dynasty, while Iran was in chaos; the Baloch chiefdom in Bampur consolidated its foundations. After the death of Mir Bahram Khan in 1921, his nephew Mir Dost Muhammad Barakzai became the ruler of the state and took some measures to strengthen its administration and gave a semblance of a nascent state to his chiefdom by appointing administrators, revenue collectors, and *Hakoms* (rulers) for different regions of Western Balochistan (Sykes, 1902). He also tried to establish relations with the Khan of the Baloch at Kalat, Sultan of Muscat and Oman, and king of Afghanistan. Attempts were also made to establish contact with the newly established revolutionary government in Russia (Janmahmad, 1987). By forging alliances with the powerful ruling families in the different principalities of Western Balochistan, he also consolidated his power base and grip on the chiefdom.

In February 1921 Reza Khan, an officer in the Iranian Cossack Division, with the help of British mission, captured political power in Tehran. In 1925, after finally overthrowing the Qajar dynasty, he declared himself 'Shah of Iran' changing his name to Reza Khan Pahlavi, claiming his ancestry to the ancient Pahlavi rulers of Iran. He also changed the name of his country from Persia to Iran. Iran was occupied by the Allied Powers during the Second World War. In 1944, Reza Khan was forced by them to abdicate. They were suspicious about his loyalties; however, the Pahlavi dynasty continued with his son Muhammad Reza Pahlavi who was installed as the new king of Iran. The dynasty ended in 1979 as a result of the rise to power by the Ayatollahs (Ayatollahs are highest among the hierarchy of the clergy in the Shiite sect of Islam and are believed to be expert on all earthly and heavenly matters).

Reza Khan after assuming power, embarked upon an ambitious program of nation building and territorial unification. One by one, the Persian army occupied all regions, which became partly independent from central authority or on the verge of declaring independence from Persia. After subjugating Gilan in 1921,

Kurdistan in 1922, Luristan in 1924 and Khuzistan in 1925, he turned his attention towards Balochistan. The situation changed for the newly independent Baloch chiefdom as Reza Khan began exploring strategies to bring the Baloch areas west of Goldsmid Line under Persian control (Baloch, 1987). In 1927, the Persian Government gave an ultimatum to the ruler of the Baloch chiefdom Mir Dost Muhammad Barakzai to accept the sovereignty of Persia (Sykes, 1902). This he refused and anticipating a Persian attack, began to improve his fortifications, building and strengthening the network of alliances he had established over the whole of Western Balochistan with ruling chiefs. He also activated religious leaders among the Baloch to mobilize them on Sunni and Shia sectarian grounds. This had been a new but useful tool of exploiting Perso-Baloch religious differences and for mobilizing the Baloch masses against the Persian hegemony (Baloch are overwhelmingly Sunni and Persians belonging to Shia sect of Islam).

The Persian army, under the command of General Amir Amanullah Jahanbani, began their advance on Balochistan in 1928 (Sykes, 1902). There began a bloody war of attrition between the Baloch and Persians which lasted for a year, resulting in the murder of thousands of the Baloch and the permanent occupation of their newly emergent chiefdom. The heroic resistance of the Baloch denied any immediate victory for the overwhelming Persian army. Fierce battles were fought between Persians and the Baloch in different regions. Persians had to fight for every fort in Western Balochistan. The Baloch resistance, however, weakened considerably with the use of air power by Persians. The Persian commander Jahanbani was astounded to see the fierce resistance of the Baloch in the face of overwhelming artillery and air superiority of his army. Observing the resistance of the Baloch during a fight for a small fort, he observed that:

> *"I was wondering how a much smaller rebellion force had the courage of resisting an army corps equipped with machine-guns and artilleries and even had no concern of being surrounded! What was their motive, personal and collective*

feelings to reach that level of bravery and self-sacrifice? Whether such a resistance was to show their valour or was the result of their defective minds and their ignorance about the rule of war? In my opinion the reason for such a futile and madly resistance was the hearing of the historical legends narrated by old people who always ridiculed the Iranian army forces very often coming to Balochistan, staying for a while, facing the Baloch resistance in their great and invincible forts, suffering high casualties and going back hopelessly while the ones with greater courage would have stayed longer until facing the hot summer and then vacated Balochistan in a deplorable condition" (Jahanbani, 1929: page 99, 100).

Comparing the Baloch fighting spirit with that of Russians, Jahanbani pointed out that it was a great surprise that a small number of Baloch fighters, who had been surrounded and suffered heavy casualties, repeatedly dared to deceive us and resist our far superior power, while hundreds of thousands of the Russian Army in the Tannenberg war fields after being surrounded and losing their morale, had no will and yielded their weapons when ordered by a single German soldier. Jahanbani thought that the refusal of the Baloch to surrender despite being surrounded by the mighty Persian army and with no hope of any victory was because the Baloch, have from childhood, been familiar and friendly with their guns, the Baloch and guns were always together, their separation was known as impossible, they love their guns as much as their lives and losing it is a great shame for them. However, the massive use of artillery and air force was no match with the primitive arms of the Baloch despite the show of extra ordinary courage and spirit in resisting the Persian onslaught.

The Baloch chiefdom collapsed because it was no match for the power of Persian state. The spirit to fight and resist are not important in modern warfare. The Baloch chiefdom lacked the structural and organizational capacity to withstand a modern army with limitless resources, artillery, and air power. Mir Dost Muhammad Khan Barakzai did not have enough time to consolidate his authority over an inherently divided tribal society where local *Hakoms* were liable to defect to powerful forces. His failure to make any connection with powerful tribes of Sarhad region was exploited by Persians to their advantage. Lack of any external support, the desertion of some Baloch *Hakoms* to the Persian side, lack of supply provisions for the besieged contingents in different forts, and lack of modern weaponry were factors which forced Mir Dost Muhammad Khan Barakzai to surrender after many months of struggle to preserve the independence of the Baloch chiefdom. He was detained in Tehran and after a year's detention, was tried and hanged by the Persian authorities in 1931 (Naseer, 1979).

RESISTANCE IN SARHAD

During the early years of 20th century, while the Baloch chiefdom in Bampur was struggling to consolidate its power base in Southern Balochistan, various Baloch tribes in Sarhad and Sistan regions were resisting Persian encroachments. In Sarhad, there was an ongoing resistance by Ghamshadzai, Yarahmadzai, and Esmailzai tribes against the Persians. However, the situation changed for the worse for the Baloch during First World War. The German attempts to create trouble for the Allied Powers in Iran were blown out of all proportion by British intelligence. They began reporting increased activities of German agents among Baloch tribes of Sarhad and Sistan and submitted reports of financial and military support for the Baloch by Germans. Although, these were not substantiated, rumours were sufficient to force the British authorities in Iran and India to take countermeasures. In order to forestall any German political or military advance in the region during the War, the British sent an expeditionary force under the command of General Dyer to deal with the Baloch resistance in Sarhad. At this time, Sardar Khalil Khan Ghamshadzai held the area around Jalk and Safed Koh, while Sardar Jiand Khan Yarahmadzai who was also the nominal head of the confederacy of the Baloch tribes of Sarhad, controlled areas west of Safed Koh.

Areas west of Khwash were under the control of Sardar Juma Khan Esmailzai. In a prolonged campaign, General Dyer and the Persian forces succeeded in defeating Baloch forces and crushing the Baloch resistance in 1920 (Dyre, 1921). The Baloch in Sarhad again rose in rebellion in 1925, but were overcome by Persian authorities in 1926 (Aitchison, 1865). From then onwards, the resistance against the Persians was only manifested by intermittent outbreaks of disorder in this part of Balochistan until the late 1930s. A rebellion of Sardar Juma Khan Esmailzai was crushed in 1931, and another uprising in Kuhak was defeated in 1938 with much bloodshed by the Persian Army under the command of General Alborz (Baloch, 1987).

With the joint efforts of the British and Persians, the Baloch resistance in Sarhad region was crushed. A reign of terror prevailed in the region and valiant chiefs such as Sardar Jiand Khan Yarahmadzai and Sardar Khalil Khan Ghamshadzai were eliminated from the scene. General Dyer and his successor General Tanner together with the Persian forces were successful in getting rid of 'the trouble' created by the Baloch tribes. Khwash, the headquarters of the Baloch resistance in Sarhad, was occupied by the British troops, and a strong military outpost was established to deter any future rebellion by the Baloch or any German activity in the region. The Barakzai chiefdom was occupied and there prevailed a period of generalized frustration throughout Western Balochistan. The Persian grip became even stronger over the Baloch with the introduction of various administrative measures. The Pahlavi dynasty began a process of cultural imperialism and embarked upon a campaign of assimilating the Baloch into the Persian national identity by implementing their plan of creating an artificial ethno-demographic unification of Iran.

RESURGENCE OF THE BALOCH RESISTANCE

It took many years for the Baloch to overcome material losses and psychological traumas which they suffered during the confrontations in the early period of Pahlavi dynasty. For a time, it appeared that the Baloch had lost their will to resist in Western Balochistan and they totally surrendered to the Persians. However, later events suggested that it is very hard to measure the resilient power of the Baloch. Soon they began to formulate strategies and a new phase of the Baloch resistance in Iran began which was more organized and along with traditional tribal leadership of the Baloch, a new element of middle class political activists joined ranks with the political and armed resistance. This phase of the Baloch national struggle in Iran was marked with the formation of an armed resistance organization-the Balochistan Liberation Front (BLF).

DAD SHAH EPISODE: THE QUEST FOR A HERO

In the context of the Baloch national struggle in Western Balochistan, the description of the Dad Shah Phenomenon is important, as it has been a controversial and much debated topic among the nationalist circles for a long time. For some, it was a story of typical Baloch personal vendetta while for many other, it became a symbol of resistance against the Persians and their allies in Western Balochistan.

Dad Shah probably born in 1914 was a resident of village Dan e Bed in Thoothan region of Nillag or Safed Koh. His father, Kamal, was the village elder or *Kahoda* having a small land holding in the village. Dad Shah, his two brothers and one cousin were among the 200 *lankbands* (volunteer soldiers) of Shirani chief Ali Khan Shirani, who was the *Hakom* or administrator of a region starting from Panouch and surrounding areas up to Laashaar region and Kerman. Dad Shah was reputed to be a sharp shooter and one of the best among the *lankbands* of Shirani chief. Ali Khan Shirani used high handed tactics in collecting revenues for the Persian government and was not a popular figure among the masses as well as among the Baloch tribal elite.

Because of a land dispute, Dad Shah's family developed some enmity with Abdul Nabi of Bunshore village and Din Muhammad Shayhak of Zurrati village. Ali Khan Shirani sided with Dad Shah's opponents, this resulted in the family members of Dad Shah leaving his service. However, the wanderings of Dad Shah began in 1943 when he murdered his wife after accusing her of illicit sexual affairs. He also went to Muscat and killed a young person Lalak, who was from his village and living in Muscat following the murder of Dad Shah's wife (Lalak was accused of have sexual relations with Dad Shah's wife). Ali Khan Shirani with the help of Khuda Dad Khan Reki, a Baloch officer of gendarmerie, tried to arrest Dad Shah on murder charges after his return from Muscat. Khuda Dad Khan Reki reportedly burned the date-farm of Dad Shah which further infuriated him and he began to attack the relatives and supporters of the Shirani chief. With the murder of Ali Khan's Cousin, Mirza Khan, an all-out confrontation began between supporters of Ali Khan Shirani and Dad Shah and his family.

At the time of Dad Shah Episode, the southern regions of Western Balochistan were administered on behalf of Pahlavi regime by various Baloch tribal chiefs or *Hakoms*. Haji Islam Khan Mubariki was the *Hakom* of Aahorran; Ali Khan Shirani was *Hakom* of Panouch and Benth; Sardar Zaman Khan Bamari was the *Hakom* of Bazman and Dalgan; Sardar Abdi Khan Sardarzai was the *Hakom* of Dashtyari; Mirza s/o Barkat was the *Hakom* of Giaban; Mir Hothi Khan was the Mir (chief) of Laashaar and Mohammad Omar Khan s/o Dost Muhammad Baraanzai was the leading figure in Bampur. All of these *Hakoms* were always busy conspiring against each other in order to weaken the other in their bid to gain greater attention from the Iranian authorities. Some of them were also involved in long standing blood feuds. Dad Shah's family was easily given protection by Mir (chief) of Laashaar as Laashaaris and Shiranis were not in good terms. This was because Nawab Khan Mubariki and Haji Ali Khan Mubariki were believed to have been murdered with the involvement of Sardar Abdi Khan Sardarzai, a close ally of Shirani tribe.

It is generally believed that acting from his secure base in Laashaar region, Dad Shah and his group killed nearly 200 people during 14 years of his conflict with Ali Khan Shirani and his supporters or affiliated families. In 1957, Dad Shah decided to shift his family members from Laashaar to Eastern Balochistan or perhaps in Karachi (Pakistan). His brother Ahmad Shah was crossing the border into Pakistan along with the women and children of the family when a mishap occurred which caused the end of Dad Shah. On March 26, 1957, near Tank e Sar, Dad Shah ambushed a convey carrying an American family attached to an aid project in Western Balochistan, mistakenly taking it as a detachment of Gendarmerie following him and his family members. Two Americans Kevin Karl, Anita Karl and a Persian guard Shams were killed. (According to some accounts which could not be verified by reliable sources, three Americans: Kevin Karl, Anita Karl, and Wilson along with two Iranians were killed). The incidence caused a diplomatic uproar in Tehran as the Iranian government came under tremendous pressure from the US government to apprehend the murderers of American citizens. It is said that one of the factors in the resignation of then Iranian Prime Minister, Hussain Ala, was this incident. Iranian authorities gave an ultimatum to the Laashaari tribe to deliver Dad Shah and his group to them, as they believed that Laashaaris are protecting him and his gang members. Ahmad Shah and other family members of Dad Shah were arrested by Pakistani authorities when they entered Eastern Balochistan and later were delivered to Iranian authorities.

The political rivalry and personal vendetta of various tribal chiefs now became a factor in the Dad Shah Phenomenon. According to supporters and relatives of Laashaari chief, the onus for handing over Dad Shah to the authorities was shifted to the Laashaari tribe because of the intrigues of Shirani, Sardarzai and Buledai chiefs. They believed that on the instigation of Haji Karim Bakhsh Saeedi, who was the head of Buledai tribe and a prominent political figure of Iranian Balochistan, the Persian Government pressurized the Laashaari chief to deliver Dad Shah to them. Saeedi was in family relations with Ali Khan Shirani and was the political opponent of Laashaari and Mubariki families. Although, the family members of Karim Bakhsh Saeedi strongly denied his involvement in any way in Dad Shah Affair; nevertheless, Laashaari sources were persistent in their claim that it was because of manipulations of an alliance of the Sardarzai, Buledai, Reki and Shirani tribal elders which was responsible for the sufferings of the Laashaari and Mubariki families.

To put pressure on Laashaari tribe, the administration arrested nearly all notables of Laashaari and Mubariki tribes including Mir Issa Khan a known Baloch bureaucrat, Mir Mohim Khan, who became the Mir of Laashaar after the death of his father, Haji Alam Khan, Haji Islam Khan, Karim Khan, Haji Mirza Khan, and Ayub Khan. With the mediations of Assadullah Alam, the court minister and General Amanullah Jahanbani (commander of Iranian forces which invaded Balochistan in 1928), Issa Khan was reportedly given an audience with Shah of Iran in which the Shah asked him to deliver Dad Shah to authorities in whatever way possible, otherwise, the consequences would not be good for the personal security of his family members. On the agreement that Laashaar elders would do their best to persuade Dad Shah to surrender to the authorities, Mir Mohim Khan and others were released from prison.

After their release, the Laashaari elders began their efforts to persuade Dad Shah to surrender and Dad Shah consented to meet a delegation of Laashaari tribal elders headed by Mir Muhammad Khan, the younger brother of Mir Laashaar. Members of the delegation included Perry Jiand, Shambe Jan Muhammad, Karim Bakhsh, Haji Dad Khuda Aziz, Din Muhammad Perry, Yar Muhammad, dad Muhammad, and Shimmel Kadir. After a prolonged discussion, Dad Shah refused to surrender on the grounds that he did not believe that the Persian authorities would show any leniency towards him. However, Mir Muhammad Khan convinced Dad Shah to meet his brother, Mir Mohim Khan, the Mir of Laashaar.

In the first meeting between Mir Mohim Khan and Dad Shah at Hasht Koh near Aab Gah, Dad Shah insisted on the release of his brother and other family members from prison in Tehran as a precondition for his surrender which Mir Mohim Khan promised to convey to the authorities. Although, there was no positive response from Iranian authorities to this demand; nevertheless, Mir Laashaar continued his efforts to persuade Dad Shah to surrender. In the final meeting, the situation became tense as Dad Shah out rightly refused to surrender while Mir Mohim Khan was insistent. When it became apparent that the meeting had failed to deliver anything, Dad Shah tried to capture the Persian driver, Mahmoodi who accompanied Mir Mohim Khan's delegation. Dad Shah tried to take the Persian hostage in exchange for the release of his family members. On this, the situation took an ugly turn. Mir Mohim Khan fired and killed Dad Shah. Meanwhile, Dad Shah's brother Muhammad Shah and others who were hiding on a nearby hilltop opened fire on the delegates, killing all except Muhammad Omar Khan and Khuda Bakhsh, and the Persian official Mirza Hassan Yadgari. Muhammad Shah himself was also killed by a wounded Mir Mohim Khan. Another version of the incident is that Mir Mohim Khan believed that Dad Shah is not in any way going to surrender, he opened fire and killed him in the beginning of the meeting. The surviving members of Dad Shah's group scattered into the surrounding regions and some went to the gulf countries. His younger brother Ahmad Shah was hanged in Tehran.

A significant section of the Baloch political activists both in Pakistan and Iran, tried to portray Dad Shah's activities as part of their national resistance against Persians as he targeted supporters and allies of the Iranian state in Western Balochistan. The Baloch in Pakistan organized rallies to pressurize the Pakistani authorities not to handover Ahmad Shah and other family members of Dad Shah to Iran. The cause of Ahmad Shah was also taken up by National Awami Party and the 'Save Ahmad Shah Committee' also filed a petition in the Supreme Court of Pakistan in Dhaka. Over a period of time, Dad Shah gained the status of a national resistance hero which the Baloch political activists needed in order to galvanize their efforts against Persian atrocities and aggressions. However, many among nationalist circles were of the firm opinion that an episode which began purely as a personal and family dispute and which was later used by rival tribal elite in their own interests must not be recognized as part of the Baloch national resistance. However, it is certain that these opposing views regarding the nationalist credentials of Dad Shah will continue for some time.

THE ARMED RESISTANCE OF BALOCHISTAN LIBERATION FRONT

After the collapse of Barakzai chiefdom of Bampur and the crushing of the Baloch resistance in Sarhad by Pahlavi regime, a new phase of organized Baloch resistance began under the banner of a clandestine organization, the Balochistan Liberation Front (BLF) in the 1960s. This resistance was different from previous ones in many ways and attracted the attention of a large segment of the Baloch society.

BLF's strategies included a total dependence on armed struggle and actively seeking external support for the Baloch Cause. Depending only on armed struggle was a rejection of classical way of developing a national liberation struggle (The prerequisite of an armed resistance in classical definitions has been the mobilization of masses in order to raise their political awareness). During 1960s and early years of 1970s, the Baloch resistance against Iran by BLF got some kind of support from the revolutionary regime of Baath Party in Iraq. That was in response to Iran's interference in affairs of Iraqi Kurdistan, where Iranians were believed to support Kurdish rebels in their activities against Iraq. The Iraqi support for the Baloch was also to find allies in the region in the wake of the announced British withdrawal east of Suez in 1968. Iran was seen, by the Arab nationalist regime in Iraq, as the major rival for influence in the gulf and an ally of imperialist forces in the Middle East. In their efforts to counter Iranian influence in the region, Iraqis supported various nationalist and anti-Shah movements in Iran to weaken the Persian state internally. Iraqi support for the Baloch resistance in Western Balochistan was in line with this Iraqi policy and the clandestine Balochistan Liberation Front was extended comprehensive support. This backing included the supplying arms and ammunition, providing military training to Baloch volunteers, and extending financial and publicity assistance to the Baloch resistance. Baghdad Radio began to broadcast Balochi programs, propagating the Baloch point of view and highlighting the plight of the Baloch in Iran. Several Baloch tribal chiefs and political activists affiliated with BLF were based in Baghdad directing the resistance from exile. Prominent among these included Mir Abdi Khan, Mir Moosa Khan, Akber Barakzai, Mir Jumma Khan and Abdussamad Amiri. Baloch youths recieved basic guerrilla tactics and training for armed insurgency from Iraqi army instructors. The armed resistance under the banner of Balochistan Liberation Front (BLF) engaged a vast number of Iranian forces mainly in southern Balochistan in guerrilla activities.

With increased armed encounters between the volunteers of BLF and the Persian security forces, the Pahlavi regime reacted with more repressive measures against the Baloch. Various military garrisons were established throughout Balochistan. The Baloch port of Chahbar was converted into a naval base. Believing that BLF volunteers might get sanctuary and assistance from their Baloch brothers in Eastern Balochistan, increased cooperation between Iran and Pakistan occurred, in order to coordinate the efforts of both countries against the Baloch resistance. Both countries were convinced that the resistance in Western Balochistan was part of the struggle for a greater Balochistan. A map was widely publicized by security establishments in Iran and Pakistan showing a liberated Balochistan reaching from the Soviet border to the Indian Ocean, showing Western Balochistan and Eastern Balochistan as part of a greater and united Balochistan. This propaganda was perhaps a tactical manoeuvre in order to warn the US and its allies and to invoke the long held fears of Western powers that an independent Balochistan might provide the Soviet Union with access to the warm waters of Indian Ocean. It was also to gain more Western support in dealing with Baloch resistance, and it practically blocked any hope of getting some kind of sympathy for the Baloch national liberation struggle from Western powers. It is noteworthy that this increased cooperation between Iran and Pakistan which began to counter the resistance in Western Balochistan also played an important role in crushing the Baloch uprising in Pakistani Balochistan during the 1970s in which the Iranian air force became significantly involved in the Chamalang operation against the Mari tribe.

The Baloch political and armed mobilization in Western Balochistan during later decades of Pahlavi dynasty was undoubtedly influenced by increased political activities and armed resistance by the Baloch in Eastern Balochistan. Many political activists which became part of the Baloch resistance in Western Balochistan during the 1960s and 1970s were initially refugees from Western Balochistan who settled in Eastern Balochistan and Sindh where they became active in nationalist movements of the Baloch and Sindhis. In 1970s, the Baloch resistance against Iran received a much needed boost with the establishment of a Baloch nationalist government in the Pakistani controlled Eastern Balochistan in 1972 under the leadership of Sardar Ataullah Mengal, Mir Gous Bakhsh Bizenjo and Nawab Khair Bakhsh Mari. However, this was a short lived as the Nationalist government was soon dismissed on charges of harming the integrity of the Pakistani state. Nevertheless, with the nationalist uprising, which began after the dismissal of the government in 1973, the Baloch in Western Balochistan took great inspiration for their political and armed resistance. The BLF continued its struggle for more than a decade but in the face of a massive crackdown on its fighters and supporters inside and outside Balochistan together with the end of external support from Iraq in 1975, reduced its potential to be a potent organization. There developed serious ideological and personal differences between its exiled leadership. The ideological and strategic differences between tribal chiefs and the middle class political cadre caused much damage to the prospects of BLF surviving as a leading resistance organization.

The Iraqi factor in the Baloch resistance came to an end on 6 March, 1975 (only to resurface in 1980s during the reign of the Ayatollahs), with the signing of the Algiers agreement between Iran and Iraq. This ended Iraqi support for the Baloch in Iran and Iranian support to Kurdish nationalist elements in Iraq (Chaliand, 1980). Some among the exiled Baloch leadership went back to Iran and surrendered to the Iranian authorities, hundreds of fighter also gave up arms, while many among the political activists scattered into Syria and various Western countries. Some of the exiled leaders and activists were hunted down by the Iranian secret police and executed in different cities in Pakistan (Hosseinbor, 2000). By 1976, the front ceased to exist as an effective organization politically or militarily.

The Baloch resistance in Western Balochistan during the Pahlavi Dynasty under the banner of Balochistan Liberation Front did not materialize in the political and cultural emancipation of the Baloch because of internal and external factors. Nevertheless, the impact of its struggle was significant. Bizenjo (2009), pointed out that the key elements of a national liberation struggle include:

- A developed and sharp national consciousness
- An intense and irresistible urge for independence
- Organization
- Objective conditions
- Dedicated leadership
- A readiness to render the supreme sacrifice for the cause

Undoubtedly, the urge for independence was there, there was no reason to doubt the dedication of resistance leaders, Baloch masses were also ready to render the supreme sacrifice for the liberation of their land. However, lack of an effective organization which could mobilize the masses and absence of favorable conditions can be cited as major causes in the collapse of resistance under the banner of Balochistan Liberation Front. Some analysts blamed the inherent infighting between the tribal leadership and the middle class political cadre of the Front for the collapse of the struggle in mid 1970s. Many observers blamed the defective strategies of BLF on an ideological front for the collapse of the movement. The Front openly rejected the idea of first mobilizing the masses under the slogan of a struggle for the Baloch cultural, economic and political rights. Perhaps this misconception of the Front leaders that they could channel the general discontent of the Baloch masses against Iran into a general armed uprising without first raising the level of their political consciousness caused much damage to the Baloch resistance, when without political mobilization and lacking a functional network of nationalist activists, the call for a general uprising fell upon deaf ears. As observed by Janmahmad (1989), the only Baloch party affiliated with the Baloch national resistance during Pahlavi regime was *Baloch Raj e Zrombesh* or the Baloch National Movement, founded in 1971. It stood, however, for an autonomous Balochistan within the framework of a federal Iran (The party became dormant or ineffective as a driving political force until it was revived in 1983 after the fall of Pahlavi regime). Although, the armed resistance by the BLF did not succeed in achieving its proclaimed goal of national liberation; it nevertheless, forced the Pahlavi regime to introduce some political and economic measures to pacify Baloch discontent. The privileges of the tribal elite and *Hakoms* were raised. Their collaboration with the regime increased through Amir Assadullah Alam, who was believed to be one of the influential figures of Pahlavi dynasty. Some economic projects were initiated in Balochistan. Schools were opened in many villages and many Baloch students were given scholarships for higher education in Iranian educational institutions.

The Pahlavi regimes' policy was to keep the Baloch politically weak by denying any access to even local power centres. The regime also cleverly manipulated personal and tribal differences of the various Baloch *Hakoms* and tribal chiefs, forestalling any united Baloch resistance against Iran. Their culture, language, and national identity were mortally threatened by the increased cultural and religious invasion from the Persian state. The use of Balochi language was ruthlessly depressed, and the Baloch were encouraged to adopt Persian dresses and public behaviour. The Persians also created some new Baloch tribes, giving them names of their choice. The Balochi personal names were forcibly replaced in official documents and Shia *Mullahs* were encouraged to convert the Baloch. Although attempts to persuade the Baloch to adopt the Shia doctrine of Islam failed, in reaction, however, it prompted some of the Baloch to become strict Sunni followers. In the coming years, this action and reaction phenomenon nearly changed the character of a secular Baloch society, and religion increasingly began its intrusion into the Baloch society in Western Balochistan.

During Pahlavi regime, the Baloch national resistance against Persian domination was manifested in three different ways. The newly emerged Barakzai chiefdom afforded a valiant resistance against the Persian invasion, the tribes of Sarhad rose in revolt and from the 1960s the Balochistan Liberation Front spearheaded a national resistance until 1975. However, the Baloch resistance in all occasions and manifestations was cruelly suppressed and they suffered tremendously under Pahlavi dynasty. Resistance by tribes of Sarhad were crushed with the mass slaughter of hundreds of the Baloch and killing of their respected chiefs. The Baloch chiefdom of Bampur was occupied and its ruler Mir Dost Mohammad Barakzai was hanged in Teheran. The resistance by BLF ended without achieving its objectives for several different reasons; nevertheless, it inspired a whole generation of youth in Western Balochistan. It rekindled the hope of Baloch nationalists, and they could see a chance of overthrowing the Persian yoke forever, following crushing defeats during the 1920s and 1930s. The ordinary Baloch were also excited and this was manifested by a generalized show of sympathy by them towards the program of the Front. With the activities of BLF, the resistance in Western Balochistan, perhaps, for the first time, got not only international attention but was able to receive material support for a brief period from external sources. The young Baloch activists based in Iraq and other countries in the Middle East began building their connections with other national liberation movements and became familiar with ideologies of various resistance struggles around the globe. Through their interactions, the Baloch nationalist cadre widened their political horizon by absorbing new ideas about nationalism, statehood and national liberation. The Baloch question became a major national and internal issue for the Pahlavi regime; however, the regime was diplomatically successful in portraying the Baloch national resistance as Soviet supported and for the ultimate fulfilment of a Russian desire to reach the warm waters of the Indian Ocean. This pre-empted any support from the Western world for the Baloch national question. After the collapse of Baloch resistance, the Pahlavi regime adopted a policy of constant suppression and assimilation to deal with the Baloch national question.

CHAPTER 6

THE BALOCH RESISTANCE AFTER THE FALL OF PAHLAVI DYNASTY

A combination of internal and external factors caused the demise of Pahlavi dynasty in 1979 and Iran came under the rule of Shiite religious leaders or Ayatollahs. With the fall of the Pahlavi Dynasty, a new phase of the Baloch national resistance began in Western Balochistan. During the last years of the Pahlavi regime, newly graduated Baloch youths and students studying in different educational institutions in Iran and Pakistan, began organizing themselves in clandestine resistance groups. Some of them formed Baloch only organizations, while others joined democratic and left wing organizations fighting against the Pahlavi regime and having manifestoes to create a revolutionary Iran in which rights of all national entities would be safeguarded. Although, organizing themselves into disciplined political organizations was quite a new phenomenon in a tribal society; nevertheless, not only did this process attracted the educated class among the Baloch but a large number of un-educated youth from different segments of the society also joined the rank and files of resistance groups within a few years. A short-lived armed resistance by various Baloch organizations during the 1980s was crushed by the new religious regime and almost all the Baloch leadership fled the country.

BEGINNING OF POLITICAL MOBILIZATION

The Pahlavi dynasty came to an end by February, 1979 and after a brief period of political, social and economic anarchy, the Persian state came under the firm rule of religious fundamentalists with Ayatollahs in control of everything. It appears that after the collapse of BLF resistance in 1976, the Baloch political activists were in a state of shock and for a while they remained dormant. However, with the available space provided by the fall of Pahlavi dynasty, the Baloch began to initiate political mobilization throughout Western Balochistan. There was an outpouring of suppressed political activities and Baloch political activists previously working clandestinely, openly announced the formation of political groups and movements.

Political activities in Western Balochistan were virtually non-existent and in the absence of freedom of expression, freedom of the press, freedom of assembly and organization, together with the ban on political activities, the Baloch national struggle in Iran remained under the leadership of tribal chiefs and *Hakoms*. Only during last decades of Pahlavi dynasty and during early years of Ayatollahs, the Baloch middle class and educated youth became prominent in the national struggle. The first observable and significant activity in Balochistan was the formation of branches of many Iran based left wing political parties whose program included the right of self-determination for nations comprising the Iranian state. The majority of the Baloch political activists were of the opinion that the Iranian state was weakening and a change was inevitable with the fall of the monarchy. They believed that there were great chances of Iran becoming a democratic federal state and this would provide the opportunity for the Baloch to get some kind of autonomous or federal status. They were of the opinion that in the given situation, where objective conditions are not favourable for another armed showdown with Persians, the Baloch could get a significant share in the power structure of the state by joining the democratic forces who were openly advocating the cause of the minority national entities in their manifestoes.

However, there was also a minority opinion among the Baloch that they should not under estimate the aims, ambitions and power of Persian nationalism regardless of the internal tussles or any political upheaval in Iran, Persians from every segment of the society irrespective of any political orientation would unite, sensing any danger to the integrity of their state. They believed that joining the Iran based parties would not serve the Baloch cause.

The left wing political organizations with which the Baloch nationalists became affiliated were *Toudeh* Party, *Fidaheen e Khalq, Mujaheedin e Khalq* and *Paikar*. The political activists affiliated with these parties began organizing mass demonstration throughout Balochistan highlighting the Baloch demand for socio-political rights. A euphoric state was created by these activities and the Baloch were hopeful of being able to get at least some share in the power structure of the Iranian state. According to Hosseinbor (2000), the Baloch began to assert their power by ousting non-Baloch officials from their positions, occupying offices left vacant by the Shah's Secret service-SAVAK. In many cities, on many occasions, they disarmed the gendarme and army units. The Balochi periodicals and magazines which began publishing during this period were loudly publicizing pro-autonomy, pro-independence and pro-revolutionary materials.

Contrary to the evaluation of the majority of the political analysts of that time, the revolution in Iran took the wrong direction. The strong perception was that following the end of the tyranny and dictatorship of the Pahlavi dynasty, the democratic and progressive forces would take over. However, with the covert assistance and overt complacency of the Western powers and because of increased divisions amongst the democratic forces, the religious elements in Iran were able to establish a dictatorship of Ayatollahs within a few months of the collapse of Pahlavi regime. This unexpected turn of events in Iran caused much confusions among rank and file of the Baloch nationalist forces. The democratic and progressive political groups to which the Baloch nationalists affiliated themselves, became the prime target of the Ayatollahs and were brutally crushed. The regime of the Ayatollahs began sending strong signals that any nationalistic activities by the Baloch would not be tolerated. An imminent clash between the Baloch and the Persian state under the Ayatollahs was on the horizon. In this perspective, there developed a broad consensus among the Baloch political activists that affiliation with the Iran based parties could not deliver any good in the forthcoming showdown with the Persian state. Many argued that the affiliation could only dilute the Baloch national question and they began to dissociate themselves from Iran based left wing parties and formed their own Baloch only organizations. However, in contrast to the fairly extensive nationalist organizational base in Pakistan, the Baloch in Western Balochistan were just beginning to acquaint themselves with the formation of political organizations after decades of brutal political repression under the Pahlavi dynasty. The number of educated Baloch was limited, as subsequent Persian regimes were following strictly a policy of keeping the Baloch educationally and economically backward. Nevertheless, even with their limited intellectual resources, various resistance organizations were established with different political or social orientations by nationalist and left-oriented middle class elements in Western Balochistan. Some of them began to form networks for future militant activities against the state. Many tribal chiefs who were earlier pacified or neutralized by the Pahlavi regime also organized themselves into resistance groups. Religious elements among the Baloch organized themselves on religious and sectarian grounds to exploit the domination of the Shia majority over the Baloch Sunni minority. Small scale guerrilla activities were also carried out by the militant wings of these organizations in south and central regions of Western Balochistan.

FORMATION OF BALOCH POLITICAL ORGANIZATIONS

Initially, the Baloch political activists began their activities under the banner of *Bam e Istar* and *Nabard e Baloch*. Later all progressive elements organized themselves in a broad based organization of *Sazman e Democratic Murdom e Balochistan*. Hosseibor (2000), noted that the *Sazman* was an umbrella organization of various left wing organizations. It participated in the democratic politics which was allowed in the beginning of the revolution. It also participated in the first parliamentary elections for the drafting of a new constitution. Active in the *Sazman* were former activists of Iran based leftist organization such as *Fidaheen Khalq* and *Paikar*. Prominent personalities in the Sazman included Dr. Rehmatullah Husseinbhor, Durra Raisi, Rahim Zard Kohi, Shafi Zaindini, Rahim Bandoi, Aziz Dadyar, Jamshed Amiri, Khusro Mubaraki, Mohammad Ali Dehwari, Abdul Malik Dehwari, Reza Shah Bux, Rustom Mir Laashaari, Mohindas Ashkani, Rehamat Khuda Banda, Ahirdad Hossienbhor, Ahmad Hassan Raisi, Abdul Ghani Raisi, Ibrahim Lashkarzai, Karan Shahnawazi, Wali Mohammad Zaindini, Dr. Dedwar, Murad Amiri, Chirag Narui, Gazabek Raisi, Chaker Chakerzai, Pir Bux Amiri, Ayub Hoshang, Rehamat Sayad Zada, Taj Mohammad Sayad Zada, Chiraq Mohamamadi, Faqir Mohammad Raisi, Ghulam Hussein Studa, Nazar Mohammad Hashimzai and Abdullah Zarpanah. These were a group of young enthusiasts, who did not have much experienced in politics but very dedicated in the achievement of the goal of Baloch salvation. In order to gain state legitimacy for their activities in Iran, the *Sazman* did not openly advocate an independent Balochistan but stressed the demand for an autonomous Balochistan within the Iranian federation. The main focus of their activities was concentrated on the political mobilization of the Baloch working class. They openly dissociated themselves from the political activities of tribal chiefs and former *Hakoms* and administrators who were affiliated with the Pahlavi regime but had now joined the national resistance. *Sazman's* demand for autonomy was to get administrative autonomy for Balochistan, recognition of Balochi as medium of instruction in educational institutions, and ownership of natural resources. This organization was soon dissolved and became ineffective during the initial phase of its formation because of the crackdown on its leaders by the Islamic regime. Its leader, Rehmat Hosseinbor was attacked and critically wounded by the Iranian secret services. Another short lived organization championing the rights of the working class among the Baloch, in the name of *Sazman e Inqilabi e Rahkargir* was founded by Ali Chakarzai, Fateh Mohammad Abadian and Ahirdad Sepahi. The religious elements among the Baloch were earlier organized under the banner of *Hezb e Ittehad al- Muslemin* which was led by a much respected Baloch religious personality, Moulvi Abdul Aziz. During the process of creating a new constitution for Iran, Moulvi Abdul Aziz vehemently advocated an autonomous status for Balochistan with the guarantees of securing the cultural, religious and economic rights for the Baloch. *Sazman e Democratic Murdom e Balochistan* and *Hezb e Ittehad al- Muslemin* jointly began a political agitation in Balochistan and tried to paralyze the functioning of the government machinery in the region after the approval of the new constitution in a referendum boycotted by the Baloch. The new constitution of Iran denied any right to the Baloch as a national entity. In the ensuing agitation against the constitution, dozens of people were killed before the Iranian forces were able to establish a semblance of peace in Western Balochistan. The religious organization was forced to disband when the state power was unleashed after the initial phase of leniency towards its demands. After the death of Moulvi Abdul Aziz, his son, Abdul Malik, made an alliance with the Sunni religious elements of Kurds in *Shura e Mili e Ahle Sunna*. This too was disbanded after the murder of Abdul Malik in Pakistan, by Iranian secret services in early 1980s. Tribal chiefs and former *Hakoms* in Balochistan, who have been involved in perpetual personal and tribal feuds, in an unprecedented move, agreed to work in coordination under the banner of an alliance called *Wahdat e Baloch* soon after the Islamic revolution in Iran. This union included Sardarzai, Maliky, Laashaari, Shirani, Narui, Ghamshaadzai, and Esmailzai chiefs. The Mubaraki chief Amanullah formed its own movement *Fidaeen Baloch*.

DEFEAT OF ARMED UPRISING AND MASS EXODUS OF BALOCH NATIONALISTS

The militant wings of various Baloch organizations and united fronts carried out serious armed activities mainly in the south of

Western Balochistan. With increased turmoil in Balochistan, the Ayatollahs blamed Western powers and the Arab neighbours for supporting these organizations. The regime reacted using brutal tactics and the full power of the state to crush the resistance. A large number of political activists and combatants were killed by Iranian forces and agents of their secret services. Thousands of the Baloch were imprisoned and the leadership of organizations was forced to flee into neighbouring Pakistan, Afghanistan and the Gulf countries. However, based in these countries they tried to reorganize their political and militant activities in and outside Western Balochistan.

While in exile, the Baloch political activists were not only involved in heated theoretical debates but also in organizing new groups, organizations and alliances. *Jumbish e Azadi Khuahan e Balochistan* formed in 1981 was mainly comprised of left wing elements among the Baloch who were previously affiliated and later became disaffected with the policies of the left wing parties regarding the national rights of the Baloch and other national entities in Iran. *Baloch Raj e Zrombesh* which was dormant after the murder of its founder, Rahim Zardkohi, was reorganized in 1983. During 1985, Laashaar chief Mir Mohammad Khan in alliance with the Narui, Ghamshadzai and Esmailzai chiefs formed *Jumbish e Mujahideen e Baloch* (renamed as *Sazman e Mubarizin e Baloch* in 1992); while Baraanzai chief formed his own organization. While in Afghanistan, the Narui chief Sardar Sher Ali created his own united front *Itehad e Milli* in 1986 but failed to receive support from other sections of the Baloch nationalists, his organization became virtually ineffective.

Concerted efforts by Iranian secret agents with the covert assistance of their counterparts in Pakistan, resulted in the murder of some of the exiled leaders of the Baloch national resistance. Some prominent tribal chiefs including Laashaari Chief Mir Mohammad Khan and his nephew Mir Amin Laashaari narrowly escaped death but sustained serious bullet injuries in assassination attempts on their lives in Pakistan. Some of the activists and tribal elite were killed in infightings between the leadership of *Wahdat e Baloch* while they were living in exile in Pakistan. As observed by a veteran of the Baloch national resistance in Iran, unfortunate murders of Mir Mouladad Sadarzai and Mir Amanullah Mubariki in the 1980s, were caused by the dispute over the running of the finances and the armed activities of the *Wahdat e Baloch*. Tragically, it was also the resurfacing of the old tribal enmity between Mubariki and Sardarzai tribes which was also believed to be a factor in the Dad Shah episode during Pahlavi regime.

During the early years of Islamic regime, the Baloch resistance groups were offered external support from many quarters. They obtained significant moral and material support from the revolutionary government in Afghanistan. The Persian authorities also blamed Iraq for supporting the Baloch armed resistance in Iran. The United States and other Western powers were similarly accused by Iranian government for supporting the Baloch insurgency. They also accused elements of former regime of Reza Shah Pahlavi for financially aiding the Baloch. However, on the ground, it was the support of the Afghan government which was visible. The increased cooperation between Pakistan and Iran to counter the Baloch activities, the collapse of the revolutionary government in Afghanistan, and the end of Iran-Iraq war caused serious blows to Baloch resistance organizations operating in exile.

After the crushing defeats during the Pahlavi rule, it appeared that there is no way of stopping the socio-political onslaught of the Persians; however, the Baloch national resistance resurfaced during the chaotic years following the fall of the Pahlavi regime. The Baloch political mobilization was only in its formative stages when Reza Shah Pahlavi was deserted by his Western friends, his army, and other supporters, paving the way for his exit in disgrace from Iranian scene. The Baloch were organized in political and armed resistance groups and a short-lived uprising of the Baloch was crushed by the government of Ayatollahs. In many ways, the Baloch nationalist mobilization in Iran during years following the collapse of Pahlavi rule was the continuation of the struggle of Balochistan Liberation Front. There were serious and dedicated efforts by the Baloch nationalist activists, tribal elite and religious elements to organize themselves in parties or alliances. With the political mobilization of the Baloch, tension increased between the Baloch and the regime of Ayatollahs resulting in bloody skirmishes between Baloch armed volunteers and Iranian security forces. After exerting their importance during the early phase of Islamic regime, the Baloch political mobilization and armed resistance could not manage to sustain their activities in Iran and became ineffective. Politically, the Baloch were organized in small disparate groups and could not form a united front. This was probably the reason why their armed resistance despite foreign assistance could not find roots and was unable to make an impression either on the Baloch masses or on the regime of the Ayatollahs. The leadership in exile became vulnerable. Fearing for their life, the exiled Baloch nationalists in Afghanistan and Pakistan migrated in large numbers to various European and North American countries. By all accounts, the Baloch political mobilization and armed resistance against the Persian state after the collapse of Pahlavi regime was a short-lived phenomenon.

CHAPTER 7

BALOCH NATIONAL RESISTANCE IN 21ST CENTURY IRAN

The 21st century Baloch political and resistance movement in Iran has two aspects. Living in exile, the Baloch nationalist leadership tried to form parties, make alliances and realign themselves according to the new realities of the Baloch resistance. They were also involved in organizing political and resistance pockets inside Western Balochistan. Another aspect was the emergence and increasing significance of the religious elements in the Baloch politics inside Western Balochistan. The Persian state under the Ayatollahs had taken stern measures to counter Baloch resistance. Their strategies included creating division, the unleashing of state terrorism, mass executions of the Baloch, collective punishment and various assimilation tactics.

TRANSFORMATION AND REALIGNMENTS OF POLITICAL ORGANIZATIONS

The majority of the Baloch nationalist leadership settled in the West after initially migrating to Pakistan, Afghanistan and the Arab countries during 1980s. During their initial years of exile, they tried to retain their organizations, created after the collapse of Pahlavi regime; however, these organizations once again underwent serious transformations from 1990s. Some of them were divided on ideological or policy differences and consequently new parties created and alliances were made. A significant section of *Baloch Raj e Zrombesh* left the party blaming the leadership of inactivity and after some years formed their own party as Balochistan People's Party of Iran in 2003. However, in the meantime, to coordinate the activities of various Baloch nationalist groups, attempts were made to form an alliance of nationalist forces. Although, Balochistan People's Party refused to join it, Balochistan United Front formed in 2003 was a serious attempt in the direction of uniting all the Baloch political organizations working in various Western countries. Prominent in the formation of Balochistan United Front were Dr. Habibullah Malik, Dr. Abdul Doshaki, Ghulam Reza Hosseinbhor, Jamshed Amiri, Aziz Dadyar, Anwer Dehwari, Dr. Noor Mohammad Maliki, Hassan Kamali and Nasser Mubaraki. The Front did not last long and disintegrated in 2005.

At present, the Baloch nationalists from Western Balochistan are carrying out political activities under banners of a number of organizations. The organizations which are most active include Balochistan People's Party led by Nasser Buledai, and *Baloch Raj e Zrombesh* with Abdullah Syahoi as its spokeperson. Their main activities include highlighting the grave human rights situation in Balochistan and advocacy for the Baloch cause among the political and humanitarian institutions of the West. In 2005, with the initiative of the Balochistan People's Party of Iran, Balochistan has been successful in gaining the membership of prestigious Unrepresented Nations and Peoples Organization (UNPO). Another aspect of Baloch activities by various organizations representing Western Balochistan is their close working with the Baloch nationalist organizations, groups and personalities from Eastern Balochistan who are also busy in highlighting the Baloch national question and human right issues in international forums. There are many other organizations of the Baloch in Diaspora which have not been particularly active in recent years. These include:

1. *Jibe Mardom Balochistan* led by Ghulam Reza Hosseinbhor
2. *Jibe Mutahida Balochistan* (Jamhori Khuahan) led by Jamshed Amiri
3. *Jibe Mutahida Balochistan* led by Dr. Abdul Doshaki
4. *Jumbish e Mubarizin e Balochistan* led by Mir Laashaar Muhammad Khan Laashaari
5. Compaign for Independent Balochistan led by Mehrab Sarjo
6. *Itehad e Milli* led by Narui chief Sardar Sher Ali

Apart from claims of having armed resistance units inside Western Balochistan, major activities of organizations and exiled leaders are centred on advocacy for the Baloch national struggle in Iran by highlighting human right violations in Balochistan and the resolution of the Baloch national question under the charter of the United Nations Organization. On various international forums, they are trying to exploit the convergence of interests of those seeing the danger emanating from the fanatical and rogue states such as Iran and Pakistan with that of the Baloch national liberation struggle. The Baloch nationalists, belonging to several different organizations of Western Balochistan and based in European capitals are hopeful that their struggle will get the required support from the international community, as Iran is increasingly being seen as a threat to world peace and internally it is racing towards economic, social and political chaos. In recent years, this perception has prompted conscious elements within various nationalist organizations to form a workable alliance of parties, organizations and personalities active inside and outside Western Balochistan. The urgency for this move has been triggered by an unexpected phenomenon, the exponential increase of religious influence, which has developed in Western Balochistan for a decade and is gaining momentum. This has created a new danger for the Baloch national struggle in general and the Baloch cause in Western Balochistan in particular. Although, some among the Baloch leadership welcome any move against the Persian state, regardless of its political, social and ideological orientation, the majority among the Baloch nationalists have shown considerable concern. They fear that this previously unheard phenomenon in a secular Baloch society if not countered with a robust alternative by nationalist forces, will ultimately change the essence of the Baloch national struggle from being a secular and democratic struggle to that of a religious and sectarian one. This could be used by states occupying Balochistan to their advantage. They believe that enemies of the Baloch can exploit this to show only the religious face of the Baloch struggle with grave consequences for the Baloch national resistance in future.

There is also an ongoing debate and discussion among the Baloch nationalist circles on how to proceed in order to achieve the objective of national salvation, bearing in mind the prevailing situation in Western Balochistan and the strength of various nationalist organizations. Some of the groups insist on an autonomous Balochistan in a federated Iran. They argue that keeping in mind the objective reality of the progress of the Baloch national resistance in Iran and the conditions and circumstances relating to it, federalism for Iran and the demand for autonomous status are the only feasible options. While for a significant section of the Baloch, an independent and united Balochistan is the sole objective of the Baloch national resistance in Iran.

EMERGENCE OF RELIGIOUS FACTOR IN WESTERN BALOCHISTAN

Religion has never been a potent political tool among the Baloch and Priests or *Mullahs* have been in a subordinate position in the social and political spheres of Baloch society. However, the *Mullahs* were able to assert themselves as an undeniable political force in Balochistan during the 1980s. This was mainly because the whole nationalist Baloch leadership had fled the country creating a leadership vacuum which the religious elements endeavoured to fill.

With the promulgation of a new constitution soon after taking control in 1979, the Ayatollahs made it clear that Iran from now on would be a totally theocratic state based on Shi'ism. Although, dating from the Safavids rule, Shi'ism became the official religion of the state; nevertheless, there was not any observable or major infringement of Shi'ism on areas where Sunnis were in majority. The Ayatollahs adopted Islam as the official religion and the doctrine of 'Twelve Imams' was declared immutable. They also created the provision of *Vilayat e Faqih* (governance of religious jurists). This was seen by Sunni leaders as totally un-Islamic and unacceptable. The Baloch religious groups, under the leadership of Moulvi Abdul Aziz, vehemently opposed these moves. Under the banner of *Hezb e Ittehad al- Muslemin*, they mobilized the masses exploiting the imbalance regarding various Islamic sects in the Iranian constitution. This peaceful uprising was also joined by the nationalist and left wing forces, mainly by supporters and cadres of *Sazman e Democratic Murdom e Balochistan*. On the face of it, the Baloch demands included guarantees to recognise the Baloch as a national entity with equal opportunities for social, cultural and economic development. This popular mobilization, apart from demands for cultural, religious and political rights, was based on awakening the masses for an ultimate struggle for Baloch sovereignty. Mass demonstrations throughout Balochistan were held, paralyzing the state machinery; however, soon the agitation became violent and dozens of people were killed in skirmishes between Baloch demonstrators and the state security forces (Hosseinbor, 2000). As the agitation gained momentum, the Baloch religious elements, afraid of being overshadowed by the nationalist forces, also began openly talking about the national rights of the Baloch. They were not however, demanding the independence of Balochistan from Iran but were asking religious, cultural and economic rights in a federated Iran. Their constant reference to constitution was significant. In a way, taking the initiative, as identified by Harrison (1981), they were presenting the Ayatollahs with an acceptable alternative to Baloch nationalist and left wing opposition in Balochistan. However, threatened by the vigour of the evolving Baloch national resistance, the Ayatollahs adopted a policy of zero tolerance towards the Baloch, regardless of them being religious, secular, left or right wing. Some of the religious leaders were persecuted by the regime and many went into exile but a significance section of the religious leaders remained in Balochistan and practically replaced the nationalist and tribal leadership of the Baloch national resistance in Iran.

From 2003, a religious group, *Jundallah*, began militant activities in many regions of Western Balochistan targeting the state security apparatus. The organization claimed to continue fighting for national and religious rights of the Baloch and to resist Shia encroachments on the Sunni Baloch beliefs. The Iranian security forces arrested its leader, Abdul Malik Reki in February, 2010 and he was later executed by the authorities in June 2010 on charges of waging war against the Islamic republic of Iran. The capture and subsequent execution of Reki along with the trials and executions of several other active members of *Jundallah* was a heavy blow to the religious faction of the Baloch armed resistance in Iran. However, the organization still carry out small-scale ambushes on convoys of Iranian security forces, assassinations and abductions of government officials or people affiliated to the government under the new leadership of Muhammad Zahir Baloch. In a bid not to antagonize the secular Baloch national resistance and to dilute the perception of being a terrorist organization, *Jundallah* included Baloch nationalism in its narratives and tried to rename itself as the People's Resistance Movement of Iran (PRMI). This was an unsuccessful effort to refute claims by Iran that it harboured an Islamist Sunni sectarian agenda. In their official statement, *Jundallah* declared that in such conditions, faced by the Baloch in Iran, it was not easy for the Baloch to live peacefully; asserting that they had a moral right to defend their community, nation and the country.

While referring *Jundallah* as a Pakistan based organization, Iran has accused Pakistan of not doing enough to counter *Jundallah* activities, which are emanating from bases in Eastern Balochistan. Indeed, it has also criticized Pakistan for supporting *Jundallah*'s religious and sectarian struggle as an effort to direct attention away from its own problem of a secular Baloch national resistance. The Iranians are also accusing the US intelligence agencies of supporting the organization and its many offshoot groups with the help of Pakistani security agencies and with funding from Saudi Arabia and Qatar. Israel and the United Kingdom are also in the Iranian list of countries supporting the Baloch religious groups fighting against them. However, on the ground there has been no substantial evidence to prove any Western involvement.

Several other Baloch religious groups have emerged in Western Balochistan since 2012. They are claiming responsibility for activities against security forces in the Sistan *wa* Balochistan province of Iran. One among them is *Jaish ul-Adl* (Army of Justice) founded by former members of *Jundallah*. After an attack on border security forces in October 2013, they claimed that this is in revenge for the execution by hanging of 16 Baloch in Zahedan. The group vowed to retaliate against oppression and crimes being committed against the innocent Sunni community in Iran including the Baloch, Kurds, and Ahwazi. Iran has accused Saudi Arabia of funding *Jaish ul-Adl* and Pakistan of turning a blind eye to this. According to Hoshang (2015), *Jaish ul-Adl* adopted a more moderate approach and to some extent has moved further towards Baloch ethnic nationalism. During 2015 and 2016, *Jaish ul-Adl* carried out many serious hit and run attacks on security forces in Western Balochistan and appeared to be the only potent armed group against the regime of Ayatollahs. *Harkat e Ansar e Iran* was another splinter group of *Jundallah*. The group merged with *Hizbul-Furqan* and formed *Ansar Al-Furqan* in late 2013. The Iranians blame Qatar, Saudi Arabia, and Pakistan of giving financial and logistic support to the group. Hoshang (2015), observed that all religious groups in Western Balochistan are in one way or another, had connections with radical groups such as *Sepah-e Sahabah* and *Lashkar-e Janguhi* and Taliban in Afghanistan and Pakistan, indicating a strong connection between Pakistani Inter-Services Intelligence agency (ISI) and the religious organizations in Western Balochistan.

Five factors can be cited as responsible for the growing power of the religious elements in Balochistan:

- the reaction against the heavy crack down on Sunni parties and organizations by a Shia regime;
- the militarization of religious elements in neighboring Afghanistan and Pakistan by the West during Afghan conflict in 1980s;
- the involvement of Saudi Wahhabism in Balochistan to settle some scores in their protracted conflict with Shi'ism;
- the involvement of Pakistan in patronizing religious elements in both sides of Goldsmid line in its adopted policy of diluting the danger of a secular national resistance of the Baloch;
- the elimination of nearly all Baloch nationalist leaders of secular orientations.

The above mentioned factors became responsible for changing the character of religious elements in Western Balochistan from being a docile, subordinate section of the society in to being an independent militant segment among the Baloch. According to an exiled Baloch leader, the Baloch nationalists are running out of time in Western Balochistan. They have to take a decision on armed resistance and political mobilization inside Balochistan very soon; otherwise the vacuum which has been created by the absence of nationalist leadership and lack of any visible political activities are attracting the Baloch youth towards religious elements.

THE BALOCH POLITICS IN 21ST CENTURY IRAN

Baloch politics can be analysed taking into consideration three different aspects of the Baloch struggle in Iran in recent decades.

1. The Baloch are continuously facing the subjugating measures adopted by the Persian state under the rule of Ayatollahs.
2. The ineffectiveness of nationalist endeavors in mass mobilization and armed resistance against the Persian state because of a state of disunity among the nationalist groups.

3. The emergence of the religious phenomenon in the Baloch society and politics in Western Balochistan.

In the 21st century, the Baloch in Western Balochistan under perpetual Persian occupation, have found themselves suppressed and oppressed to varying degrees. They are deprived of their cultural, social and economic rights. Treated as third class citizens, the Baloch in Iran are struggling to preserve the basic elements of their national identity. They are forced to adopt Persian names and are deprived of using their mother tongue as the medium for instruction at schools. The use of the Balochi language in public places is being discouraged. Policies of the Ayatollahs regarding the Baloch and other national minorities are clear manifestations of a chauvinistic Persian nationalism. The regime is carrying out policies of previous regimes including demographic manipulations in order to make the Baloch a minority in their own homeland. With the influx of Persians, cities such as Zahedan (Duzzap) and Chahbar are increasingly losing their characteristics as Baloch cities.

Circumstances have never been favourable for the Baloch to achieve their desired goal of overthrowing the Persian yoke, nor has their resistance been able to secure any constitutionally sanctioned degree of autonomy as a result of their political or armed resistance. While talking to the author, a veteran nationalist activist from Western Balochistan observed that after the fall of Pahlavi regime, the ineffectiveness of the Baloch national resistance was because of disunity and distrust among the nationalist circles. This together with the lack of a visionary personality able to lead the struggle to its cherished goal of emancipating the Baloch from the yoke of Persian imperialism. No central figure or personality was identified which the tribal elite and the middle class Baloch nationalist leadership could rely on. This was because nearly all tribal chiefs and *Hakoms* affiliated with the Baloch resistance were either killed, imprisoned or neutralized by successive Iranian regimes. The prevailing situation in Western Balochistan was not favourable for the middle class to develop a leadership cadre, as political activity of any kind by the Baloch was not tolerated by successive Persian regimes.

A disconnect has been created between the Baloch leadership in exile and those acting inside Western Balochistan as a result of the long absence of leadership. A difference of opinion on strategy can be observed between Baloch organizations operating in exile and those participating in the political process of the Persian state inside Balochistan. All nationalist movements and political parties involved in the political processes of Iran have moreover, if only for pragmatic reasons, accepted the political incorporation of Balochistan into the Persian state, demanding federalism and moderate forms of self-rule or autonomy under the charter of the United Nations Organization. Justifying their stance on the demand of federalism, a prominent leader of the Baloch national struggle in Western Balochistan told the author that a genuine federal arrangement would grant the Baloch political institutions the legitimate right to resolve the Baloch national question with the Persian state. He asserted that a reduction in the power of central government in Tehran would give the Baloch much needed political space without having to demand full sovereignty.

Despite being divided, weak and seeing no help from relevant quarters of the international community for their national cause, the Baloch parties, groups and personalities from Western Balochistan living in exile, hope to achieve their objective of overthrowing the Persian yoke. They believe that it is only a matter of channelling the Baloch nationalist sentiments in a united organization to launch an effective resistance. They believe that soon the Baloch nationalist parties will engage the Persian state in a meaningful political and armed resistance. Some of the Baloch nationalist groups in exile also claim to have their armed resistance units inside Balochistan, but in a dormant state in order to save their strength for a future showdown with the Persian state. According to a prominent leader of the Baloch national resistance in Iran, this is a tactical and strategic decision and they are waiting for the proper time to engage the Persian state in an armed resistance for the ultimate victory. Internal divisions within Iranian society and state is an encouragement for the Baloch nationalists as there has been observable deterioration in all spheres of the Persian state during the last three decades. The imposition of the Shi'ism on a society which is a mosaic of various Islamic sects and national entities with their own socio-cultural beliefs has proved to be divisive and disruptive. Some of the nationalist leaders believe that the protracted war with Arab Wahhabism; the attempts to export its political Islam into the Middle East; the patronage of various international terrorist groups; the confrontation with the West on the nuclear issue, and the brutal handling of national questions have considerably weakened the foundations of Persian state.

The nationalist political and tribal groups in Western Balochistan have not been able to provide strong resistance except in some instances of political agitation and armed skirmishes between the Baloch and security forces, during the early years of Ayatollahs takeover of Iran. After the collapse of the political and armed resistance led by the nationalists and tribal elite during the last decades of 20th century, any significant resistance activity has only been carried out by the Baloch religious groups. The religious elements are also aware of the situation, in order to gain sympathy and support from nationalist circles, they are now mixing religious and nationalist demands to their narratives. A section of the Baloch youth has undoubtedly been attracted and increasingly affiliated with the religious and sectarian led Baloch resistance in Iran. With these developments, clear signs of frustration are visible among the Baloch nationalist circles. They are well aware of the fact that the vacuum which was created by the absence of a nationalist leadership and lack of any visible political activity will attract the Baloch youth towards religious radicalisation.

Inside Western Balochistan, nationalists are carrying out their low profile political activities either clandestinely or by joining Iran based political parties. During contacts with nationalist circle inside Iran, there were three views among Baloch nationalists:

1. Some of them calling themselves national democrats believe in participating in the so-called democratic process of the state in order to gain opportunities for the greater political mobilization of the Baloch masses.

2. Those who call themselves federalists believe that the Baloch should accept being a federating unit of Iran as a first step in their struggle for national self-determination.

3. The pro-independent groups believe that there is no point in joining any state political process, as it is counterproductive for the Baloch national struggle and brings opportunistic tendencies among nationalist cadres.

PERSIAN STRATEGIES IN DEALING WITH THE BALOCH NATIONAL QUESTION

The Persian state has employed classical colonial strategies in order to counter 'the menace' of the Baloch national struggle in Iran. The methods and tactics include creation of divisions among the resistance groups and personalities, unleashing of state terror in various ways, socio-cultural discrimination, bringing about demographic changes and endeavours to assimilate the Baloch into a non-existent wider Iranian national identity.

CREATING DIVISIONS

Since the time of Qajar rule in Iran, it has been the policy of the state to create divisions among the Baloch tribal chiefs who were in the forefront of Baloch resistance against Persian incursions in Balochistan. The policy was also continued by Pahlavi regime which was successful in creating personal, political and tribal animosity among major tribes and *Hakoms*. The policy of divide and rule has not been changed in the Iran of the Ayatollahs. However, with the changing dynamics of the Baloch resistance in Iran, where the influence of tribal elite is weakening; the Islamic republic is now concentrating its divisive policies on sectarian parameters. In recent decades, the armed resistance against the Persian state is mainly carried out by the religious elements among the Baloch. The regime of the Ayatollahs is reportedly supporting or creating a chiasm among various Sunni sectarian militant organizations operating in Balochistan. Some of the observers on the affairs of Western Balochistan also see the active involvement of the Iranian government in the endemic state of disunity among secular and nationalist organizations and personalities. As prominent nationalist leader from Western Balochistan considered, in an interview with the author, that there was covert support for the religious elements from the Iranian establishment, despite facing armed resistance from them, which is understandable. According to him, it has been the policy of the Iranian establishment to replace the secular leadership of the Baloch resistance with a religious one. This is in line with the state policy of diluting the national and secular aspect of the Baloch resistance.

The secular element in the Baloch national struggle of Western Balochistan is being led by the exiled leadership and is divided into numerous groups, organizations and parties. During the 1970s, the Pahlavi regime in order to weaken the Baloch resistance based in Iraq, tried to create differences between middle class political activists and tribal elite who were working together under the banner of BLF. Among the reasons for the collapse of this resistance, many Baloch intellectuals have identified the distrust created among the Baloch leadership in Iraq by infiltrators sent by the Pahlavi regime's secret services. Continuing the policy of Pahlavi regime, the present government in Iran, is also encouraging those elements among the Baloch Diaspora who believe that the tribal elite has no positive role in the Baloch national struggle in Iran. Whether it is due to lack of political vision or because of state manipulations by Iran, the Baloch leaders are working under the banners of several groups and are unable to unite in order to fight the common cause of liberating their people from a long period of subjugation.

The arrest of *Jundallah* leader, Abdul Malik Reki, in a very successful operation was a clear manifestation of Iranian infiltration into the rank and file of the Baloch resistance led by religious groups. A brother of Abdul Malik Reki was also killed by Iranian secret services in Quetta (Pakistan). During the 1980s and 1990s, several Baloch leaders from Western Balochistan were killed in Karachi (Pakistan) by agents of the Iranian State, believed to be operating within ranks of the Baloch nationalists.

STATE TERRORISM

Iran has broken all records of brutality. Mass executions, torture, detention without trials, extra-judicial killings and murder by summary trials are the norms in dealing with the Baloch national resistance.

The state response to the political and armed activities of different Baloch groups in Western Balochistan has been the disproportionate use of force. The state security agencies have adopted a policy of combating the Baloch armed fighters as if they were dealing with armed drug dealers or highway robbers. A special security force in the name of *Mersad* has been deputed to harass the Baloch population indiscriminately. This force based in Kerman and Zahedan has carried out kidnapping, torture and killings of Baloch political and social activists. A new military base '*Rasoul-e-Akram*' has been established in Zahedan. *Mersad* forces operating from the *Rasoul-e-Akram* base have clear instructions to execute 'bandits' (a term usually used by the Persians for the Baloch nationalists and resistance fighters) whenever they are captured. The commander of the *Rasoul-e-Akram* base is quoted by official *Rudbar Zamin* publication in August 2006, as saying, that in order to strengthen the intelligence system, several forward operating bases have been established in the region, paramilitary (*Basij*) camps, and friendly tribes will also be used.

Arbitrary prosecution by speedy trial courts, is another aspect of the crimes against the Baloch by the Persian state. Summary executions became a regular feature in Iran after the takeover of Ayatollahs in early 1980s. A special court set up in Zahedan is exclusively dealing with cases of Baloch nationalists. The deputy governor responsible for security affairs was quoted by the official IRNA news agency in 2006 as saying that following the establishment of *Rasoul-e-Akram* base, the operation of the brigades under its command in their decisive fight against lawless elements and those who undermine security, the activity of a special court dealing with security offences, the judicial system's firm stand against crime and the intensification of security measures, have all contributed to make people feel more 'secure and tranquil'. This clearly showed the intensity of the persecution the Baloch nationalist forces through summary trials.

Amnesty International (AI) reported various cases of arrest and murder of the Baloch nationalist and religious leaders in revenge killings by security agencies in response of casualties suffered by them in 2006. The use of helicopter Gunships and aerial bombardment have been reported near Bam in Kerman against reported Baloch insurgents. Mass arrests and summarily executions of suspected *Jundallah* supporters have been reported by various international agencies in 2007. Amnesty International (AI), in its annual report entitled 'The Human Right Abuses Against the Baluchi Minority', published in September 2007, showed great concern over the increasing human rights violations by the state authorities of Iran in Western Balochistan. In the south Kerman region, the arrest of 174 armed civilians, murderers and fugitive thieves was confirmed by the Interior Minister and reported by the Fars News Agency on 24 April 2007 (These terms are usually used by Iranian authorities for Baloch resistance activists). The head of a registered NGO 'The Voice of Justice People's Society, Yakub Mehrnehad, was arrested by the authorities and summarily prosecuted in Zahedan and executed in 2008. There was a period during 1990s when the number of the Baloch executed by the authorities fell considerable. However, as observed by the Amnesty International (AI), from the beginning of 21st century, the number of the Baloch executions has risen dramatically.

The violation of basic human rights of the Baloch by Iranian state has been a deliberate and continuous policy. The 2011 report of UN Secretary General on the situation of Iran at the Human Rights Council in Geneva, was a clear indictment of the Persian state by affirming that the past 30 years were characterized by the persistent violation of human rights in Iran (HRC, 2011).

MASS EXECUTIONS

In 2008, according to Baloch and Iranian sources, 1100 Baloch activists were executed in Zahedan. The Human Rights Watch in its World Report 2016, blamed security agencies and intelligence forces for perpetrating gross human rights abuses in Western Balochistan. The report discovered that 830 prisoners who were executed in 2015, the majority of whom were charged with drug related offences (HRW, 2015). In February 2016, the Iranian Vice President for women and family affairs, Shahindokht Mowlaverdy, claimed that all men in a village in the province of Sistan wa Balochistan were executed for drug offences. The claim was later confirmed by Mohamad Javad Larijani, secretary general of Iran's High Council for Human Rights. On 26th October, 2013, Iranian authorities executed 16 Baloch political activists in Zahedan in order to avenge the killing of security personnel during an ambush by the Baloch religious group *Jaish ul-Adl* (Gulati, 2013). On 4 January 2015, Baloch sources claimed the abduction of 30 people by the Iranian Security Forces in the village of Nasirabad in Sarbaz region and they are still missing. It has been the norm of the state authorities in Iran to carry out punishments that violate the prohibition of torture and other cruel, inhuman or degrading acts. These acts of state barbarism are sometimes carried out in public and included flogging, blinding and amputations.

SOCIO-CULTURAL DISCRIMINATION

The United Nation Charter and its various covenants and resolutions clearly state that persons belonging to national or ethnic, religious and linguistic minorities have the right to enjoy their own culture, to profess and practice their own religion, and to use their own language, in private and in public, freely and without interference or any form of discrimination. However, in Iran, the Baloch and other national entities are facing serious socio-cultural discriminations.

A US state department report in 2010, graphically mentioned that the ethnic minorities were discriminated against in the Iran of the Ayatollahs. The report pointed out that in practice minorities did not enjoy equal rights and the government consistently denied their right to use their national language in schools. The Amnesty International report in 2012 observed that: "Iran's ethnic minority communities, including Ahwazi Arabs, Azerbaijanis, Baluch, Kurds and Turkmen, continue to suffer discrimination in law and in practice. The use of minority languages in state-controlled workplaces and for teaching in schools remains outlawed. Religious minorities face similar discrimination and marginalization. Activists campaigning for the rights of minorities face threats, arrest and imprisonment, as do activists campaigning against the pervasive discrimination which impacts severely on women in law and in practice" (AI report, 2012, page 7). Iran's treatment of ethnic minorities has also been a subject of discussion during the UN's Universal Periodic Review process (UPR). In the first round of the UPR in 2010, 5 recommendations relating to racial and ethnic discrimination were made to Iran, with a further 15 made in 2014 (UPR Info, 2015). Of these 20 recommendations, none was accepted by the Iranian authorities. Amnesty International in its annual report 2015 on Iran mentioned that Ahwazi Arabs, Azerbaijani Turks, Baloch, Kurds and Turkmen are systematically being discriminated against socially, politically and religiously by authorities. Those who called for greater cultural and linguistic rights faced arrest, imprisonment, and in some cases the death penalty (Amnesty International, 2016).

In 2014, a United States' report on the human rights situation in Iran pointed out that the selection procedure limited employment opportunities and political participation of *Sunni* Baloch and caused them to be underrepresented in government positions. The report also noted that Baloch journalists and human rights activists faced arbitrary arrest, physical abuse, and unfair trials (US Department of State, 2014). In 2015, a United Nation report detailed human rights violation of ethnic and religious minority groups. The report pointed out discriminations which included arrest, torture and imprisonment, the denial of economic opportunities, expulsion from educational institutions, deprivation of the right to work, and closure of businesses etc. Political activists from the minority nationalities seeking greater recognition for cultural and linguistic rights risk facing harsh penalties, including capital punishment.

COLLECTIVE PUNISHMENT

The Persian state has employed a policy of collective punishment as a tool in the battle against the Baloch. As mentioned earlier, during 2013, 16 Baloch political prisoners were summarily executed as an act of official revenge for the death of a dozen soldiers belonging to the Iranian Revolutionary Guards together with the whole male population of a village in Western Balochistan hanged by the Iranian authorities. Many Baloch sources affirm that there were other instances of execution of male members of whole communities. The easiest way of diluting their barbarism is to claim that the executed Baloch were drug peddlers. In June 2015, the authorities announced that they have hanged 10 Baloch prisoners in Zahedan on drug-related crimes. According to Nasser Buledai, the leader of Peoples Party of Balochistan, as a result of such atrocities, many of the villages in Western Balochistan have been emptied of young males. They have either been killed systematically or fled to safety elsewhere. The population in several districts of Western Balochistan has decreased considerably since the takeover of the Ayatollahs in Iran.

ASSIMILATION

To 'persianize' the whole Iranian plateau had been the dream of successive Persian regimes in Iran. Perceiving the Baloch national resistance as a grave threat to its integrity, the Persian state has followed a policy of ruthless coercion, in order to force the Baloch to merge themselves into a non-existing Iranian nation. Assimilation measures include systematic attacks upon their cultural identity, suppression of the Balochi language and the portrayal of the Baloch as being merely tribes of wider Persian national identity, thus denying the national status of the Baloch in Iran.

To implement their policy of assimilation, the authorities have resorted to gross violation of human rights such as kidnapping, torture and often simple assassination of Baloch writers, intellectuals and political and religious leaders who have resisted the assimilation policies of the state. Politically, the state is not ready even to consider the demand for broader autonomy within the frame work of the Iranian constitution raised by the Baloch political and religious groups participating in the political process of the state. The state establishment is convinced that demands for greater autonomy by the Baloch for Western Balochistan are tactical moves designed to secure a forward position in their fight for national independence.

Assimilation of 'others' has been the tool of various Persian dynasties as part of their strategy in the development of a Persian national identity. Since the establishment of the modern Persian state by Safavids, every regime has attempted to assimilate or bring the components of country's national minorities into line, and force them to conform to a narrow conception of Iranian identity. The regime of the Ayatollahs since 1979 has followed the same policies as their predecessors regarding the Baloch and other national entities. Ayatollah Khomeini in one of his policy speeches in 1981, declared that the talk of racial character and nationhood by members of any ethnic entity was a plot hatched by the agents of Western imperialism in order to create disputes amongst Muslims. He emphasized that nationalism against other Muslims contradicts Islam, the holy Qur'an and the sayings of the great prophet.

The state is promoted an image that there are no national issues in Iran and all national minorities were part of the Iranian nation. Beck (1992) and Zamani (2014), pointed out that using the education system, the regime has been successful in instilling in Persian youth a sense of Iranian identity, which in practice meant the continued denial of existence of other national entities with their particular cultural, linguistic and historical identity. The definition of being Iranian has been heavily based on Shi'ism, Persian culture and historical traditions. This Iranian identity has been used as a tool to counter challenges from minority national entities. For the Persian establishment whether secular or religious, the establishment of the Persian language over other national languages in Iran has become a sacred goal. The desire to eliminate differences in customs, clothing, and other cultural manifestation has always been an objective of the Persian state.

CHANGING THE DEMOGRAPHY

Persian regimes irrespective of their political orientations, have been systematically bringing demographic changes in Western Balochistan. During the Pahlavi regime, the Baloch city of Duzaap (now renamed as Zahedan) was flooded by non-Baloch settlers and the overwhelming Baloch majority of the city was changed, thus during the regime of Ayatollahs, the Baloch in Duzaap are now in the minority. The same fate is awaiting the Baloch in the port city of Chahbar. In Kerman and Sistan many Baloch townships either have lost or are increasingly losing their identity as Baloch settlements. According to a leader of the resistance, the Baloch are on the verge of being extinct as a national entity.

The Iranian state is bringing demographic changes to make the Baloch a minority in Balochistan and to dilute the Baloch national question in Iran. The Baloch see recent development projects in Chahbar as the beginning of their cultural extinction. The perception among the Baloch is that with the completion of these port projects, millions of non-Baloch from Persia proper will settle in these cities, bringing drastic demographic changes by converting the Baloch into a minority in Western Balochistan. Thousands of acres of land surrounding these towns was already acquired by Persians businessmen. This ethnic influx will change the social-cultural and political landscape of Western Balochistan forever.

On the one hand, there has been no respite for the Baloch in Western Balochistan; on the other hand, from the beginning of 21st century, the Baloch national resistance in Iran faced a multitude of problems. Almost all the nationalist leadership is living a life of exile in different Western countries. This limited their contact with the people in Western Balochistan, creating a leadership vacuum which is filled by religious elements. The chronic lack of resources is impeding any meaningful political or armed activities inside Iran. Lack of unity among the nationalists is casting dark shadows on their resistance against the Persian state. A process of political realignment and regrouping among the nationalists in exile who have been active in highlighting the socio-political and human right situation in Western Balochistan failed to make impact. A milieu of distrust has prevailed among the personalities and groups affiliated with the Baloch national struggle in Western Balochistan. The inherent mistrust between the tribal elite and the middle class activists has been the obstacle in the formation of a united front for the national resistance. Although, a serious attempt was made for unity among the Baloch with the formation of the Balochistan United Front. This however, failed to achieve its objective and subsequently became ineffective.

From the beginning of this century, a quite new development in Western Balochistan was observed and that is the militant resistance to Iranian domination by the religious sectarian elements among the Baloch. Inside Balochistan, the vacuum created by the absence of the nationalist leadership is increasingly being filled by religious elements. In reaction, the state authorities have unleashed a terror of great magnitude, having various dimensions. The Persian state in its counter measures against the Baloch national resistance has been successful in creating divisions among the Baloch political organizations and nationalist personalities. Their assimilation efforts are endangering the national identity of the Baloch. The state tactic of mass executions and collective punishment contributed to the sense of social and political suffocation prevailing in the life of every Baloch in Western Balochistan.

CHAPTER 8

PAKISTAN IN CONTEXT

The devastations of the two Great Wars drastically changed the world political scenario in 20th century. Empires began to crumble and new powers emerged. The status of Great Britain, Germany, France and Japan as super-powers changed. The increased momentum for national liberation in Asia and Africa, the changing internal dynamics and new social realities within their own societies forced imperial powers such as Spain, Portugal, France and Great Britain to draw up strategies for granting independence to colonized people. However, the process of decolonization was not smooth and it was fairly unjust in the majority of cases. These powers in order to safeguard their interests in regions where they had ruled, divided nations, and created artificial states. In the post-colonial era, because of the mess created in the process of giving independence to subjugated nations, several regions of Asia and Africa became zones of never ending conflicts and turmoil. Although, after the Second World War, Britain emerged as one of the victorious powers, it became impossible for the British to rule its vast colonial empire directly and granting independence to India which was once the most precious of its colonial possessions became imperative. At the same time, it also became important for the British authorities to formulate strategies in order to safeguard their interests in the region after their withdrawal. The emergence of the Soviet Union as a superpower after the war and prospects of India under nationalist Congress

Party with a progressive and anti-imperialist outlook, were seen as threats to the British and Western interests in South Central Asia and the Gulf region with newly discovered oil fields in the Arabian deserts. Building a geographical and political wall against the expanding wave of socialism was another consideration for Great Britain. In this context, plans for division of India and creation of a client state of Pakistan were put into action. The phenomenon of political Islam was successfully used in the creation of Pakistan by the colonial authorities in New Delhi, and London. In official narratives of the state and in the text books, Pakistan is described as the 'Allah given country'; however, in reality it is a British created state. Ignoring the far reaching consequences of this strategy, the immediate aim was to build a geographical and political wall against the ambitions of the Russians who were supposedly trying to encroach on British colonial interests in the Indian Ocean and the Middle East.

THE USE OF ISLAM AS A POLITICAL TOOL

After gaining total domination over India during 19th century, maintaining the British rule over the richest of her colonial possessions became of foremost importance for the colonial administrators in New Delhi. Following the mutiny or rebellion of 1857, (where followers of different religions joined against the rule of East India Company) concerted efforts were made to disrupt the communal unity, as seen in 1857. Although, Pakistan was created in a hurry in 1947 in a post-second world war perspective, the seeds of division had already been sown and from 1857, the colonial administration in India had been fomenting religious divisions by encouraging the theory of Muslims being a separate national entity in India. Indians belonging to two nations (Hindus and Muslim) was thought to be the most acceptable theory for dividing India on religious ground. In order to establish the religious differences of Indians as the basis for 'two-nation theory', writers were commissioned. Their task was to present Indian history, pointing to the religious beliefs of the dynastic rulers of India.

The British colonial authorities helped establish various religious schools in different parts of India. In 1888, Syed Ahmad Khan, a retired clerk and spy of the East India Company was financed to open the famous religious school in Aligarh and he was officially portrayed as a great Muslim intellectual (Janmahmad, 1989). Later, the colonial administration assembled all the loyal persons among the Muslims in an 'All India Muslim Conference'. The network of religious schools and the All India Muslim Conference were the institutions from where the ideology of Pakistan (ideology of Pakistan is the official doctrine of Pakistani State, which states that followers of Islamic faith in India form a separate nation so they have the right of having a separate state) was propagated. From religious schools and the All India Muslim Conference, the future activists and leaders of the religious party-the Muslim League-were recruited. The party was later given the task of demanding a Muslim state by the division of India.

It was not only India where the British needed Islam as a political tool, it was also felt useful in the long standing British conflict with the Russians in Central Asia. Alarmed by fast reaching Russian moves towards the Indian borders, plans were made to stop the menace before it reached the precious colonial possession. As the population of the Central Asian Khanates was Muslim by religion, it was thought by the colonial administration to use the religious sentiments in order to encourage the population to oppose Russians or to seek support for the British cause. Thus, for nearly a century, using Islam as a political tool, was included among the strategies in the famous 'great game' played by the Russians and the British spies and diplomats for the control of Central Asia. From late 19th century, all efforts were made to politically mobilise Muslims of Central and South Asia, the Middle East and North Africa in the name of fighting the infidels (Russians). Later on, the target became the atheist socialists; when the prime objective of the British Empire was to counter the ever growing danger of Bolshevik revolution. This revolution was mesmerizing not only for the European masses, but also a significant section of Muslim society was influenced by its anti-imperialist rhetoric.

Emergence of Pan-Islamism of 19th century was a very influential and effective political and religious phenomenon. Its objective was to use the ever present desire of Muslims to establish true Islam as a political weapon in the British efforts to mobilize Muslim masses against the increasing Russian threat of gaining grounds in Western and Central Asia. The slogan of Pan-Islamism was created, and the terminology of Islamic *Umma* was re-manufactured to create a transnational Islamic movement, which could serve the British colonial interests. Writers from different parts of Asia were commissioned for that purpose, and political activists were hired from India, Turkey, and Egypt for the propagation of Pan-Islamism. They were handsomely financed by the colonial administration in India and Egypt. One of the British agents, was Jamaluddin Afghani. There is much controversy regarding his origin; born either in Kabul or Asadabad in 1839, Afghani was the son of an East India Company representative in Afghanistan (Keddie, 1972; Dreyfuss, 1981). There was also a lot of controversy regarding his social background; whether he had Jewish or Persian Shi'ite connections, Afghani became the powerful tool for spreading Islamic fundamentalism, and in many ways was the founder of political Islam in the contemporary world.

Controlled by the British experts on affairs of the East, Wilfrid Scawen Blunt and Edward G. Browne, Afghani was given different assignments and appointed to various important positions in Afghanistan, Turkey and Iran with active British scheming (Dreyfuss, 1981). He was installed as the Prime Minister of Afghanistan in 1866 for some time (Dreyfuss, 1981). In 1869, he was sent to India to coordinate intellectual efforts on the "two-nation theory" front with other British agents like Syed Ahmad Khan (Kia, 1996). Syed Ahmad Khan and many other religious leaders and academics, allied with the colonial administration in India, were tasked to propagate the "two nation theory" which was based on the notion that as Muslims and Hindus are two separate religious entities, so they cannot live together in one country. However, Afghani was withdrawn from India as he developed serious personal differences with Syed Ahmad Khan and his group. For a short period beginning in 1870, Afghani became a member of the Board of Education in Istanbul (Kiddie, 1968; Landau, 1990), and according to Dreyfuss (1981), this became possible only through active manipulations in the Istanbul court circles by British officials. After his expulsion from Turkey, he was based in Cairo where he was directed to intensify his efforts in the formation of a network of activists and to unite them under the slogan of Pan-Islamism. The Prime Minister of Egypt, who was a known protégé of the British, gave Afghani an important position in Al Azhar University. Here using his position, he was able to recruit young students for his cause—famous among them was Muhammad Abduh—who later became the founding ideologue of Muslim Brotherhood Movement. A majority of radical movements in today's Middle East are the direct offspring of the Muslim Brotherhood Movement. During 1879, Afghani became overtly involved in the British and French efforts to depose Khedive Ismail of Egypt; however, instead of rewarding Afghani, the newly installed Khedive of Egypt, Taufiq, suddenly ordered him to leave Egypt and according to Kiddie (1968, page, 21), this was either because of inflammatory speeches or the unwanted political intrigues of Afghani. After his expulsion from Egypt, Afghani was installed in Paris where he established a French language journal and an Arabic journal called *Al-Urwah al-Wuthkah* (Landau, 1990). Among his Pan-Islamist circles in Paris were Egyptians, Indians, Turks, Syrians, and North African propagandists; mostly recruited by the British military establishment in Egypt and India. In 1885, with British connivance, the King of Persia, Nasir ad-Din Qajar, appointed Afghani as the Prime Minister of Iran for a year (Dreyfuss, 1981). After being expelled from Iran on charges of plotting to kill the Persian monarch, he was installed in London in 1886. From his London headquarters, he was instrumental in the destabilization of the Qajar Dynasty by recruiting and handsomely financing Ayatollahs and other religious personalities (some of the powerful Ayatollahs and religious leaders ruling Iran since 1979 are the direct descendants of Afghani's recruited people). The immediate objective of his endeavours was to build up an uprising in Persia led by his recruited Ayatollahs to blackmail the Qajar Dynasty in order to gain commercial favours for British companies, curtailing Russian influence in Persia and accepting British demands of strategic importance (Keddie, 1972). Another target, which was given to Afghani in London, was to champion vigorously the formation of a military pact between Britain, Turkey, Persia, and Afghanistan against Russia (Landau, 1990).

Afghani's efforts, although, did not produce tangible results in Central Asia and there occurred no real religious resistance against the Russian occupation of Central Asia. Nevertheless, his clandestine web of writers and religious leaders played important role in the consolidation of British efforts to divide India on religious grounds. The "Pan-Islamic Movement" and the terminology of the "Nation of Islam" or Indian "two nation theory" were effectively used by strategic planners in London and New Delhi for the division of India in 1947. Some of the Muslim religious leaders and an elite group of Muslims—affiliated with East India Company and the colonial administration in India— were organized into a political party, the Muslim League, and were given the task of demanding a state out of India on religious grounds. The so-called demand of creating an Islamic state of Pakistan got its ideological foundation from the Pan-Islamic movement of Jamaluddin Afghani. Khimjee (2013) observed that Muslim religious element in India influenced by Afghani's 'Pan-Islamism' soon became the dominant factor in the Muslim politics of India. Afghani's magazine '*Urwat al-Wuthkah*' was continuously urging Indian Muslims to reclaim their territory (*Dar al-Islam*) as a religious obligation, describing Muslim presence in India as living in *Dar al-Harb* (Dar al Harb literally means the place of war; however, in an Islamic perspective, the term is used for areas of the world where non-believers or infidels live*)*. Although, the main objective of creating the religious state of Pakistan was to safeguard British interests in the Middle East and Central Asia after its withdrawal from India in 1947; it did nevertheless, provide a strong base for the propagation of fundamentalist Islam in the region for the coming decades.

PAKISTAN: THE PURPOSELY CREATED STATE

With the end of colonial setup in India in mind, the British were planning to safeguard their long-term interests in South-Central Asia and the Middle East. In the changing political scenario where the Soviet Union emerged as the second super power after Second World War, where China and India were eventually to be ruled by communists and nationalists, creating a client state was thought to be imperative by the planners and strategists in Whitehall and New Delhi. The creation of such a state was also felt necessary to safeguard British interests in the Middle East with its newly found vast oil reserves. The Muslim League under the leadership of Mr. Muhammad Ali Jinnah and a host of other leaders who had been on the pay-roll of the British colonial authorities for generations-was ready to serve the purpose of safeguarding British interests. The eventual creation of Pakistan was to establish a British base in the region after the withdrawal.

Long before, the British already had a blue print of their future actions in India and that was the partition of the Bengal province in 1905. Azad (1988), believed that although, the immediate objective was to weaken the nationalist forces, the partition of Bengal became the model for future division of India. The true picture of the colonial policies of separating Muslims from Hindus came into open when the colonial establishment created Muslim League in 1906. This was a political party composed of loyal Muslims, spies of the British administration in India and personalities whose families had been on the pay-roll of East India Company for many years. To bolster the image of the League, the British in 1909 introduced separate electorates for Muslims and Hindus at the provincial level. The Communal Award in 1932 was the next step, which enhanced the communal divide (Azad, 1988). The open rebellion on the part of the Indian National Congress enhanced the position of the Muslim League in the eyes of the British authorities enormously because of its compliant stance during the 'Quit India Movement' of 1942-1943. While Congress leaders were imprisoned during the movement, the Muslim League offered Britain its open support. However, the League was never accepted as their representative political party by the majority of Muslims in India. Its leaders were not trusted by Muslim masses because of their open connections with the colonial administration. In elections held in 1937, the League failed to secure a majority vote in any of the Muslim majority provinces of India (Azad, 1988). As the British authorities failed to muster enough support for the Muslim League party among the Muslims of India for its division on religious grounds, they decided to impose the partition and to do it fast.

After World War II, the British hurriedly put into action their well chalked out plan of dividing India and then quitting. The British Prime Minister Winston Churchill in 1940 was quoted by many Indian politicians-including G.M.Syed from Sindh-as having assured the pro-British Indian politician Sir Skindar in Cairo that a country would be created for the loyalists of the British administration in India (Janmahmad, 1989). During the same period in 1940, the leader of Muslim League, Mr. Muhammad Ali Jinnah, proposed the creation of Pakistan at the Lahore Muslim League convention in 1940. As a result a resolution was passed demanding the partition of India and creation of a religious state for Muslims. The resolution was believed to have been drafted in the Whitehall. Lord Zetland, the then secretary of state for India discussed fully and endorsed the resolution, when Muslim League leader Choudhry Khaliquzaman met him in London to deliberate on the Lahore meeting of the Muslim League (Sarila, 2006).

The British objectives in the creation of Pakistan were summarized in a memorandum for the Prime Minister, by the military establishment of the Great Britain as follows (Sarila, 2006, p. 26):

- *We will obtain important strategic facilities [such as] the port of Karachi and air bases in North West India and the support of Muslim manpower.*
- *We should be able to ensure the continued independence and integrity [of] Afghanistan.*

- *We should increase our prestige and improve our position throughout the Muslim world, and demonstrate, by the assistance Pakistan would receive, the advantages of links with the British Commonwealth.*

- *Our links with Pakistan might have a stabilizing effect on India as a whole, since an attack by Hindustan on Pakistan would involve Hindustan in war, not with Pakistan alone, but [also] with the British Commonwealth.*

- *The position on the Frontier might well become more settled since relations between the tribes and Pakistan would be easier than they could be with a united India.*

Lord Mountbatten, the last Viceroy of India, in an unsigned memorandum summarized the crux of the British view for the creation of Pakistan (Sarila, 2006, p. 28):

> *"The Indus Valley, western Punjab and Baluchistan[the northwest] are vital to any strategic plans for the defence of [the] all important Muslim belt...the oil supplies of the Middle East. If one looks upon this area as a strategic wall (against Soviet expansionism) the five most important bricks in the wall are: Turkey, Iran, Afghanistan and Pakistan.*

> *Only through the open ocean port of Karachi could the opponents of the Soviet Union take immediate and effective countermeasures. The sea approaches to all other countries will entail navigation in enclosed waters directly menaced by Russian air fleets...not only of the sea lanes of approach, but also the ports of disembarkation.*

> *If the British Commonwealth and the United States of America are to be in a position to defend their vital interests in the Middle East, then the best and most stable area from which to conduct this defence is from Pakistan territory.*

> *Pakistan is the keystone of the strategic arch of the wide and vulnerable waters of the Indian ocean."*

On February 26, 1947, the British Government made the important policy announcement regarding India. It declared its intention to quit India by June 1948 and transfer the authority from British to Indian hands. On 3 June 1947, Viscount Louis Mountbatten, the last British Governor General of India, announced the partitioning of British India into India and Pakistan. With the speedy passage through the British Parliament of the Indian Independence Act 1947, on August 14, 1947, two provinces of Punjab and Bengal were divided and with the merger of Sindh and North-Western Frontier Province, the religious state of Pakistan was created out of India. In a controversial referendum, British Balochistan was also merged with the newly created state (British Balochistan consisted of leased areas of the Baloch state of Kalat and some regions of southern Afghanistan which were ceded to the British India with the drawing of Durand line).

PAKISTAN: A UNIQUE PHENOMENON

'Divide and rule' had been employed by imperial powers throughout history and the division of the people being ruled was considered one of the most practical strategies for the safeguarding of rulers' interests. Pakistan was created to safeguard the multi-faceted strategic interests of the British Empire who was at that time the guardian of Western Imperial interests in the region. However, the genesis of Pakistan is a unique experience in the history of political science in that it was the first country created on the grounds that people of one religious faith cannot live with the people of another religious faith. It is also unique in that it gave an ideological base for the creation of the state, a new theory 'Two Nation Theory' was manufactured. It was based on the perception that people of different cultural, historical and linguistic background can form a nation only upon the basis of their religious faith denying all established definitions of a nation. Janmahmad (1989), commented that this ideological foundation of Pakistan was superfluous and without any historical truth. The people who invaded, ruled and settled in India since the 9th century were a medley of various Middle Eastern and Central Asian nations and tribal groupings who never constituted a nation. A national identity is based essentially on a common race, common language, common social values and traditions, a common history and a territory which are completely missing in the case of Pakistan.

There are many other unique features of this 'Allah given-British created' state. The speed in which the creation of Pakistan was finalized is unprecedented in the history of colonialism. In 1940, a resolution was passed at a meeting of a party demanding the division of their country on religious grounds, and within six years, they achieved what they demanded. It was also unique in the history of political science, that a country was created without any movement on behalf of the general population and without even a nose bleed, in the struggle to liberate a people from colonialism. It was unique that the entire national leadership of this newly independent state was exported from elsewhere, its ideology was created by the colonial power, its national language was not the language of any national entity of the country, and the population of regions, which now comprised Pakistan, was overwhelmingly against the creation of Pakistan.

With the baggage of its artificial creation, its superfluous and fallacious founding philosophy and later developments in international polity, Pakistan was bound to become a satellite state subservient to the wishes of the Western Bloc. A vital component behind the stability of the Pakistani state came from its strong relationship with Great Britain and the United States. Both states became patrons of Pakistan, and sources of military and economic aid (Haqqani, 2005). This special relationship was vital in the consolidation and stabilization of this artificially created state and its superfluous religious ideology. It was also vital for the UK and the US, as it was to become an important part of the physical 'Islamic barrier' against presumed Soviet socialist advances towards the warm waters of Indian Ocean. Pakistan was not created because of any demand from the people of the region, but because the colonial power wanted a state for their protégé in order to use it for the protection of its vital interests in the region following its withdrawal from India.

The colonial administration of British India in New Delhi and Whitehall were ever-ready to counter any move endangering the security of precious British colonial possessions in India, and presumed Russian advances towards warm waters of the Indian Ocean. Tragically, it was the Muslim desire for re-establishment of true Islam which was used as one of their tools in efforts to safeguard colonial interests in Indian Ocean, Central Asia and the Middle East. The creation of the client state of Pakistan by dividing India in the name of Islam, is one among many artificially created states by colonial powers for safe guarding their long-term strategic interests in regions they ruled for long times.

For the people of regions, which now comprised Pakistan, creation of a religious state came out of blue; however, the British decision of partitioning India and creating a religious state was the culmination of a long standing and unrelenting policy of the colonial administration in India and policy planners in London for Middle East and Central Asia. The occupation of India, the rivalry of Czarist Russia with Britain in Central Asia, the emergence of the Soviet Union on the horizon of world politics, and discovery of oil reserves in the Middle East can be cited as causative factors in the creation of Pakistan. Pakistan is a unique case of exploiting a people's religious or mythological beliefs in the division of a country and the creation of a state by powerful forces in the political history of the world.

CHAPTER 9

INDEPENDENCE AND FALL
OF THE BALOCH STATE

With the British announcement of their withdrawal from India following the end of Second World War, the Baloch state of Khanate of Kalat prepared for independence after a prolonged British occupation. Efforts were made to regain territories which had been incorporated in the province of British Balochistan and a group of lawyers was hired by the Khan of the Baloch to plead his case on the sovereignty of these areas, once the British has gone. The Baloch state itself proclaimed its independence on August12, 1947. Elections were held for a bi-cameral parliament. However, it became a short-lived independence and Pakistan occupied the Baloch state only 9 months following the declaration of its independence.

BALOCHISTAN AT THE TIME OF BRITISH WITHDRAWAL

At the time when preparations were being made for the creation of Pakistan and eventual British withdrawal from India, Eastern Balochistan under British control was divided into British Balochistan and the Khanate of Kalat. British Balochistan comprised of Afghan areas ceded to the British under the Treaty of

Gandamak in 1880 and areas of the Khanate of Kalat including, Quetta, Marri-Bugti Agency, Sibi and Chagai, which were leased out by the Khan of Kalat to the Government of British India with the signing of various accords in 1883, 1899, and 1903 (Naseer, 1979). Dera Ismail Khan and Dera Ghazi Khan regions of Balochistan were already included in the province of Punjab. British Balochistan was part of British India and ruled by an Agent to Governor General, while the Khanate was in treaty relationship directly with Whitehall. With the division of Balochistan during the last decades of 19th century by the Goldsmid, Durand and McMahon lines, and with the collapse of the Baloch resistance against Qajar and Pahlavi regimes, Western Balochistan was already under the full control of the Persian state.

BALOCHISTAN PREPARES FOR INDEPENDENCE

During 1930s, the Baloch state was struggling to convince the British authorities that they should implement the treaty obligations signed with the Baloch state of Kalat following its occupation in 1839. However, a new development in the Indian political scene adversely affected the endeavours of the Khan for regaining some autonomy for the Khanate. In 1935, a Government of India Act was promulgated, which introduced far-reaching constitutional and administrative changes in British India. Besides formally establishing the province of British Balochistan under the Government of India Act, the Khanate of Kalat itself was declared as part of British India. This was in clear violation of the Treaty of 1876, which committed the British to recognize and respect the independence of Kalat under its various Articles. The treaty was signed between the Khan and the Viceroy of India, Lord Lytton, at Jacobabad in July 1876 (Aitchison, 1929). It was the renewal and reaffirmation of the treaty which was concluded on the 14 May 1854 between the British Government and Khan Naseer Khan. It affirmed the perpetual friendship between the British Government and Khan of Khelat, his heirs, and successors.

Article 3 of the treaty explicitly mentioned that: *"whilst on his part, Meer Khodadad Khan, Khan of Khelat, binds himself, his heirs, successors, and Sirdars, to observe faithfully the provisions of Article 3 of the Treaty of 1854, the British Government on its part engages to respect the independence of Khelat, and to aid the Khan, in case of need, in the maintenance of a just authority and the protection of his territories from external attack, by such means as the British Government may at the moment deem expedient"* (Aitchison, 1929). However, it appeared that Treaty of 1876 was only on paper, and the British never fully honoured its treaty obligations with the Khanate of Kalat. With the promulgation of Government of India Act 1935, the Khanate was reduced to the rank of an Indian princely state, at least *de facto* if not *de jure*. According to Bizenjo (2009), the Khan did realize the importance of settling the issue of the status of his state with the British authorities in the wake of developing changes. However, he was not strong enough to take a robust and workable attitude toward the issue. He hired a known protégé of the British authorities, Mr. Muhammad Ali Jinnah, as the lawyer to represent the interests of the Khanate in New Delhi, a move which later became an important factor in the demise of the Baloch state. Mr. Muhammad Ali Jinnah, when appointed as the first Governor-General of Pakistan in 1947, played a key role in the occupation of Balochistan by Pakistan. The Khan neither had grasped the reality that the Great Britain planned to create a country by dividing India nor was he able to realize that his state by its geographical location and its contiguity with the proposed new country would be vulnerable.

In preparation for independence after an imminent British withdrawal, the Khan of Kalat, Mir Ahmad Yar Khan put forward the following demands to the British authorities with reference to various treaty agreements between the British and the Khanate (Baloch, 1975; Naseer, 1979):

- The British must honor all their commitments, and the treaty of 1876 must be fully honored.

- All leased and tribal territories such as Quetta, Chagai, Bolan, Nasirabad, and Mari-Bugti areas should be returned to the control of the Khanate.
- The Khan should be allowed to announce the establishment of a parliament, which should comprise of two houses.
- The right to appoint the prime minister of the Khanate should be given to the Khan with the consultation of the British Government.
- Instead of the tribal chiefs, the Khan should exert control on Jhalawan and Sarawan without the interference of the British political agents.

Receiving no positive response from the British authorities, the Khan, in 1939, called a "Consultative Jirga. (assembly) of all tribal chiefs and elders from all over the state in which he announced the establishment of a cabinet and a Council of State without prior consultation with British officials. The cabinet comprised of twelve independent ministerial members of equal importance, and the *Wazir-e-Azam* (prime minister) was to be responsible to the Council of State. Axmann (2009), observed that the British vehemently opposed the administrative reforms. They became irritated and alarmed by the unilateral actions of the Khan.

At a time, when the Baloch state was expecting that, upon the cessation of British power in India, its pre-1876 full independent status would be restored and it would regain sovereign rights over all its territories held or leased to Britain; things were moving fast towards the creation of Pakistan. A three member Cabinet Mission was sent from London in 1946 to devise the methodology for the transfer of power in India. The Khan decided to raise the status of his state and presented a memorandum to the Cabinet Mission. The salient features of the memorandum were as follows:

➢ The Kalat is an independent and sovereign state, its relation with the British Government being based on various mutual agreements and treaties.

> ➤ The Kalat is not an Indian state, its relations with India being of only a formal nature by virtue of Kalat's agreements with the British.

> ➤ With the ceasing of the agreement of 1876 with the Kalat Government, the Khanate of Kalat should regain its complete independence as it existed prior to 1876.

> ➤ All such regions as were given under the control of the British in consequence of any treaty would return to the sovereignty of Kalat state and resume their original status as parts of the Kalat state.

> ➤ On the lapse of the British sovereignty, the agreements in respect of the parts under their control should cease to have any legal binding; and the rights hitherto vested in the British shall automatically be transferred to the Kalat Government (Baloch, 1975).

On April 11, 1946, the Khan, during his meeting with Indian Viceroy Lord Wavell, also explained the Khanate position after the British withdrawal from India. After the announcement of the plan for partitioning of British India into India and Pakistan on June 3, 1947, the Kalat Government had a series of meetings and presentations with representatives of the Viceroy and officials of the future Government of Pakistan in Delhi. On August 4, 1947, a tripartite meeting was held in Delhi, chaired by Viceroy Lord Mountbatten and attended by his legal advisor Lord Ismay. On the Baloch side, Khan Ahmad Yar Khan, and his Prime Minister Barrister Sultan Ahmad were present. Mr. Muhammad Ali Jinnah and Mr. Liaquat Ali Khan represented Pakistan. In the meeting, a consensus was reached upon regarding the future of Balochistan and it was agreed that the Baloch state of Kalat would be independent enjoying the same status as it originally held in 1839 before the British occupation. It was also agreed that in case, relations of Kalat with any future government of divided India become strained, Kalat would exercise its right of self-determination, and the British Government should take precautionary measures to help the Khanate of Kalat in the matter as per the Treaties of 1839 and 1841 (Bizenjo, 2009). A "Standstill Agreement" was signed by Mr. Muhammad Ali Jinnah and Mr. Liaquat Ali Khan on behalf of future state of Pakistan and Mr. Sultan Ahmad on behalf of the Khanate of Kalat on August 4, 1947 (Baloch, 1975). In the agreement, the Government of Pakistan recognizes the Khanate as an independent sovereign State, in treaty relationship with the British Government, with a status different from that of an Indian princely states. It was also agreed that regarding areas of the Khanate leased out to the British in 19th century, legal opinion would be sought as to whether or not the agreements of leases made between the British Government and the Khanate of Kalat would be inherited by the Pakistan Government.

BALOCHISTAN BECAME INDEPENDENT

After the formal declaration of Balochistan as an independent state on August 12, 1947, the Khan appointed Nawabzada Muhammad Aslam Khan as the first Prime Minister of the independent state and Mr. Douglas Fell as the Foreign Minister. The Prime Minister and Foreign Minister of Balochistan visited Karachi to negotiate with the Government of Pakistan on modalities for concluding a treaty of friendship on the basis of August 4, 1947 Standstill Agreement, including matters relating to the areas held under lease with British authorities. The response by Pakistani authorities for a friendship treaty was not promising which later proved their malicious designs towards the Baloch state.

With the promulgation of Government of Kalat State Act 1947, the new constitution of newly independent Baloch state established some kind of a representative system of governance. According to the constitution, a council of ministers was constituted, headed by a Prime Minister. The ministers were appointed by the Khan and held their office at the discretion of the Khan. The function of the council was to aid and advice the Khan of the Baloch, in the exercise of executive authority of the state. (Naseer, 1979). A bi-cameral legislature was enacted composed of an upper and a lower house. The Upper House (*Darul Umara*) was composed of tribal chiefs from Jhalawan and Sarawan. It had forty-six members, ten of whom were appointed by the Khan. Eight of these ten members were to be selected from the Lower House as well as from the Council of Ministers, and the other two members were to be selected from the minority groups. The members of the cabinet were allowed to participate in debates in the house but were not allowed to vote. The Lower House (*Darul Awam*) was composed of fifty-five members, of whom fifty were to be elected and the Khan to nominate the remainder. Elections were held for both houses of the parliament under the Government of Kalat Act 1947. The majority of the members in the House of Commons were elected from candidates nominated by the nationalist organization, the Kalat State National Party (KSNP). The first session of the *Darul Awam* was held at Shahi Camp, Dhadar, on December 12, 1947.

EVENTS LEADING TO THE FALL OF THE BALOCH STATE

Soon after the declaration of independence of the Baloch state, unexpected events began to unfold, leading to second demise of the Baloch state. After the occupation of Kalat in 1839, the newly independent Baloch state once again faced another occupation in 1948.

The Khan was unable to take any positive step to regain the possession of the Baloch areas of British Balochistan as the British in collaboration with the new administration of Pakistan had other plans for the future of Balochistan. The first blow to the newly independent Balochistan came with the merger of British Balochistan with Pakistan, using unfair means by the British authorities in Quetta. Janmahmad (1987), observed that in a sham referendum, the authorities pressurized members of *Shahi Jirga* of Quetta Municipality, who were the nominees of the colonial administration to vote for the merger of British Balochistan with Pakistan. However, they were unable to muster the support of the majority of members of the *Jirga*. The date of the referendum was brought a day earlier, and without voting, it was announced that members of *Shahi Jirga* voted for the annexation with Pakistan. Earlier, the British authorities rejected out rightly the demands of the Baloch tribal chiefs in Mari, Bugti, and Derajat regions to re-join the Khanate of Kalat after the British withdrawal. The Baloch state was powerless to do anything on the loss of its precious territories.

Sensing the real intentions of the Pakistani state which was basking in the glow of all out British support, the Government of Kalat invited the Indian Government to enter into an agreement of friendship and cooperation. A request was also made by the representative of the Khan, Sir Sultan Ahmad, for permission to establish a trade agency in New Delhi. The congress government in New Dehli was not interested (for reasons still unknown) and the Khanate's representative was informed that the request could not be considered. It appears that the refusal of Pakistan and perhaps also of India to conclude friendship treaties with Balochistan was consistent with the British designs of drawing a new map of the region after their formal withdrawal. Dashti (2012), believed that a viable Pakistan was the aim of the British and without Balochistan, it was difficult to give a proper geographical and strategic viability to it as a country. The British authorities impressed upon the Pakistani leaders the need to take practical action for the incorporation of the Baloch state into the newly created religious state. Mr. Muhammad Ali Jinnah, who was hired and handsomely paid by the Khan of the Baloch to represent the case of the leased areas of the Baloch state before the colonial administration in New Delhi was now playing the role of Brutus. To the astonishment of the Baloch, Mr. Jinnah and the Pakistani authorities were openly encouraged by the British administration in India to deal with (the danger of) an independent Balochistan. An extract from a secret memorandum prepared by the British Minister of State for The Commonwealth Relations Office on September 12, 1947, is clearly indicative of the master-mind role of the British Government in future development of events leading to the occupation of the Baloch state by Pakistan in 1948 (Baloch, 1987):

> *"Pakistan has entered into negotiations with Kalat on the basis of recognizing the state's claim to independence and of treating the previous agreements between the crown and Kalat providing for the Lease of Quetta and other areas, which would otherwise lapse under section 7 (I) (6) of the Indian Independence Act, as international agreements untouched by the termination of paramountcy. The Khan of Kalat, whose territory marches with Persia, is, of course, in no position to undertake the international responsibilities of an independent state, and Lord Mountbatten, who, before the transfer of power, was warned of the dangers of such a development, doubtless passed on this warning to the Pakistan Government. The United Kingdom High Commissioner in Pakistan is being informed of the position and asked to do what he can to guide the Pakistan Government away from making any agreement with Kalat which would involve recognition of the state as a separate international entity" (p. 257).*

Pakistan began pressurizing the Khan of the Baloch to merge his state with the religious state. Mr. Muhammad Ali Jinnah, the Governor General of Pakistan, in October 1947, menacingly proposed the accession of Khanate of Kalat to Pakistan. The Khan summoned his parliament in December, 1947, during which the *Darul Awam* (House of Commons) debated the issue of Khanate relationship with Pakistan and the consequences of any move by Pakistan against the Baloch state. The House of Commons rejected any form of merger with Pakistan and resolved to protect the sovereignty of the Baloch state at any cost; unanimously rejecting the proposal for accession of the Baloch state into Pakistan. The *Darul Umarah* (House of Lords) during its session on January 2–4, 1948, endorsing the decision of the *Darul Awam*, also rejected the accession proposal. Both houses of Kalat Parliament once again rejected any merger proposal with Pakistan during their sessions held on the last week of February, 1948 (Naseer, 1979; Baloch, 1987; Janmahmad, 1989).

After failing to pressurize the Baloch parliament, the Pakistani authorities now openly adopted an aggressive policy towards the Baloch state. They successfully manipulated Kharan and Lasbela, — the two subordinate regions of the Khanate — for their "merger" with Pakistan directly. Similarly, Makuran, another province of the Khanate, was forced to declare its "independence" from the Baloch state on March 17, 1948 and a day later announced its merger with Pakistan (Naseer, 1975). Lacking resources to counter the Pakistani moves, the Government of Kalat could only issue a press statement declaring Kharan, Lasbela, and Makuran inalienable parts of Balochistan. The Khan, in a press interview, expressed his desire for an amicable settlement of the dispute with Pakistan over the accession of three constituent units of his state. The Pakistani government did not bother to respond. In his memoirs, the Khan lamented on the loss of territories by stating that the Pakistani Cabinet was working on the scheme to break up the centuries old Baloch state. The taking over of Khanate provinces of Makuran, Kharan, and Las Bela, was tantamount to the political castration and geographical strangulation of the Khanate of Kalat (Baloch, 1975).

Attempts to put up any meaningful resistance against the Pakistani aggression came to an end when the British government flatly refused to supply any arms and ammunition to Balochistan when the Commander-in-Chief of the Khanate forces, Brigadier General Purvez approached the Commonwealth Relations Office and the Ministry of Supply during his visit to England in December 1947 (Bizenjo, 2009). On February 2, 1948, Muhammad Ali Jinnah, the former hired attorney of the Khan and now the Governor General of Pakistan, in a letter to the Khan, forcefully repeated the Pakistani demand for a merger. The parliament of the Khanate was then finally informed by the Prime Minister of the Baloch state that Pakistan had refused to enter into any treaty relationship and had extended an ultimatum for unconditional accession (Naseer, 1979). The Baloch state was helpless against the Pakistani aggression and the Khan of the Baloch could only threaten to appeal to the International Court of Justice and the United Nations. After gaining possession of the Khanate provinces of Makuran, Las Bela, and Kharan, the

Pakistani authorities were now openly threatening the use of force against the capital of the Baloch state. The tribal chiefs and various political parties and groups, including Kalat State National Party (KSNP), advised the Khan that since it was not possible to face the might of Pakistan Army in a head-on confrontation, in the given situation, the only option to defend the country was to wage a defensive guerrilla war. The Khan was advised to proceed to Afghanistan and from there to approach the United Nation, while Baloch fighters waged the war against the invaders. However, the Khan could not muster enough personal courage, and under the influence of his Foreign Minister and advisor Mr. Douglas Fell, he decided to hand over the Baloch state to Pakistan (Bizenjo, 2009). The Khan of Kalat, Mir Ahmad Yar Khan, after hearing the news that the Pakistani troops had moved into southern coastal towns of Pasni and Jiwani, eventually succumbed and affixed his signature to the Agreement of Accession on March 27, 1948, terming his action as a "dictate of history":

> *"I confess, I knew I was exceeding the scope of my mandate . . . [but] had I not taken the immediate step of signing Kalat's merger, the . . . British Agent to the Governor-General could have played havoc by leading Pakistan into a fratricide war against the Baluches (Baloch, 1975, p. 162)."*

The occupation of their country by Pakistan was unexpected and came out of blue for the Baloch. It was totally unacceptable for them, but they were unable to offer any meaningful resistance. On the one side, there was the might of the Pakistan army and on the other side, the Baloch were unarmed and disorganized, whose symbol of unity and strength - the Khan of the Baloch– had betrayed them. In the words of Mir Ghous Bakhsh Bizenjo, who was the leader of House of Commons in the Baloch parliament at the time of occupation, in taking such a step—in gross violation of the will of Baloch people as expressed unanimously by members of both Houses of Parliament—the Khan rendered himself guilty of an act of great injustice to them by his act of cowardly submission to invaders (Bizenjo, 2009). According to Bizenjo, at the crossroads of history, Balochistan was unfortunately without any robust leadership; a leadership, which was needed to consolidate the newly achieved independence after a long and dark period of colonial rule. At this crucial period of Baloch history, the Khan of the Baloch was a broken man, and the grit and conviction to defend the independence of the Baloch state was no longer in him (Bizenjo, 2009).

The Pakistani authorities resumed the full charge of the Khanate on April 1, 1948 by appointing a political agent for the administration of the Khanate. A short-lived and ineffective resistance against the occupation led by younger brother of the Khan was crushed by Pakistan, political activities were banned, and KSNP was declared illegal and its leaders were arrested. The Baloch dreams of an independent and honourable status were shattered by the grand designs of an imperialist power safeguarding its interests in the region, disregarding all its treaty obligations with one of its colonial protectorates.

The independence of the Baloch state after nearly a hundred years of colonial control was short-lived as after nine months it was occupied by a newly created religious state. The creation of Pakistan was among the mishaps of history, which ultimately led to the demise of the Baloch State of Kalat, causing one of the most tragic events in the history of the Baloch. Events taking shape in the remote and faraway lands caused occupation, division and misery for the Baloch. The British occupation of Balochistan in 1839 and its subsequent division was one of the casualties of 'the great game' between Russia and the British Empire during 19th century. The 'cold war' (fought between Soviet Russia and the Western powers headed by the US and the UK in the aftermath of Second World War), caused the occupation of the Khanate of Kalat by the newly created state of Pakistan. From a cold war perspective, it became imperative for the British to strengthen its client state of Pakistan as it was of great importance for safeguarding Western interests in the Persian Gulf and other long-term strategic interests of Britain and the West in the region. In the achievement of this target, Great

Britain ignored its treaty obligations made with the Baloch state after its occupation in 1839. The occupation of Balochistan by Pakistan is a typical example of a collateral damage to a people orchestrated by external political developments and having nothing to do with the Baloch. The Baloch leadership was caught unawares by the fast moving developments of international politics. They could not formulate robust policies to safeguard their independence and in the process of making Pakistan viable, their land was taken away from them, and a protracted and bloody conflict ensued between the Baloch and Pakistan.

CHAPTER 10

THE RESISTANCE AGAINST PAKISTAN AFTER THE OCCUPATION

After the occupation, the Baloch reacted with a short lived armed resistance and political mobilization against the loss of their land and sovereignty. The Khan of the Baloch also became active after remaining silent for many years and began organizing and mobilizing different tribes of Jhalawan and Sarawan. However, the initial armed resistance, the later political mobilization efforts and the activities of the Khan ended in 1958, when Martial Law was declared in Pakistan. All political activities were banned and the Palace of the Khan in Kalat was bombarded and he was arrested on charges of conspiring with Afghanistan to dismember Pakistan.

THE SHORT-LIVED ARMED RESISTANCE

The Baloch soon recovered from the effects of the devastating shock and aftershocks of suddenly losing their independent status, and began formulating strategies to regain their lost sovereignty. The younger brother of the Khan, Prince Abdul Karim was the first person to begin an armed resistance against Pakistan. He issued a manifesto in the name of Baloch National Liberation Committee disavowing the unconditional accession agreement signed by the

Khan, proclaiming the independence of the Baloch state of Kalat, and demanded fresh negotiations with Pakistan. On April 15, 1948, he crossed the border to get help from Afghanistan along with his close companions, prominent among them was Muhammad Husain Unqa, Malik Muhammad Saeed, Abdul Wahid Kurd and Muhammad Khan Raisani and Qadir Bakhsh Nizamani. Unfortunately, there was no positive response from Afghans. The Afghan Foreign Minister, Muhammad Ali Khan, told Malik Muhammad Saeed, the emissary of the Prince that the Afghan government was not in a position to extend any kind of material help to the Baloch except giving members of the Baloch delegation refugee status in his country (Dehwar, 1994). After the refusal of help from the Afghan government for his struggle against Pakistan, the Prince decided to return to Balochistan where he established a resistance camp near Kalat and volunteers from various tribes began to pour into the camp. Skirmishes began between Pakistani forces and the Baloch fighters; however, on July 12, 1948, Prince Abdul Karim and over one hundred others were surrounded and arrested by Pakistani armed forces. They were tried in a special *Jirga* and sentenced to various terms of imprisonment. According to Bizenjo (2009), with poorly equipped and a resource-starved volunteer force, Prince Abdul Karim could not have stayed across the border for long. The success of his mission of organizing an effective armed resistance movement against Pakistan without solid external support became impossible. As material support neither from Afghanistan or from any other external source, ever came; the armed resistance of Prince Abdul Karim was doomed to fail. However, the uprising headed by the Prince and its sad ending is important in the Baloch history of national liberation struggle as it established that the Baloch did not accept the occupation of their land. It symbolized the beginning of the Baloch national resistance in Pakistan, it also made it obvious that the Baloch resistance in order to be effective against the occupation needed more organization and resources.

Pakistan, besides taking stern and draconian military actions against the Baloch resistance, in order to neutralize the Baloch reaction against the occupation, in 1952, created an administrative unit 'Balochistan States Union' (BSU), comprising former constituent regions of the Khanate. This was to give a false perception of giving Balochistan some kind of autonomous status within Pakistan. The Khan of Kalat was chosen as President of the BSU, a constitution was drafted and early elections and the formation of a government were promised. However, nothing materialized and in 1954, the Khan and the puppet rulers of the states comprising BSU, were forced to sign an agreement to be part of 'One Unit' of West Pakistan (One Unit was another administrative unit combining all provinces and territories of West Pakistan into one administrative unit). This was a project aimed firstly to counter the majority of Bengalis and secondly to begin a process of assimilation of minority nationalities into Pakistan's artificial state national identity). The Balochistan States Union ceased to exist from October 14, 1955. This was the ultimate demise of any semblance of an independent status of Balochistan in Pakistan.

POLITICAL MOBILIZATION AFTER OCCUPATION

The knee jerk reaction by the Baloch against the occupation was manifested by armed resistance and after the collapse of the resistance by Prince Abdul Karim, the Baloch as a whole were traumatized for a period. However, after recovering from the initial shock, nationalist activists and leaders began mobilizing politically.

Historically, the Baloch political struggle, following the occupation of Balochistan by Pakistan, was the continuation of political mobilization, which began after First World War. The first quarter of the twentieth century can be mentioned as the founding years of the Baloch political awakening. During the First World War, a small youth group began to mobilize the masses by establishing clandestine groups and formal political organizations, a phenomenon which was unprecedented in the history of the Baloch. These efforts culminated first in the formation of *Anjuman-e-Itehad-e-Baloch wa Balochistan*, and finally in the Kalat State National Party (KSNP) in 1937 (Naseer, 1979; Baloch, 1987; Janmahmad, 1989; Bizenjo, 2009). The *Anjuman* was not only the formation of a structured open political organization but it also marked the beginning of a secular, non-tribal nationalist movement in Balochistan.

The *Anjuman* and KSNP became the nuclei of a long-drawn Baloch national struggle against subjugation and exploitation. When Mir Ahmad Yar Khan became the new Khan of the Baloch on September 20, 1933, the Baloch nationalists tried to influence him in favour of their demands for political reforms and tried to embolden him into making preparation for the eventual independence of Balochistan (Naseer, 1979). They were conscious of the rapidly changing scenario in India and anticipated the impending British withdrawal from the region.

Under the auspices of the *Anjuman*, the convening of the First All India Baloch Conference in Jacobabad from 27-29 December 1932 was a major political event regarding the Baloch political mobilization (Naseer, 1979). The conference reiterated *Anjumans'* demands for democratic and social reforms in Balochistan and the re-unifications of all Baloch regions into the Khanate of Kalat. The next year, this conference was followed by a similar conference named as 'All India Baloch and Balochistan Conference' in Hyderabad (Sindh). This conference also reaffirmed the resolution of establishing a constitutional government in Balochistan and the unification of all Baloch lands (Baloch, 1987).

On February 5, 1937, at Sibi, Baloch nationalists and activists affiliated with the *Anjuman* convened a conference and the first Baloch political party, the Kalat State National Party (KSNP) was founded which became the progenitor of many political organizations and resistance groups in coming decades. The political mobilization of the Baloch during last decades of colonial rule was spearheaded by leaders and activists of Kalat State National Party. The objectives of the party were-on broader front, to struggle against colonialism and imperialism and on the internal front, against the oppressive hegemony of tribal chiefs (*Sardars*). However, the end of colonial rule for Balochistan was the expressed or unexpressed primary goal of the party (Baloch, 1987). According to Bizenjo (2009), the manifesto of the KSNP published on April 1, 1937 contained mainly points for solidarity among the Baloch, unification of the Baloch land, preservation of the Baloch national identity besides mobilizing the masses for an anti-colonial struggle. The manifesto pointed out that despite having a glorious past under the Khanate of Kalat, the Baloch have been denied their national rights under the colonial setup. It called for ending of tribal feuds among various tribes and stressed unity among the Baloch. It demanded internal reforms in the Khanate with the status of the Khan to be converted as a 'Constitutional Head'. It asserted that historically, Balochistan was as much an independent state as Iran and Afghanistan and the British and Baloch relations were under treaty obligations; hence, the national identity of the Baloch and the territorial integrity of Balochistan should not be compromised and the Khanate of Kalat should assert itself as the custodian of Baloch traditional and historical heritage in order to play a significant role in the family of nations in the region.

From its formation, the KSNP played hide and seek with the British administration in Quetta on the one hand and with the Khan of the Baloch in Kalat on the other hand. During its life time, it faced bans from the administration of the Khan, imprisonments and persecution of its leaders by the administration of British Balochistan. On other occasions, it was rehabilitated by the Khan and many of its leaders and activists were inducted in the administrative setup of the Khanate. The KSNP despite basic differences, adopted a policy of cooperation with the Khan on national issues. In the first ever elections in the short-lived independent Balochistan, it emerged as the most powerful political force by taking majority of the seats in the Lower House of Parliament. It attempted to persuade the Khan to adopt feasible and practical steps in order to protect the newly won freedom. On its initiatives, both houses of the Baloch Parliament rejected any idea of compromise on the sovereignty of the Baloch state in the face of the belligerent attitude of Pakistan. Although, the party was not able to foil Pakistani aggression against the Baloch in 1948; nevertheless, its activists became torch bearers of the Baloch national struggle in coming years.

In the aftermath of the occupation and the collapse of the armed resistance by Prince Abdul Karim, the KSNP was banned by the Pakistani authorities. After a brief period in the political wilderness, the Baloch political activist began to reorganize themselves in order to carry on the resistance struggle on a political front. Veterans of the banned Kalat State National Party established a new organization named as *Ustaman Gal* (Party of the nation) in 1955. Prince Abdul Karim who had been released from prison by Pakistani authorities at that time was elected as President and Muhammad Husain Unqa as Secretary of the party. The party adopted a policy of joining the struggles of other nationalist and progressive parties in Pakistan. This was perhaps a tactical decision in order to gain support from a wider section. Being a part of the political process of the state was to decrease the intensity of the coercive actions of the state on the Baloch political activists who were branded by the state establishment as anti-state elements. *Ustaman Gal* was merged with Pakistan National Party (PNP) on December 2, 1956. The salient policy points of the PNP included the struggle for the dissolution of One Unit, national rights for the national entities of Pakistan, protection of fundamental rights of all citizens and an anti-imperialist and non-aligned foreign policy for Pakistan. After a year, with the merger of a section of Bengali nationalists and progressive elements into PNP, on July 25, 1957, a new party – the National Awami Party (NAP) - was established in Dhaka. Among the aims of National Awami Party was reorganization of provinces on linguistic, cultural and historical basis; maximum provincial autonomy for the provinces in a federal structure, with only defence, foreign affairs and currency to be left with the Federal Government and all other powers to rest with autonomous units (Rashiduzzaman, 1970). The NAP provided a progressive alternative to the religious narrative of Pakistani establishment and it became the voice of the oppressed nationalities by advocating autonomy for the federating units of Pakistan. The Baloch leadership saw no alternative but to use the platform provided by NAP to further the political aims of the Baloch national resistance in Pakistan.

TRIBAL MOBILIZATION UNDER THE LEADERSHIP OF KHAN

Soon after its creation, Pakistan became a country full of intrigue and political manipulation between the various contenders for power within the ruling alliance of Military, *Mullahs* (the religious elite) and *Muhajirs* (refugees from north Indian provinces). A widely propagated left oriented military takeover bid of the state political apparatus was foiled on 9th March 1951 and several senior army officers and a large number of progressive intellectuals from all over the country were arrested. They were tried by a special tribunal and the case became known as the Rawalpindi Conspiracy Case. In the same year, on 16th October 1951, the first Prime Minister of Pakistan, Nawabzada Liaquat Ali Khan, was shot dead in Rawalpindi, under mysterious circumstances, but it was widely believed his murder was ordered by the military establishment. From then onwards, Pakistani politics became a game of musical chair orchestrated by the powerful military establishment. Several Prime Ministers were changed during the first decade of its existence as a state. On October 27, 1958, the army came into open, Martial Law was declared, replacing the so-called democratic system with a prolonged military dictatorship.

In Balochistan, after some years of remaining silent, the Khan of the Baloch, Mir Ahmad Yar became active and tried to mobilize tribes of Sarawan and Jhalawan. In 1957, he initiated a public campaign for the restoration of the former status of his Khanate by organizing tribal assemblies and rallies. Subsequently, he headed a delegation of forty-four tribal chiefs belonging to several tribes of Balochistan in a meeting with Iskandar Mirza, the President of Pakistan. The Baloch delegation in the meeting put forward the demand of restoration of the Khanate within the federation of Pakistan. Bizenjo (2009), observed that for the Pakistani authorities, the activities of the Khan were in practice the beginning of a struggle for the dismemberment of their country. The Baloch demands were rejected and the delegation return to Kalat empty-handed. This further infuriated the Baloch tribes and a situation of violent confrontation was created. The Baloch tribal chiefs of Sarawan and Jhalawan began a general mobilization, while the Pakistani army strengthened its position in Balochistan to pre-empt any mass uprising by the Baloch. On October 5, 1958, the army moved into Kalat under the command of Brigadier Tikka Khan. Tanks entered into premises of the Khan's Palace firing indiscriminately. The troops also fired on agitating people outside the Palace, killing several of them (Ahmad, 1992). The Khan was arrested, taken to Punjab, accused of secretly negotiating with Afghanistan for a full-scale Baloch rebellion against Pakistan and interned in Lahore. Nearly a thousand Baloch activists were arrested in the follow up of the military operation.

On October 7, 1958, President Iskander Mirza proclaimed martial law throughout Pakistan, the constitution was abrogated, assemblies and governments were dismissed, political parties were banned and political leaders and activists were arrested in their thousands. One of the major reasons for proclaiming Martial Law was the danger posed to the integrity of the state as a result of the rebellion in Balochistan. Within three weeks of the imposition of martial law, i.e. on October 27, 1958, President Iskandar Mirza was sacked by his army chief, General Ayub Khan and he himself became Chief Martial Law Administrator. A reign of terror was unleashed in Balochistan by the military rulers of Pakistan. Prince Abdul Karim was arrested again, tried under martial law and sentenced to 14 years' rigorous imprisonment. The arrest of the Baloch political leaders and activists, the humiliation of the Khan and the mass arrest of tribal people paved the way for another confrontation between the Baloch and Pakistan.

After the occupation, the armed resistance under the leadership of the younger brother of the Khan was a short-lived affair and collapsed without achieving its objectives. The nationalist forces organize themselves in parties and alliances to lead the political resistance and mobilize the Baloch masses. Later they became engaged in the formation of new political alliances with representative parties of other national entities in Pakistan to broaden the scope of their struggle. After many years of keeping silent, the Khan of the Baloch became involved in mobilizing the tribes of Jhalawan and Sarawan regions; however, the situation changed with the declaration of Martial Law in Pakistan in 1958 with the banning of all political activities and arrest of the Khan on charges of conspiring to threaten the integrity of Pakistan. In a situation of mounting tension, a confrontation became imminent between the Baloch and Pakistan.

CHAPTER 11

THE BALOCH NATIONAL STRUGGLE FROM 1958 TO 1970

From 1958 onward, the dynamics of the Baloch resistance underwent drastic changes. The arrest of the Khan, persecution of Prince Abdul Karim and a ruthless crackdown on political activists belonging to the NAP prompted a mood of resistance among the Baloch. Mengal, Zehri and other tribes of Sarawan and Jhalawan were already in a state of agitation with the call of the Khan for mobilization. They were soon joined by the powerful Mari and Bugti tribes. The nationalist political workers under the banner of the NAP began to mobilize the masses. This period saw the emergence of the phenomenon of a guerrilla warfare against Pakistan and a general state of unrest prevailed throughout Balochistan. The armed resistance and political mobilization continued for nearly a decade and ended with the announcement of political reforms in 1969 by the new military rulers in Pakistan who also extended a reconciliatory gesture towards the Baloch.

BEGINNING OF THE ARMED RESISTANCE

Pakistani rulers accused the Khan of the Baloch and the leaders of the NAP of seeking help from foreign countries, in order to harm

140

the integrity of Pakistan. As a result, the state began to mobilize and strengthen its troops on strategic locations in Balochistan and soon fighters from various tribes and Pakistani army units came face to face in a confrontational situation. The Mengal tribe began to attack military and government facilities in Jhalawan region in defiance of government orders to surrender their arms. House-to-house raids were conducted by the army and the people were asked to deposit their arms with the authorities. In military action against the Mengal tribe, scores of Mengals were jailed and persecuted. With the increased activities of the Zehri tribe, the whole region of Jhalawan was in turmoil. On the political front, NAP stepped up the agitation in Balochistan and the Government responded by arresting all active members of NAP and throwing them into the notorious Quli Camp under the custody of the army. A fully fledged army operation dealt heavy blows to the Baloch fighters in Jhalawan but the spirit of resistance grew and many fighters from other tribes joined the Mengal and Zehri fighters.

In a bid to neutralize the Baloch tribes involved in the resistance, the government began negotiations with the Zehri tribe. The Zehri chief Nawab Noroz Khan agreed to suspend militant activities, while the Government promised under oath on Holy Qur'an that issues would be resolved through talks. However, in May 1959, he and his companions were taken into custody and put on trial under Martial Law on charges of treason. Nawab Noroz Khan was sentenced to life imprisonment (he died in Kohlu prison in 1962) and his six companions and family members were sentenced to death in Hyderabad prison. Several others were sentenced to jail terms ranging from 5 to 14 years and sent to different jails in the country.

A new dimension was added to the Baloch resistance when two of the most powerful tribes Mari and Bugti joined the resistance after chiefs of both tribes became involved in nationalist politics and joined National Awami Party. The joining of these tribes gave a much needed boost to the resistance after the collapse of Zehri uprising. Politically, with the support of these powerful tribal chiefs, the workers of NAP became more vocal and nationalists became the dominant political force in Balochistan. Armed conflict of the Baloch and Pakistani forces reached its peak. This resulted in the arrest by the military government of Sardar Ataullah Mengal, Nawab Khair Bakhsh Mari, Nawab Akber Bugti and Mir Gous Bakhsh Bizenjo along with many other Baloch leaders. Armed resistance also became more effective as the powerful tribes of Mengal, Mari and Bugti were now leading militant activities in many parts of Balochistan. The Pakistani government responded to increased political and armed activities from the Baloch nationalist activists and tribal fighters by issuing a decree, replacing Mengal, Mari and Bugti chiefs with government appointed tribal chiefs. However, this action further infuriated these tribes and the government nominated tribal chiefs were murdered when they tried to enter into their tribal homes. With the hanging of Nawab Noroz Khan's companions in 1962, the arrest and imprisonment of Baloch political workers, removal of Sardar Ataullah Mengal, Nawab Khair Bakhsh Mari and Nawab Akber Bugti as chiefs of their respective tribes, a state of general uprising prevailed in Balochistan for many years. Mir Ali Muhammad Mengal, Mir Sher Muhammad Mari, Mir Luang Khan Mengal and Mir Mewa Khan Bugti became prominent leaders of armed resistance during this period. Mir Hazar Khan Rahmakani also emerged as a guerrilla commander and played important roles in later decades. The army began to create a web of military cantonments throughout Balochistan increasing its presence exponentially during the period of 1958-1971. For several years, the Pakistani army was engaged by Baloch fighters in classical hit and run activities in many parts of Balochistan. The Pakistani establishment responded with indiscriminate use of excessive force, including aerial attacks, killing of civilians and burning of hundreds of Baloch settlements. Harrison (1981), observed that in fact, although, there were large scale casualties among the Baloch, massive use of air force by Pakistan made the Baloch fighters die-hard. During this period, the first use of Napalm bombs by the Pakistani air force was reported. The Baloch resistance was mainly concentrated in Jhalawan, Sarawan and Mari-Bugti regions. The last of the major encounters of the Baloch fighters with army units was witnessed in 1968 in Mari region, Pat Feeder and the adjoining areas of south eastern Balochistan and upper Sindh regions (Ahmad, 1992).

On the political front, an important happening during this period was the split in the ranks of NAP in 1968 between Wali and Bhashani groups. As NAP was the political face of the Baloch resistance, the split directly affected the national struggle of the Baloch and other national entities in Pakistan as well as the democratic and progressive forces in Pakistan. The Baloch leadership decided to join the NAP Wali group.

During 1958-1969, Pakistan was in the full grip of a military dictatorship. Political parties and political activities were banned during early years of Martial Law. In 1962, the military dictatorship was given a civilian façade by conducting controlled elections under an indirect electoral mechanism enshrined in a new constitution for the religious state. However, several prominent politicians including the Baloch nationalist leader Nawab Akber Bugti were barred from participating in the political process. The limited war with India in 1965 resulted in many ruins and much devastations in Pakistan. This accelerated the beginning of the end of the prolonged military dictatorship. By 1968, Pakistan was in turmoil. A robust democracy movement sprang up calling for free elections and the return of civilian rule. Protests occurred throughout East and West Pakistan. The army moved into Karachi, Lahore, Peshawar, Dhaka, and Khulna to restore order; however, so great was the intensity of the movement that in rural areas of East Pakistan, the curfew imposed by authorities became ineffective (Baxter 1998). Under mounting public pressure, the President, General Ayub Khan invited the politicians to a round table conference held in Rawalpindi, promised a new constitution, and announced that he would not stand for re-election in 1970 (Baxter 1998). However, the army had other plans and on March 25, 1969, the much discredited General Ayub Khan stepped down as President of Pakistan and power was transferred to another General. The chief of army staff, General Yahya Khan became the Martial Law Administrator and president of Pakistan.

The fighting between the Baloch and the Pakistani army was suspended with the fall of Ayub Khan. The new dictator, General Yahya Khan, pledged to restore a federal setup in the country. He also promised to restore previous units in West Pakistan, abandoning the One Unit. Soon a democratic process was initiated in the country. The imprisoned Baloch leaders were released. For the Baloch armed resistance, it was a breathing space during which they tried to reorganize, and train their cadre, garner equipment and establish communication links. It kept a low profile after the fall of the Ayub regime for some years. Personalities which emerged as undisputed representative of the Baloch national struggle included Nawab Khair Bakhsh Mari, Sardar Ataullah Mengal, Nawab Akber Bugti and Mir Gous Bakhsh Bizenjo. These personalities would dominate the Baloch national struggle for the next several decades and they were to become a source of inspirations for upcoming generations of Baloch nationalist activists and fighters in the national resistance.

INCORPORATION OF GWADAR INTO PAKISTAN

A development in 1958 which according to Baloch nationalists was a serious blow for their future struggle was the taking over of the southern port city of Gwadar by Pakistan. During the 18th century, the revenue income of Gwadar port was gifted by Khan of the Baloch, Mir Naseer Khan 1, to a member of Muscat's royal family when due to a family feud he came to Kalat and sought asylum in Balochistan. In later decades, with the occupation of Balochistan by the British and weakening of the Khanate of Kalat, the royal family of Muscat refused to surrender the sovereignty of Gwadar back to Balochistan and it was declared as an integral part of the Sultanate of Muscat and Oman for nearly two centuries. On September 6, 1958, under the pressure from British authorities, Sultanate of Muscat and Oman sold Gwadar to Pakistan for 3 million pounds (Ahmad, 1992). With Gwadar in control, Pakistan became able to have all out control over the coastal regions of Balochistan while the Baloch lost their political presence and importance in Sultanate of Oman which was strategically a very important country in the Gulf region. This was also the end of significant Baloch socio-political connections with the Gulf which could have been vital in their national liberation struggle in the coming decades

FORMATION OF BALOCH STUDENTS ORGANIZATION (THE BSO)

Another significant political development regarding the Baloch nationalist politics during 1958-1970 was the formation of the Baloch Students Organization which in later decades played pivotal roles in the Baloch national liberation struggle.

During 1960s, the Baloch students began their socio-political activities under *Warna Waninda Gul* which was mostly patronized by the Baloch leadership of NAP. In 1968, under the auspices of NAP, the Baloch students held a convention in Karachi and formed the Baloch Student Organisation (the BSO). The BSO worked in coordination with the NAP and become identified with its nationalist politics and drawn into its operational orbit. It also served as a political nursery for the youth to develop their leadership potential and provided second tier leadership to NAP. However, alarmed by the development, the establishment of that period tried to divide the Baloch students from the very beginning and a small number of Baloch students formed the BSO (*anti-sardar* group) with an anti-NAP program. The BSO (*anti-Sardar* group) became affiliated with Pakistan People's Party and was renamed the BSO-*Awami* in 1972. It claimed to be progressive in its ideology and against the *Sardari* system in Balochistan which upholds the primacy of the tribal chiefs. However, it actively supported the Pakistani establishment during the upheavals of 1970s, campaigning against the Baloch leadership. It termed the Baloch national resistance as a struggle not for national rights of the Baloch but only for safeguarding the personal interests of tribal chiefs. The Pakistani establishment using this section of the

BSO, was able to create suspicion about real aims and objectives of the resistance. The majority of its former leaders continued as staunch supporters of the state establishment of Pakistan and were active in many Pakistan based parties, getting privileges from the establishment and being patronized by the intelligence agencies. Some are blamed by resistance groups of actively supporting security forces operating in Balochistan against the contemporary Baloch resistance. Nevertheless, active support by the establishment, made it very difficult for this group of the BSO to gain respectability among the Baloch students and masses. Many disserted its ranks. Some of its leaders including Mir Abdul Nabi Bungulzai and Wahid Kamber joined the ranks of the Baloch People's Liberation Front (BPLF) which was the armed wing of the Baloch national resistance during 1970s. They spent years in exile during 1980s and played pivotal roles in the armed resistance of 21st century.

Despite its division into various groups, the BSO played a pre-eminent role in the Baloch national liberation struggle in the last many decades. During the 1980s, the two factions of the BSO merged together and the organization emerged as the harbinger of the Baloch people's hopes and aspirations. The BSO soon turned into more of a spirited political forum rather than a run-of- the-mill student organization. With the emergence of many nationalist political groups and organizations in 1980s, the BSO also faced divisions and its various factions supported different nationalist political parties. Janmahmad (1989), observed that in spite of its shortcomings, miscalculated political decisions, and the penetration of state agents in its ranks, the BSO remained the strongest force among the Baloch youth. Its importance cannot be dismissed easily in the Baloch national struggle. It has produced many devoted activists for the Baloch resistance. The majority of the contemporary leaders of the Baloch national resistance in Pakistan are the product of the BSO, one way or the other.

The Baloch national resistance from 1958 to 1969 against Pakistan was comprised of armed resistance by tribal volunteers and political mobilization by the NAP. Militant activities during

1958-1970 were carried out by tribesmen belonging to Mari, Mengal, Zehri and Bugti tribes and mainly concentrated in the Jhalawan and Mari- Bugti regions. During this period, the Baloch resistance was not able to make a major impact in Pakistan and internationally. However, politically, the NAP became the *de facto* representative of the Baloch masses, armed resistance became more mature and many tribes became involved in the resistance. The strategies of the Baloch resistance included resorting to political as well as militant means. In the former arena, the Baloch under the political umbrella of the National Awami Party (NAP), agitated for political and fiscal autonomy and opposed One Unit, which was the amalgamation of the provinces of the west wing of the country into a single entity. During this period, the Baloch resistance began to transform from being a tribal oriented movement into a relatively broad-based Baloch nationalist movement involving many segments of the Baloch society. Baloch students with the formation of the BSO, became actively involved in the nationalist politics. Although, the Baloch nationalists suffered a lot; they nevertheless, showed unprecedented resilience especially from some of the tribal chiefs and leaders. These tribal chiefs became the symbol of the Baloch courage and dignity in the face of brutal measures against them by the Pakistani state.

CHAPTER 12

THE BALOCH NATIONAL
RESISTANCE DURING 1970S

After a prolonged military rule, the discredited military establishment tried to begin an era of democracy in Pakistan by holding parliamentary elections in December 1970. However, it soon became clear that the actual intentions of the army was not to relinquish absolute power but somehow to share it with its own puppet political parties and personalities. The reluctance on the part of the establishment to respect the verdict of the people which they gave in support of political parties of choice in the general elections, caused the eruption of violent hostilities in East Pakistan and later in Balochistan. In the process, East Pakistan seceded and became an independent Bangladesh after facing a severe blood bath from the Pakistani army. Following the dismissal of the first elected nationalist government in Balochistan, the Baloch and Pakistani state became engaged in a bloody conflict in which the Baloch were brutally subdued by military aggression and political manipulations. The consequences of this defeat were devastating, one of them was the division in the ranks of the Baloch leadership.

DISINTEGRATION OF PAKISTAN

With the fall of General Ayub's military rule, a new era of democratic dispensation began in Pakistan. On November 28, 1969, the military ruler General Yahya Khan called for a return to a constitutional government and announced a plan for electing a constitutional assembly and provincial assemblies. Elections were scheduled to be held in October 1970, but a cyclone hit the coast of East Pakistan and the elections were postponed until December. The One Unit was dissolved and with the issuance of the Legal Framework Order (LFO), four provinces in West Pakistan were re-established. Balochistan got the status of a province in the federation of Pakistan. In the general elections held in December, 1970, in the Punjab and Sindh provinces, the Pakistan People's Party (PPP) won the majority seats, the National Awami Party won the elections in Balochistan and it became the single majority party in the North West Frontier Province (NWFP). The Awami League under the leadership of Sheikh Mujib ur-Rahman became the majority party in the national assembly by winning a landslide victory in East Pakistan on its manifesto advocating a 'Six Point' agenda for a federated republic of Pakistan (Baxter 1998). The six points were:

1. *Pakistan should be a federation under the Lahore Resolution of 1940, which implied the existence of two similar entities. Any new constitution according to the Bengalis had to reflect this reality.*
2. *The federal government should deal solely with defense and foreign affairs.*
3. *There should be two separate but freely convertible currencies. East Pakistan would have a separate banking reserve as well as separate fiscal and monetary policies.*
4. *The federated units would have the sole power to tax. The central government should be granted funds to meet its expenditures.*
5. *Separate accounts from foreign exchange earnings would be maintained. The federating units would be free to establish trade links with foreign countries.*

6. *East Pakistan would have a separate militia* (Abbas 2005: page, 58).

The electoral results were against all the predictions of the Pakistani intelligence agencies and were a blow to the actual designs of the military establishment in Pakistan. The political parties supported by the establishment were nearly wiped out. The military establishment perceived the election victory of the nationalist forces in the national assembly and in three provinces together with Awami League's six point agenda as the end of their objective of permanently ruling the country through their proxy political parties. Although, shocked by the unexpected election results; it was not ready to transfer power to the elected representatives of the people and defined the six-points as treasonous and inspired by India to disintegrate the country. Bizenjo (2009), observed that after all, the Punjab-dominated ruling alliance of religious elements and the Urdu-speaking north Indian refugee (*Muhajir*) elite had exercised unchallenged control over Pakistan since its birth, and could not digest even the thought of giving up power or even sharing it with people's representatives. When, in late January 1971, the Awami League announced the finalization of the draft constitution on the basis of its Six-points, but 'ensuring the indivisible unity between the two wings of Pakistan', the NAP announced that it would extend its cooperation to the Awami League in constitution-making.

The military at first refused to call the elected assemblies into session and finally decided to do away with democracy and a public representation façade. At midnight on March 25, 1971, the Pakistani army in order to suppress the popular demand for the transfer of power to representatives of the people, as expressed in the general elections, began a reign of horror in East Pakistan. The hall mark of this was random rape, arson, murder of Bengali intellectuals, teachers, doctors and political activists (Abbas, 2005). Bizenjo (2009), noted that on the night of 25th -26th March 1971, all hell broke loose on Dhaka. The city was on fire. The armed forces had launched their macabre operation against the people of East

Pakistan. The mass slaughter was on. Millions of Bengalis fled to India. A bloody guerrilla war ensued between Bengali fighters under the banner of *Mukti Bahini* (Liberation Army) and the Pakistani armed forces in which thousands were killed. Unprecedented violations of human rights and war crimes were committed by the Pakistani security establishment. In November, 1971, the Indian army directly became involved in the fighting and the Pakistani army surrendered on December 16, 1971. With that, East Pakistan became Bangladesh and a truncated Pakistan in the west survived to be comprised of Punjab, Sindh, Balochistan and NWFP.

THE FIRST NATIONALIST GOVERNMENT IN EASTERN BALOCHISTAN

With the loss of East Pakistan and the surrender of 90 thousand soldiers, the Pakistani Army had suffered a blow to its collective pride and prestige. Internal dissents in the army began to surface, forcing generals to hand over power temporarily to a civilian setup. The leader of the Pakistan People's Party, Mr Zulfiqar Ali Bhutto, a long term close associate of the military establishment, was sworn-in as the President and Chief Martial Law Administrator of Pakistan on December 20, 1971.

Civilian dispensations were established in Sindh and Punjab, where elected members began to exercise transferred powers. Meanwhile the government refused to hand over power to elected representatives of the people of Balochistan and NWFP. However, under huge public pressure and after protracted negotiations, the federal government in Pakistan agreed to transfer the provincial powers to NAP government in Balochistan. On April 28, 1972, the President of Pakistan administered the oath of office to Mir Gous Bakhsh Bizenjo as Governor of Balochistan. The National Awami Party (NAP) government in Balochistan headed by Sardar Ataullah Mengal took office on May 1, 1972. It was a momentous event in the Baloch national struggle in Pakistan. The first elected Baloch government in Balochistan after its occupation in 1948 raised high hopes for economic, social and cultural emancipation among the political workers and masses. Throughout the world, the Baloch were jubilant and a near euphoric state prevailed among the Baloch both in Eastern and Western Balochistan.

The nationalist government in Balochistan introduced various policies which were not appreciated by the establishment of Pakistan. It began a process to indigenize the administration by replacing non-Baloch with sons of the soil. The nationalist government also tried to recruit Baloch on various administrative positions previously held by non-Baloch from Punjab. In order to minimize dependency on federal law enforcement agencies, a rural force known as *Dehi Muhafiz* was created to tackle the law and order situation which has been exclusively controlled by federal security forces in the province. To develop a standard writing system for Balochi language, efforts were made to introduce Roman script for Balochi. Pakistani establishment and the ruling alliance were not in favour of Roman script in place of Arabic script and perceived this move as a conspiracy against Pakistan and Islam. The rural force, *Dehi Muhafiz* was also termed as a para-military force of Baloch nationalists.

Soon it became apparent that the establishment was not ready to allow the Baloch nationalists to rule Balochistan despite having a mandate from the people. The Pakistani establishment saw in the nationalist government a threat to national integrity and fearful of a repeat of the Bangladesh situation. This fear was heightened by the fact that many in the Balochistan government had been fighting the Pakistan Army in recent years. The federal government accused the NAP government of repeatedly exceeding its constitutional authority and alleged that actions of Balochistan government were part of a plot to dismember Pakistan. The central government in Islamabad accused Chief Minister of Balochistan Sardar Ataullah Mengal of recruiting 1600 former militants into the police, levies and newly created rural levies (*Dehi Muhafiz*). By a massive media campaign of maligning the Baloch leaders of conspiring to destroy the state, the ground was prepared for the dismissal of the first elected Baloch nationalist government. This was timed with the disclosure of a cache of 300 Soviet submachine guns and 48,000 rounds of ammunition, found in the house of the Iraqi Defence Attaché in Islamabad allegedly consigned to Baloch separatist elements.

For the first time, Iran became directly involved in the Baloch conflict with Pakistan. Iranian pressure was supposed to be among the factors causing the dismissal of the Baloch government. The Iranian government considered a nationalist government in Eastern Balochistan dangerous for Iranian national security and the integrity of the Persian state. The Shah of Iran promised extensive military and financial assistance to Pakistan in dealing with the Baloch problem. According to then Pakistani President Zulfiqar Ali Bhutto, quoted by Selig Harrison, King Reza Shah Pahlavi of Iran was not only persistent in his demand for the dismissal the Baloch nationalist government in Eastern Balochistan, but on some occasions he was also threatening (Harrison, 1981).

Early in 1973, the government controlled press brought up stories implicating the NAP leaders of conspiring to fragment Pakistan during their stay in London. Pakistani media called this conspiracy as the 'London Plan' for the break-up of Pakistan. They were quoting the estranged Baloch leader Nawab Akber Bugti that Baloch and Pashtun leaders of the NAP had revealed to him their plan to gain independence with the help of external forces. On February 10, 1973, it was announced by the government of Pakistan that they have discovered a cache of Soviet arms and ammunition from the Iraqi embassy in Islamabad. According to government of Pakistan these were destined for secessionist forces. The Balochistan government was accused of being involved in a conspiracy to dismember both Pakistan and Iran with the help of Soviet Union and Iraq. The Baloch government in the province was short-lived and after nine months was dismissed by Pakistani government. The stage was ready for a showdown with the Baloch nationalist forces.

THE BALOCH RESISTANCE DURING 1970S

The Baloch leaders tried their best to avoid a direct confrontation with Pakistan and despite increased provocation, and the dismissal of their elected government, they tried to resolve issues by a process of political dialogue. In this context, they became part of constitution making process. A constitution by the elected parliament in the history of Pakistan was promulgated on August 14, 1973. The constitution provided a federal structure for the state and residuary powers were given to provinces. Although, the Baloch leaders had their reservations about the constitution, as they believed that this did not manifest the wishes of the Baloch and other nations in the federation of Pakistan, by not providing maximum autonomy to the provinces; nevertheless, they accepted the constitution to show that they are still willing to participate in the political process of the state.

Following the dismissal of their government, the Baloch leaders, Mir Gous Bakhsh Bizenjo, Sardar Ataullah Mengal and Nawab Khair Bakhsh Mari, were soon put behind the bars. With military action in various parts of Balochistan, a political and armed resistance by the Baloch began lasting for many years. The Pakistani army units were deployed in all corners of the province and Balochistan presented a picture of a war zone. Soon bloody hostilities erupted between the Baloch fighters and the army units in central Balochistan and Mari region. The armed struggle continued over many years with varying degrees of severity; however, by the end of 1977, there was no any armed activity by the Baloch against security forces showing the collapse of the armed resistance.

At the height of the resistance war, Pakistan deployed more than 80,000 troops in Balochistan. The fighting between the Baloch and the Pakistani army was more wide-spread than it had been in 1950s and 1960s. It was of large scale; however, Mari and Mengal regions were worst affected. By July 1974, Baloch guerrilla units succeeded in cutting off most of the main roads linking Balochistan with surrounding provinces and rail communication were paralyzed. However, the military was able to restore a semblance of centralized control by killing thousands of militants. Tragically, military action also claimed hundreds of civilian lives, including women and children. The armed resistance was mainly coordinated by an umbrella organization, the Balochistan People's Liberation Front (BPLF). Formed in early 1970s, the organization tried to create discipline in the armed resistance movement and to convert it from tribal or semi-tribal fighting groups into a disciplined and united modern guerrilla war machine; ready to fight a prolonged armed struggle for the liberation of Balochistan, observed Janmahmad (1989). The militants under the discipline of BPLF avoided direct confrontation with the Pakistani army and whenever possible, their primary tactic remained ambushing army convoys and harassing its supply lines. The armed resistance was organized into three principal areas of insurgency- the Mari-Bugti, Sarawan, and Jhalawan regions. The prominent leaders of the armed resistance during 1970s were Mir Safar Khan Zarakzai, Agha Salman Ahmadzai, Mir Hazar Khan Rahmakani, Mehrullah Mengal, Khair Jan Baloch (Chairman Baloch Student Organization), Mir Hammal Bizenjo, Rahim Bakhsh Muhammad Hasni and Aslam Gichki. According to Harrison (1981), during four years of insurgency, there were one hundred seventy eight major engagements and one hundred sixty seven lesser incidents between Pakistani forces and the Baloch fighters.

The Pakistani response to the Baloch militant activities was massive and very brutal. Employing a scorched-earth policy, the army destroyed settlements, standing crops and grazing fields, as well as guerrilla hide-outs. In 1975, the Pakistani authorities proclaimed that they had broken the back of the Baloch fighting forces and had dealt them serious blows. This was partly true, as in Central Balochistan, several commanders of the resistance had been killed including several veterans of 1960s guerrilla war. But the blow in Chamalang was so devastating for the Baloch that, according to some Baloch analysts, it took nearly two decades to recover from this massive defeat suffered by Mari guerrilla forces under the banner of Baloch People's Liberation Front (BPLF).

Supported by Iranian helicopters, the Pakistani army launched the famous Chamalang Operation in Eastern Balochistan in September, 1974 (Ahmad, 1992). According to Pakistani claims, 120 prominent fighters were killed during three days of pitched fighting in which air strikes played a devastating effect.

A new and unprecedented development in the conflict between the Baloch and Pakistan was the direct involvement of the Iranian air force in fight between the Baloch and the Pakistani forces. Iran was seriously worried about the developing situation in Eastern Balochistan and ready to undertake vigorous, appropriate measures for the prevention of any threat to its own stability and to prevent any uprising by the Baloch in Western Balochistan. The Shah of Iran, more than once, declared that the Baloch question remained a strategic problem, being interwoven with the national security of Pakistan, but it simultaneously have close connections with the national interests of Iran. In September of 1974, Iranian helicopter gunships were combined with F-86 and Mirage fighter jets, as well as Pakistani ground forces inflicted heavy casualties among the Baloch fighters in Chamalang.

For many analysts of the 1970s conflict, the Chamalang tragedy was the watershed for the Baloch armed resistance. A pitched battle continued for three days between the Baloch fighters and the combined forces of the Pakistani infantry, air force and Iranian gunship helicopters. While most of the prominent guerrilla leaders and commanders evaded capture, the official Pakistani accounts of the battle claim that 120 Baloch fighters were killed, several thousand civilians were arrested and nearly a thousand armed activists was forced to surrender to the army authorities. It was nearly a total route of Baloch forces in the eastern regions of Balochistan and forced the Baloch resistance fighters to abandon their bases in Balochistan and seek refuge in southern Afghanistan. After the Chamalang debacle, there were no more 'liberated areas' as was claimed previously by the Baloch resistance. During 1975, the Pakistan army admitted only a hundred or so skirmishes in the eastern regions of Balochistan and some in the central and southern regions. This was to show the end of an effective armed resistance by the Baloch.

In the beginning of the armed resistance, it is estimated that nearly 50,000 Baloch fighters participated in the fighting. In four years of active confrontation, both sides suffered heavy losses. It is estimated that more than 4 thousands Pakistani troops were killed and nearly 10,000 Baloch fighters and civilians became the victim of Pakistani counter insurgency measures. A prominent casualty of the 1970 resistance was Mir Assadullah Mengal, son of Sardar Ataullah Mengal who was believed to be coordinating the armed resistance activities in Jhalawan and Sarawan regions. He was picked up along with his friend Ahmad Shah by Military Intelligence (MI) in Karachi on February 6, 1976. After some years, the military authorities admitted that both were tortured and murdered; however, their bodies were never handed over to their family members. Other prominent personalities killed by the army included veterans of 1960s resistance movement Mir Luang Khan Mengal, Mir Ali Mohammad Mengal, Rahim Bakhsh Muhammad Hasni and Mir Safar Khan Zarakzai.

Although, the armed resistance continued for several years after the battle of Chamalang; the resistance was clearly weakened and the fighting that ensued after the Chamalang episode was increasingly uncoordinated and ineffective. During 1975, after it became impossible to maintain bases in Balochistan because of mounting pressure from the Pakistani army, the Baloch People's Liberation Front (BPLF) fighters abandoned their camps, crossed the border and began operating from sanctuaries in southern Afghanistan. Several guerrilla commanders and fighters from Sarawan and Jhalawan also moved into Afghanistan.

HYDERABAD CONSPIRACY CASE AND BANNING OF NAP

Beginning in 1956, the political face of the Baloch national struggle in Pakistan had been the National Awami Party (NAP). It was an alliance of progressive and nationalist forces from all nationalities of Pakistan. As part of the strategy to crush the Baloch national struggle for ever, it was felt necessary for the establishment to eliminate the NAP. On February 10, 1975, the Pakistani authorities banned the National Awami Party declaring that the party was operating in a manner prejudicial to the sovereignty and integrity of the state (Awan, 1985). After the banning of the party, 89 leaders of the party were charged with conspiring to break Pakistan and were tried by a tribunal on treason charges. The case became famous as 'Hyderabad Conspiracy Case'. The tribunal was to persecute nearly all top Pashtun and Baloch nationalist leaders and prominent political activists affiliated with NAP. Nearly all of the top Baloch leadership including Mir Gous Bakhsh Bizenjo, Nawab Khair Bakhsh Mari and Sardar Ataullah Mengal were among the accused. The charges were those of condemning the creation of Pakistan, and waging war against the Islamic state (Janmahmad, 1989). The trial continued for nearly four years; however, after the overthrow of Mr Zulfiqar Ali Bhutto's government by the army, the new Martial Law Administrator of Pakistan on January 1, 1978, disbanded the tribunal and Baloch and Pashtun leadership was released.

POLITICAL MOBILIZATION IN BALOCHISTAN

Besides armed resistance, during the initial period of the conflict in the 1970s, the Baloch national resistance was successful in mobilizing a large segment of the Baloch population against the aggression of Pakistani state. Workers of NAP and activists of BSO were in the forefront of political agitation in Balochistan. Activities like taking out rallies, arranging political gatherings in various parts of Balochistan, using the available media to highlight the sufferings of the Baloch and the atrocities committed by the armed forces in Balochistan were carried out. However, with the banning of the party, mass arrests of political and student activists, the arrest of the top and second tier leaders of NAP, and with harsh restriction on political activities, the resistance on political front came to a standstill after some years.

On the face of it, in their political gatherings and rallies, the NAP and the BSO activists were identifying the armed resistance not as a struggle for the liberation of Balochistan but a kind of agitation for the release of NAP prisoners; the restoration of the NAP government in Balochistan; greater political autonomy for Balochistan; and a greater share from the resources of Balochistan. In many instances, the political activists were also expressing their desired goal for a confederation of states within Pakistan on the basis of the Lahore Resolution of 1940 in which the central government would be responsible only for defence, foreign affairs, communications, and currency while all other authorities including the exploitation of natural resources would rest with the confederating states. However, in their secret meetings, they were declaring the resistance as the continuation of the Baloch national struggle for the liberation and unification of all Baloch people in Iran, Pakistan and Afghanistan. Slogans for the granting of right of the self-determination under the United Nations charter, were also raised during the political mobilization during 1970s. But things took an ugly turn for workers and activists operating on the political front with the collapse of armed resistance. The situation was not promising for the Baloch political mobilization. Their party had been banned, the leadership was facing treason charges in the Hyderabad Conspiracy Case, and political activities had been severely restricted by authorities in Balochistan. A situation of impasse was created in Balochistan when the political agitation and armed resistance came to a full stop in 1977.

CAUSES AND CONSEQUENCES OF THE DEFEAT

Various reasons can be cited for the defeat of the Baloch resistance during 1970s, including political, strategic, and social as well as lack of external support for the cause of an independent Balochistan. The consequences of the defeat were far reaching as severe divisions occurred in the ranks of the Baloch leadership.

WEAKNESSES OF POLITICAL STRATEGIES

As the political process under parties or organizations was a relatively new phenomenon in the tribal, semi-tribal and agro-pastoralist Baloch society, the national struggle whether it was political mobilization or armed resistance, was purely dependent on tribal chiefs. The educated political cadre consisted of a very few student leaders from the BSO, which was also a new organization and the majority of the second tier of political leadership was not mature enough to carry on the burden of leadership after the banning of the NAP and whole sale arrest of the top Baloch leadership in 1974. Strategically, the political and armed resistance was not capable of channelizing the support of a broad section of population and the local leadership of the agro-nomadic segment of the Baloch society whose unwavering support was very vital for the movement. The Baloch writer and intellectual, Janmahmad (1989), pointed out that although many of the village heads sided with the struggle; due to the inherent weaknesses of the movement, in many regions, such support was not properly mobilized.

Socially, the NAP and the BSO activists failed to mobilize the all-important middle class which was mainly watching from a distance, the developing situation, refusing to commit itself wholeheartedly with the national struggle whole heartedly. The establishment hired a group of so-called intellectuals and writers to present the resistance as the struggle of Mari, Mengal and Bizenjo tribal elites for gaining privileges from the state which the political wing of the movement did not counter effectively. With meagre resources and the extreme high-handedness of the state towards the NAP cadres and other social figures affiliated with the struggle, the Baloch national resistance was unable to counter the nefarious designs of the powerful establishment of Pakistan. Hired intellectuals and writers were able to create mistrust and confusion among a large section of the Baloch middle class regarding the goal of the national resistance. The division between Nawab Bugti and other leaders also caused much psychological and material damage to movement.

INFILTRATION IN THE RESISTANCE

Pakistan's counter-insurgency efforts included creating and nurturing alternate political and tribal leadership to replace the nationalist leaders and tribal elite. The Infiltration of the ranks of Baloch nationalists was another cause of a mortal blow to the resistance. The establishment through its planted people, was successful in creating divisions in the ranks of nationalist leadership which proved to be the final nail in the coffin of the Baloch resistance in the 1970s. Exploiting the fundamental weaknesses of an open society like the Baloch, the state security establishment was successful in penetrating the ranks and files of the national struggle with ease. This included not only the armed resistance but also within the policy making structures of NAP which was the face of the struggle in public. The establishment planted some non-Baloch Punjabi and Indian origin *Muhajirs* into the ranks of BPLF in the guise of revolutionary solidarity with the Baloch struggle. Many among them were instrumental in supplying security agencies with much needed information on the internal organizational structure and weaknesses of the resistance forces. These so-called revolutionaries were also able to exploit minor differences in strategy among the Baloch leadership, in such a way that these became unresolvable and the Baloch had to bear the shock of division within their respected and trustworthy leadership.

LACK OF MODERN ARMS AND AMMUNITION

Lack of modern techniques and equipment was another factor in the collapse of armed resistance. The Baloch fighters used their classical method of hit and run encounters with army units. Their fighting units were equipped with traditional bolt action rifles and homemade grenades. On Pakistani side, the extensive use of air power was mostly responsible for causing havoc among the resistance ranks. The use of gun-ships enabled the Pakistani army to force the Baloch fighters out of their previously secure mountain hideouts into relatively open areas where they became more vulnerable to Pakistani infantry attacks. The Iranian military involvement in the conflict was another factor in the defeat of Baloch resistance during 1970s. Collective punishment for the area where some kind of armed activity was reported and mass displacement of people from their settlements was another effective tool in the Pakistani anti-insurgency strategy against the Baloch.

LACK OF EXTERNAL SUPPORT

The lack of external support and the antagonistic attitude of the Western powers towards the Baloch national struggle was another factor in the collapse of the movement. The 1970s was the era when the Cold War was in its peak. Any national liberation struggle was seen by Western powers as an extension of Soviet influence. Suppression of such a struggle was one of their strategic goals in order to counter the Soviet advance. Unfortunately, as the Baloch national struggle from the very beginning has been anti-imperialist and left oriented, it was comfortably exploited by the Pakistani establishment, who gained vital diplomatic, and military assistance from the West to crush it. On the other hand, no support was extended to the political or armed resistance of the Baloch by the Soviet Bloc countries. In the initial stages of the movement, Afghanistan did offer refuge to Baloch activists and Kabul Radio broadcasts propagated the Baloch and Pashtun point of view but no commitment was given for the continued support of 'Baloch Cause' neither there was any military help of substance given to the Baloch resistance. When the Pakistani leader Mr. Zulfiqar Ali Bhutto and President Sardar Muhammad Daud Khan of Afghanistan agreed to stop supporting opponents of each other in 1976, the meagre support was also stopped and many Baloch refugees were asked to leave the country. Lack of any support from the international community contributed significantly to the defeat of the resistance in the 1970s.

DIVISIONS WITHIN BALOCH LEADERSHIP

The collapse of the 1970s movement was unfortunate for the Baloch national resistance in Pakistan as it resulted in far reaching social, and political consequences which adversely affected the Baloch national struggle in coming decades.

ESTRANGEMENT OF NAWAB BUGTI

There occurred two divisions among the Baloch national leadership during and after the collapse of the struggle. The first division appeared between Nawab Akber Bugti and the rest of the Baloch leadership in 1972. Nawab Bugti was one of the stalwarts of the 1960s Baloch resistance. He was banned from political activities by the military dictator General Ayub Khan under an Ordinance along with many Pakistani politicians. He was however considered to be one of the top leaders of the NAP in Balochistan and his role was pivotal in the electoral victory of the NAP in the 1970 elections. Different explanations and reasons have been given regarding the differences which developed between the top leadership of the Baloch struggle soon after their electoral victory in 1970. It appears that the differences were both of a personal and a political nature but unfortunately they became so sharp that they were almost transformed into personal animosity. Nawab Akber Bugti abandoned his long term friends and tried to destabilize the NAP government in Balochistan by demanding the resignation of his younger brother, Mir Ahmad Nawaz Bugti from the provincial cabinet. He then openly blamed the Balochistan government and the Baloch leadership of working for the establishment of an independent Balochistan under the banner of a clandestine 'Baloch Liberation Organization' (BLO). He claimed to be the treasurer of that secret organization, working for the liberation of Baloch lands using the umbrella of the NAP. Nawab Bugti accused the Baloch leadership and the Balochistan government of acquiring arms and ammunitions from foreign countries for militant activities against Pakistan. Using Nawab Bugti's allegations as proof of a conspiracy to dismember Pakistan, the nationalist government in Balochistan was dismissed. Nawab Bugti was appointed as the Governor of Balochistan. Nawab Bugti's allegations were not only exploited by the Pakistani authorities in the dismissal of the nationalist government in Balochistan after a brief period of nine months, but were also used in initiating a devastating military operation against the Baloch, and the banning of the NAP. While facing the military operation in Balochistan and treason charges in the Hyderabad Conspiracy Case, the Baloch leadership denied the existence of any secret organization. However, while in exile, in 1983, Sardar Ataullah Mengal admitted the existence of BLO with the objective of organizing and supervising the armed struggle in Balochistan towards the aim of an independent Balochistan (Lifschultz, 1983). Nawab Akber Bugti soon retreated from his stance against the Baloch leaders and tried for a patch up with them but much damage was already done and it took many years for Nawab Bugti to re-enter the fold of the Baloch national resistance. It is universally believed in the Baloch nationalist circles that Nawab Bugti episode was extremely devastating for the Baloch national struggle in the 1970s.

DIVISION AMONG NAP LEADERSHIP

Another division occurred between the Pashtun and the Baloch leadership of NAP when they were being tried in Hyderabad Conspiracy Case. Differences which were political, strategic and ideological in nature were never resolved and the nationalist politics of Pashtun and the Baloch took their separate paths for ever. This in later years caused the overall weakening of the struggle of minority nationalities in Pakistan. Two efforts on behalf of Sardar Ataullah Mengal in the 1980s and 1990s to bring the struggle of the various oppressed nationalities onto a single political platform failed to achieve its objectives.

The division which had far reaching consequences for the Baloch national struggle was between the top three towering figures of the Baloch national struggle. Mir Gous Bakhsh Bizenjo parted his political ways with his long term colleagues, Sardar Ataullah Mengal and Nawab Khair Bakhsh Mari. Differences in strategy of continuing the struggle developed between the Baloch leadership when they were in prison facing treason charges from the Pakistani authorities in Hyderabad Conspiracy Case. According to Bizenjo (2009), senior members of NAP from Balochistan, called a meeting in jail to take a final decision on what should be the future course of action regarding political and armed resistance. Two viewpoints emerged: (1) Fight for national rights within the framework of Pakistan; suspend the resistance movement which has taken the path of much violence; call the men back from the mountains; (2) Upgrade the present movement into a full-fledged struggle for separation from Pakistan; those who were in the mountains would be asked to stay there and reorganize themselves for this mission. Nawab Khair Bakhsh Mari, Sardar Ataullah Mengal and three other comrades were of the opinion that the Baloch or for that matter any other small nationality has no future in Pakistan. Their argument ran as follows:

> 'Punjab will not let any other nationality live with honour and dignity. If East Pakistan, despite its numerical and electoral majority, could be exploited and oppressed with impunity to the extent that they were left with no option but to secede, who is going to pay heed to the wailings of the Baloch with their miniscule size in terms of numbers? The blood and sweat we will squander in the futile exercise of seeking to reform Pakistan should be saved for the noble cause of the liberation of Balochistan. Therefore, no move should be made to bring back the men who are still in the mountains or in Afghanistan'.

Nawab Khair Bakhsh Mari and Sardar Ataullah Mengal were of the opinion that as there was no point in wasting energy being part of the Pakistani political process, the Baloch should work openly for the liberation of their land. They were of the opinion that an outright call for independence should be given to the Baloch masses. While on the other hand, Mir Gous Bakhsh Bizenjo thought that objective conditions were not in favour of a successful attempt to regain independence by the Baloch. Mir Bizenjo reached at the conclusion that the expressed aim of the resistance should not be independence in the given situation. He believed that the West would never allow the dismemberment of Pakistan while it was still available for safe guarding Western interests in the region. He was convinced that presently the aim of the Baloch struggle should be the fight for national rights within the frame work of Pakistan. He was of the opinion that, as apparently there was no external support and internally the Baloch need time to reorganize themselves politically and militarily, the only option left for them was to participate in the political process of the state. Unfortunately, the differences could not be patched up and the leaders parted ways. The majority of Baloch political activists became disgruntled because of the divisions and some of them dissociated themselves from any political activity for a long time. With the division in ranks of the leadership, in the student wing of the movement-the BSO, there began a destructive process of division which still continues. In the absence of the leadership and absence of any political alternative of the NAP, different factions of the BSO took up the task of acting as a guide for the masses and behaved as political parties, forgetting the actual role of a student organization. After some years, they began to dictate their immature strategies to nationalist parties and movements when they tried to reorganize themselves in 1980s.

MILITARY TAKEOVER IN PAKISTAN

While the Baloch nationalist politics was in turmoil after the collapse of the movement, and development of divisions in its ranks, in Pakistan, the so-called democratic dispensation under the government of Zulfiqar Ali Bhutto became increasingly autocratic and the role of the army once again became prominent in politics. The Army was given charge of the Baloch national question and Balochistan came under *de facto* control of the army. As observed by Bizenjo (2009), four and a half years of military action in Balochistan got Mr. Bhutto nowhere. The banning of NAP, the arrest and trial of the entire NAP leadership and activists were not the only reasons for turmoil in Pakistani politics, but many of his other mistaken policies resulted in wide-spread discontent in the whole country. During Mr. Bhutto's so-called civilian rule, everyone was in one way or another harassed, humiliated, imprisoned, tortured or cheated. Using the widespread discontent in the country, the army planned a takeover. Under the patronage of secret agencies, an alliance of opposition parties began agitating after 1977 elections, accusing the government of massive riggings. Ultimately the Chief of Army Staff, General Zia-ul-Haque, seized power on July 5, 1977. Mr. Bhutto and most of his cabinet colleagues were taken into 'protective custody'. Mr. Bhutto was later prosecuted on murder charges in a concocted trial and executed by hanging. The Pakistani army under the leadership of General Zia-ul-Haque introduced a policy of Islamization, known as *Nizame-e-Mustafa* (rule of the prophet). It transformed the country's traditional Islamic beliefs to the Wahhabi views of the Saudi version of Islam.

The 1970s was the period when the Baloch witnessed the formation and dismissal of the first nationalist government in Balochistan after its occupation by Pakistan. To resist the military aggression, the Baloch tribal and political activists fought a resistance war for many years. For various reasons, the resistance movement collapsed and did not produce any tangible result despite enormous sacrifices of the leaders and masses. The collapse of the armed resistance and the failure to continue the political mobilization brought far reaching consequences not only for the Baloch-Pakistan relations, but it also changed the internal dynamics of the Baloch national struggle for ever. The Baloch resistance of 1970s was so important that the strategies and after-effects of this movement are still being debated in the Baloch nationalist circles.

The message from the Pakistani military to the Baloch nationalists was clear that it would see their total destruction if they did not mend their ways. Thousands of the Baloch were killed in a 5 year armed and political confrontation with the state. Thousands were displaced internally and thousands migrated to Afghanistan. Sardar Ataullah Mengal, Nawab Khair Bakhsh Mari and Mir Gous Bakhsh Bizenjo emerged as undisputed leaders of the Baloch national struggle in Pakistan. The Baloch national resistance lost the services of one of its towering figures Nawab Akber Bugti because of differences he developed with other Baloch leaders. The NAP which was the political face of the Baloch national struggle in Pakistan was banned, its leaders remained in prison for many years. The BSO, the student wing of the NAP, with the banning of the party and imprisonment of its leadership performed as a political party, with far reaching negative consequences on the future Baloch nationalist politics. The defeat of the movement caused much political upheaval in the ranks of the Baloch nationalists. A process of division and disunity was initiated which is still haunting the Baloch national struggle. A disconnect developed between the leadership and political activists in consequence of divisions, which caused political anarchy in nationalist circles for many years. In the beginning of the conflict, a wide section of the Baloch society became involved in the political mobilization and armed resistance. Subsequently it was joined by the Baloch intellectuals, students and the very small and emerging Baloch bureaucracy, and supported by Marxists and socialists of the Pakistani left. However, for all practical purposes, the resistance was wholly dependent on the leadership of the tribal chiefs of the two major tribes in Balochistan. Sardar Ataullah Mengal and Nawab Khair Bakhsh Mari held almost the total control of the armed resistance. The Baloch resistance of 1970s not only widened the already existing gulf between Pakistan and the Baloch people, but also caused unprecedented changes in the Baloch polity.

CHAPTER 13

1980S AND 1990S: THE
PERIOD OF POLITICAL AND
INTELLECTUAL CONFUSION

The last two decades of 20th century were important in the history of the Baloch national struggle. This was the period when Baloch nationalists after the crushing defeat of the 1970s movement, were trying to regain the lost momentum. Student leaders became engaged in uniting and disintegrating the BSO and political leaders formed new movements and parties. It was also the period of intense and heated political debates among the nationalist circles regarding future strategies of the Baloch national struggle in Pakistan. Sardar Ataullah Mengal and Nawab Khair Bakhsh Mari went into exile and Nawab Akber Bugti successfully managed to re-enter the folds of the Baloch nationalists. The division in the top leadership that developed during the last years of 1970s, filtered down to political workers and student activists. Once regarded as the father of the Baloch nationalist politics, Mir Bizenjo was severely criticized and accused of abandoning the Baloch national cause by the BSO activists. After a decade of political upheavals, nationalists once again participated in the political process of the state and also formed two short-lived governments in Balochistan during 1988 and 1997.

THE GENERAL AMNESTY

In a general amnesty announced by Pakistani military ruler, General Zia-ul-Haque, in 1978, thousands of Baloch political prisoners were released from different detention centres. The Baloch political activists who had gone underground re-surfaced and many fighters who had immigrated to Afghanistan returned to their homes. A process of reflection on the events of the past years began among political workers and leaders. Intensive and heated debates began in the political circles about the causes of the defeat and the division within the leadership.

At first, the new military setup in Pakistan expressed its intension to initiate a process of negotiation on the Baloch question with three Baloch leaders Mir Gous Bakhsh Bizenjo, Sardar Ataullah Mengal and Nawab Khair Bakhsh Mari, who commanded the overwhelming support of the Baloch people. The Baloch leadership showed its willingness to join a negotiated process with General Zia's government to resolve the issues between the Baloch and Pakistan. Their initial demands were the withdrawal of the Pakistani Army from Balochistan, the release of Baloch prisoners and compensations for those who had suffered during the resistance movement. Although, political prisoners were released and some families were compensated; nevertheless, it soon became apparent that the Pakistani army establishment was not interested in any negotiation of serious nature on the Baloch national question. It was not ready to give any political concessions to Baloch nationalists. Nevertheless, Balochistan became relatively calm as Army units in Balochistan had been ordered to maintain a low profile and the Baloch armed resistance was still struggling to recover from the shock and aftershocks of the defeat suffered during 1970s. The Baloch Political activists became engaged in a process of long and bitter discussion on the losses and gains of the movement and how to form new and feasible strategies for the national struggle.

PAKISTAN NATIONAL PARTY

When the NAP was banned in 1975, and the party leadership was in jail facing treason charges. In order to hold together its members, political activists and sympathizers, a new party 'National Democratic Party' (NDP) was founded under the leadership of Sardar Sher Baz Mazari. Mazari belonged to a Baloch tribe from Punjab and had political and personal relations with the Baloch and Pashtun leaders of the NAP. However, after their release from prison, Baloch leaders declined to join the NDP and some of the Baloch political activists under the leadership of Mir Gous Bakhsh Bizenjo, formed the Pakistan National Party (PNP) as the alternative to the NAP. In the beginning, Sardar Ataullah Mengal was also involved in the party but soon dissociated himself from it. To attract and mobilize political workers affiliated with the banned NAP, the party adopted a manifesto calling for greater autonomy for the provinces of Pakistan as enshrined in the Lahore Resolution of 1940. The resolution, which became the founding document for Pakistan, called for the creation of a group of 'independent states' for Muslims in north-western and eastern zones within British India. In the resolution it was demanded that the constituent units or states were to be autonomous and sovereign (Malik, 2001). Although, the party failed to gain the support of the majority of former political activists of the NAP and the Baloch Students Organization; nevertheless, Mir Bizenjo still commanded respect and a significant following of educated and a rising middle class, during the 1980s. While his former colleagues and young followers were debating whether to initiate an all-out struggle for the liberation of Balochistan from Pakistan, Mir Bizenjo was adamant in his opinion that the objective conditions for an independent Balochistan are not there and the only option left for the Baloch is to struggle within the frame work of Pakistan. Although, the majority of the conscious elements in Balochistan did agree with Mir Gous Bakhsh Bizenjo; nevertheless, a significant section of students, youth and former activists of the NAP became alienated with Mir Bizenjo and his party. The party suffered a crushing defeat in the first democratic elections held in 1988, after the end of military rule. Mir Bizenjo himself could not secure a parliamentary seat. In 1996, the party was merged with the newly founded Balochistan National Party of Sardar Ataullah Mengal.

LEADERS IN EXILE

After their release from prison with the disbandment of Hyderabad Tribunal in 1978, Nawab Khair Bakhsh Mari and Sardar Ataullah Mengal left Pakistan following a brief stay and went into exile in Afghanistan, and the UK. Under the instructions of Nawab Khair Bakhsh Mari, thousands of Mari tribesmen also migrated to Afghanistan. While in Europe, Sardar Mengal and Nawab Mari apart from having medical treatments, began to analyse new developments regarding the Baloch national resistance and to explore the prospects of gaining international support for the Baloch cause. They also explored the possibilities of strengthening the organizational framework of the Baloch resistance in preparation for a possible resumption of hostilities with Pakistan. Sardar Ataullah Mengal remained in the UK while Nawab Khair Bakhsh Mari after spending some time in Europe, settled in Afghanistan for a long period.

MENGAL IN LONDON: THE CONFEDERATION FRONT

While in London, Sardar Ataullah Mengal became active highlighting the Baloch national question in Europe and North America. He repeatedly expressed his lack of confidence in a solution of the Baloch national question within Pakistan. "If the Baloch are to survive, then we must struggle for an independent Balochistan, outside the framework of Pakistan." Sardar Mengal told Lifschultz in an interview in 1983. He explained that had Pakistan accepted the concept of nationalities and rights of those nationalities as partners within the boundaries of Pakistan, one could have said that adjustment was possible. However, right from the creation of Pakistan, there has been a denial of the rights of nationalities. Sardar Mengal on various occasions, pointed out that, to prevent unnecessary bloodshed, at an earlier stage, a confederation of nations comprising Pakistan could have been a feasible option. Sardar Mengal played a prominent role in the formation of World Baloch Organization in 1981 which was to consolidate the political activities of the Baloch Diaspora in Europe and North America. In 1985, he joined hands with Sindhi and Pashtun leaders in the formation of the Sindhi-Baloch-Pashtun Front. The alliance popularly known as the 'confederation front' was a political platform of oppressed nations in Pakistan demanding a confederation of nations comprising Pakistan. He was also instrumental in the formation of a discussion group 'Sindhi-Baloch Forum' in order to initiate political debates on the national struggles of these nations.

The Confederation Front strongly deplored the supremacy of the ruling nationality of Pakistan (meaning the dominant Punjab); and injustices and highhandedness against other national entities. The Front was of the opinion that Sindh, Balochistan, Seraiki and the Pashtunkhwa are mere colonies, controlled by armed forces and its paramilitary outfits, and by civil bureaucrats from Punjab. The Front sought fundamental rights for the Sindhis, Baloch, Pashtuns, and Seraikis according to the principles of democracy and justice. According to the Front manifesto, the only solution for a viable Pakistan was the establishment of a democratic and just system where all national entities had equal rights. No one nationality should have supremacy over another, and the language of every nation should be their administrative language and the medium of education. For the achievement of this goal, the Front advocated that all the smaller nations should receive full autonomy in a confederal frame work according to the 1940 Lahore Resolution. The Front resolved that it would facilitate the struggle of the people belonging to smaller nations in overthrowing the hegemony of Punjab and in their struggle for the attainment of their fundamental rights.

MARI IN AFGHANISTAN: THE GUEST OF REVOLUTION

The socialist revolution in Afghanistan led by People's Democratic Party in 1978 was a milestone in the history of the region. Its fallouts are still observed in the societies and politics of South and Central Asia. Afghanistan has been a buffer state between Czarist Russia and British India from the era of the 'great game' during 19th and early 20th century. This status was also maintained after the formation of Soviet Union. Afghanistan was considered to be a neutral zone after the Second World War and following the withdrawal of the British from India. Afghanistan kept equal relations with both Western and Soviet Blocs during the protracted cold war. The socialist revolution in Afghanistan was seen by the West as the end of Afghanistan as a buffer. This was unacceptable to them as they saw in it the Soviet temptation to reach the Indian Ocean thus threatening their monopoly in the oil rich gulf region and giving unprecedented strategic advantage to Russia in the Middle East and South Asia. With the Soviet backed government in Afghanistan, the equation has changed. The Western powers began to counter this apparent Soviet move to change the balance of power in the region. They organized a massive insurgency in Afghanistan in order to destabilize the pro-soviet government in Kabul. Islam was again found to be useful in this new confrontation with Russia. Thousands of Jihadists from all over the world were encouraged to participate in the "holy struggle" to oust the atheist and infidels from Afghanistan. At the behest of the Western alliance and with money from Arab countries, Pakistan began training Islamic Jihadists on its territory and funnelling arms to insurgents inside Afghanistan. On the other side, the support to revolutionary government of Afghanistan proved to be a divisive factor in the Soviet power corridors. Neither Afghanistan was given the proper help, nor was there any substantial move made against Pakistan, who became the frontline state against Afghanistan. Lack of a feasible and sustained policy by the Soviet leadership regarding Afghanistan caused uncertainty in Afghanistan and considerably weakened the revolutionary government in Kabul. A protracted Jihad was fought by the West in Afghanistan, until the collapse of the Soviet backed revolutionary government in 1992.

For the Baloch and other subjugated nations in the region and for secular and liberal forces, the Afghan revolution was a welcome phenomenon. For them, the revolutionary Afghanistan was a beacon of hope in the dark sea of fundamentalism in which the fanatical regimes of Pakistan and Iran were fomenting all kinds of religious hatred and extremism. The Afghan government extended the hand of friendship to the Baloch and Pashtun nationalists who were struggling for their national rights in Pakistan. Many Baloch activists from Pakistan and Iran took refuge in Afghanistan. Thousands of Mari tribesmen were given shelter. Several of the BSO leaders also crossed into Afghanistan after the revolution. The Baloch exiles were not only given refuge, but were also given access to the educational institutions of the Soviet Bloc countries and hundreds of the Baloch youth were educated in Russia and other socialist countries in Eastern Europe.

It is believed that under Soviet pressure, the Baloch were merely treated as the guests of the Afghan people and no commitment was made to recognize the Baloch resistance as a legitimate national liberation struggle. Perhaps the Soviets were not in a position to stretch their resources by bringing the conflict to the shores of Indian Ocean. In an interview with Lawrence Lifschultz in 1983, Sardar Ataullah Mengal opined that if circumstances compelled an alternative approach regarding the Afghan situation, then the Soviet Union might initially prefer a pro-Soviet Union Pakistan rather than to have an independent Balochistan or a Balkanized Pakistan (Lifschultz, 1983).

Nawab Khair Bakhsh Mari and his tribesmen remained in Afghanistan until the collapse of revolutionary government but many of the BSO leaders and other political activists returned during 1980s to participate in the political process after the end of the Martial Law regime in Pakistan. One of the unfortunate happenings during Nawab Mari's sojourn in Afghanistan was the parting ways of his close associates, Mir Sher Muhammad Mari and Mir Hazar Khan Rahmakani. These two personalities played significant roles in the Baloch struggles of 1960s and 1970s. Their dissociation with Nawab Mari proved to be the beginning of an unending dissent within Mari tribe which only came into open after the return of Mari tribesmen in Balochistan during 1990s.

MURDER OF HAMEED BALOCH

The execution of a BSO activist by Pakistani military authorities in 1981 was among major events after the collapse of the armed resistance of 1970s. It left a significant impact on the Baloch nationalist movement especially on the politics of the BSO during 1980s.

A student of Quetta Polytechnic Institute, Hameed Baloch went to Afghanistan in 1978 and joined the University of Kabul. He became a strong believer in the solidarity of the people's movements for national liberation. Solidarity of oppressed nations was one of the elements of the Baloch national struggle and the BSO activists were at the forefront of showing solidarity with national liberation struggles in Asia and Africa. The people in the Dhofar region of Sultanate of Oman were struggling for independence from Oman. A guerrilla war for many years waged there against the Omani government. Under an agreement signed at the time of taking over of Gwadar by Pakistan, Oman recruited Baloch mercenaries to fight against the Dhofar insurgency. The BSO has been expressing its opposition to the recruitment of the Baloch mercenaries as part of their principle stance against colonialism and international solidarity of liberation movements. On December 9, 1979, Hameed Baloch led a group of the BSO activists to disrupt a recruiting assembly of Baloch mercenaries for Oman, being held in Turbat. He was arrested and tried in a military court on charges of murder and attempted murder and executed on June 11, 1981 in Mach Central Jail.

His ultimate sacrifice to uphold the principle stance of the Baloch national struggle for international solidarity with all oppressed nations, and his courage and boldness while facing the death became legendary. His last minute will or testament before being hanged became the 'Bible' of Baloch students and youth. His confidence, as was expressed in his testament, in an independent Balochistan in the life time of his daughter, inspired thousands of the Baloch youth to devote themselves for the national cause. His appeal for a united struggle for the Baloch national rights prompted moves for the unification of all factions of the BSO.

THE BSO: UNIFICATIONS AND DIVISIONS

On the very day of its formation in 1967, the Baloch Students Organization split into two. The Establishment then was successful in dividing the potential youth force of the National Awami Party from the very beginning. The BSO (*anti-Sardar*)-the section affiliated with the establishment-began its campaign of open opposition of the Baloch national struggle and the maligning of Baloch national leaders. Many attempts were made for unification but it became difficult for the Baloch leaders to bring these two groups of students into the fold of a single organization because of the role played by the state establishment.

The section of BSO which was affiliated with the NAP and the Baloch national struggle played an active role in the political agitation and the armed resistance during 1970s. Many of its leaders including the Chairman of the organization, Khair Jan Baloch, went to the mountains and headed guerrilla units in Sarawan and Jhalawan regions. Hundreds of its activists were arrested and many faced inhuman torture from security agencies. Although, the BSO had been the student wing of the NAP, it was given the highest consideration by the Baloch leadership of the Party. However, with the long imprisonment of the Baloch leadership and the subsequent traumas of the defeat and divisions among leaders, a high degree of disillusionment developed in the BSO cadre. They began to think that the national leadership was not capable of leading the nation to the goal of national liberation. They began to believe that their student organization could function as a political party and could lead the nation in the struggle for national liberation. Many among the Baloch analysts and intellectuals believed that the development of this illogical thought was the work of planted elements of the state secret agencies in the organization. Janmahmad (1989) pointed out that the government and many other elements outside the government started manipulating the organization and courting its leaders in order not only to confuse the rank and file of the BSO, but also to secure an estrangement with the Baloch national leadership and its mother organization, the NAP.

The collapse of the 1970s resistance movement was believed to be the main factor which exacerbated the illusions and delusions of the BSO activists. They blamed the policies of Baloch leaders responsible for the defeat and called for the continuation of the armed resistance. The decision to end armed activities after the release of leaders in 1978 was believed by a section of the BSO activists as a great betrayal of the Baloch cause. For many years, the BSO got out of crosscurrents of the Baloch national policies and they adopted a hostile attitude towards the Baloch national leaders especially with Mir Gous Bakhsh Bizenjo who talked about taking a realistic view of the prevailing situation facing the Baloch national struggle. From the beginning of the 1980s, the BSO was transformed from an educational organization, affiliated to the nationalist politics of Balochistan as the student wing of the NAP into a political organization on its own. This caused much damage to nationalist politics, and caused an unending process of division and fragmentation of the organization which continued into 21st century. Although, heavily infiltrated by the state security agencies; nevertheless, the BSO during the 1980s remained the strongest political force and attracted the sympathies of a large number of students and youths.

The role of the BSO leadership of both groups in Hameed Baloch episode put them into tremendous pressure from their activists and workers. Many of the activists accused the BSO leadership of cowardliness by doing nothing to prevent the execution of Hameed Baloch. The activists also pointed out that there was no effective protest against the execution and nearly all the leadership of the BSO were in hiding, fearing for their own lives. This reaction of activists and the call of unity from Hameed Baloch in his last minute testament before marching to the gallows, put the leaders under heavy pressure to merge the two groups of BSO. Both groups of the BSO held a joint convention in 1984 and a united BSO was created. With the unification of the BSO, its leaders formed a clandestine resistance organization, Balochistan Liberation Movement (BLM), for carrying out armed struggle as they believed that the Baloch national leaders were not sincere in carrying out national resistance struggle. This organization never came into the open, although they tried in vain to secure meaningful assistance from the revolutionary government in Kabul.

The unity of BSO was not long lasting and in 1986, it again split into two factions led by Dr. Yaseen Baloch, and Dr. Kahur Khan Baloch. This division also resulted in the disintegration of the BLM, nothing was heard of BLM afterward. In later years, from two newly emerged groups (Yaseen group and Kahur group), emerged two youth movements and both groups of the BSO remained affiliated with these youth movements. They abandoned their previous stance of considering the BSO as a political organization capable of leading the national struggle on their own. Nevertheless, the division of the BSO and disintegration of their armed wing resulted in much violent infightings resulting some casualties also. A prominent activist of the BSO (Yaseen group), Fida Ahmad was murdered in Turbat on May 2, 1988 by the rival faction of the BSO (Kahur group) to revenge an attack on one of their activists, Mullah Sattar.

The division of the BSO did not end and with the formation of new alliances and parties by the Baloch nationalists; the BSO also underwent similar divisions and bifurcations. By the end of last century, the BSO was mainly divided into two groups; one supported the BNM headed by Dr. Abdul Hayee, the other supported the Balochistan National Party headed by Sardar Ataullah Mengal.

THE PHENOMENON OF YOUTH MOVEMENTS

After the disbandment of Hyderabad Tribunal and the release of the Baloch leadership, a process of reflection on losses and gains of the struggle began involving the leadership, the political and student activists. However, this process stopped when Sardar Ataullah Mengal and Nawab Khair Bakhsh Mari went into exile. Nawab Akber Bugti was not in the folds of the national struggle at that time and Mir Gous Bakhsh Bizenjo alienated a significant section of political and student activists. In the 1980s, the leaders of the Baloch Student Organization tried to fill the gap created by the absence of the Baloch leadership by forming their own political group and to keep the control of BSO themselves. Their manifesto was no to the participation in the political process of Pakistani state. They believed that participation in the state political process dilutes the Baloch national struggle. They believed that the struggle should only result in an independent and united Balochistan and not for provincial autonomy within Pakistan. As the slogan was very attractive for the Baloch youth after the debacle of 1970s, for a while it appeared that a new popular political leadership had arisen on the Baloch political scene with a significant following. The new youth leadership vehemently opposed the line adopted by Mir Gous Bakhsh Bizenjo and his party the 'Pakistan National Party' which demanded the resolution of the Baloch national question within Pakistan according to 1940 Lahore resolution.

The former leaders of the BSO and some of the NAP activists became involved in a process of forming a youth organization which in another way was to replace the established leadership of the Baloch national struggle. However, the process of creating a youth movement and the organizing inexperienced and sentimental youths into a formal political arrangement was not smooth. Differences surfaced and two separate youth movements were created in 1987. The group under the leadership of Dr. Hayee and Sardar Akhtar Mengal was named as Balochistan National Youth Movement (BNYM) while two former chairmen of the BSO, Razique Bugti and Habib Jalib, founded their own group

180

named as Progressive Youth Movement (PYM). These two youth movements commanded the support of divided sections of the BSO. Soon these factions began to hurl various accusations at each other and activists of their student wings became involved in violent clashes. This division from the very start diminished the respect of these youth leaders, which they commanded among the Baloch masses.

The phenomenon of youth movements did not last long. Not only the political philosophy of their leaders changed diametrically but the two youth movements affectively became dissolved within a few years. The BNYM which was against any participation in the political process within Pakistan became a component of a nationalist alliance called Balochistan National Alliance (BNA). This was formed to jointly contest the general elections in 1988 held after the death of Pakistani military ruler General Zia ul Haque. In 1989, BNYM was transformed from a youth movement into a formal political party and renamed as Baloch National Movement (BNM). In 1990, BNM split into BNM-Mengal headed by Sardar Akhtar Mengal and BNM-Hayee headed by Dr. Abdul Hayee. The PYM which was supposed to be a radical and progressive nationalist organization with the objective of a revolutionary armed struggle for the liberation of Balochistan merged itself with the PNP following the death of Mir Bizenjo in 1990. These short-lived youth movements did not play any significant role in the Baloch politics; however, the violent infighting between their affiliated student organizations caused much damage to the credibility of these movements to be of any substance in leading the nation. During the brief life span of these youth movements, much damage was also inflicted on the degree of respect the BSO commanded among the Baloch masses as a trustworthy organization devoted to the Baloch cause.

BALOCHISTAN NATIONAL ALLIANCE AND FORMATION OF SECOND NATIONALIST GOVERNMENT

With the announcement of general elections in Pakistan in 1988, the Baloch nationalist groups and individuals formed an alliance in the name of Balochistan National Alliance (BNA). The main political organization in the BNA was Baloch National Youth Movement (BNYM) but it was supported openly by Sardar Ataullah Mengal and covertly by Nawab Khair Bakhsh Mari and led by Nawab Akber Bugti as both Sardar Mengal and Nawab Mari were living in the United Kingdom and Afghanistan respectively. In the context of the broadened political rift which developed during the second half of 1970 decade, Mir Gous Bakhsh Bizenjo's Pakistan National Party (PNP) was not included in the alliance. Nawab Akber Bugti as the leader of Balochistan National Alliance again emerged as one of the main leaders of the Baloch national struggle after his unfortunate split with the Baloch leaders in 1972.

The election in Balochistan was mainly fought between BNA and PNP. The PNP was heavily defeated with the BNA winning a large number of seats in the Balochistan Assembly. The towering figure of the Baloch national struggle, Mir Gous Bakhsh Bizenjo himself was defeated in two parliamentary seats. The alliance formed the government in Balochistan with Nawab Akber Bugti as Chief Minister in November, 1988. The BNA government was dissolved on August 6, 1990 when Prime Minister Benazir Bhutto's federal government and all democratically elected federal and provincial assemblies were dismissed by Pakistani President Ghulam Ishaque Khan on corruption charges. This move was orchestrated by the army establishment of Pakistan. With the formation of an alliance of nationalists and the inception of a second nationalist government in Balochistan after 17 years, new hopes were raised among the Baloch masses. However, neither the alliance nor the government was long lasting. BNM, the party emerged from the dissolution of BNYM, soon dissociated itself from the government of the national alliance. With the withdrawal of the only political party in the alliance, the BNA ceased to exist as a political entity. The government of the alliance was for a brief period and its functioning created no impact on the masses.

DEATH OF MIR BIZENJO

Death of Mir Gous Bakhsh Bizenjo in 1990 was one of the important happenings in the context of the Baloch national struggle in Pakistan. Popularly known as Mir Sahib, Bizenjo became involved in nationalist politics in 1938 as a member of Karachi based Baloch League. He became active in the politics of the Khanate of Kalat during the turbulent years before the independence, during independence and after the occupation of the Baloch state by Pakistan. Following the occupation, he became one of the prominent personalities of the Baloch struggle in Pakistan by joining the *Ustaman Gal* and later the NAP. During his political life, he was imprisoned for more than 14 years by Pakistani authorities and faced immense hardship during his detention in the notorious Quli Camp detention centre in Quetta. With the installation of first nationalist government in Balochistan, Mir Sahib became the Governor of Balochistan for nine months before he was dismissed by federal government on charges of acting against the integrity of Pakistan.

Mir Gous Bakhsh Bizenjo was among the prominent leaders of the Kalat State National Party (KSNP). As the leader of House of Commons in the newly elected parliament of an independent Balochistan, he vehemently opposed any thought of merger of the Baloch state with the religious state of Pakistan. His famous speech in the parliament became the founding document for the Baloch national resistance in Pakistan. He was a bitter critic of the handling of the situation with Pakistan by the last Khan of the Baloch and believed that the Khan was not qualified to lead the Baloch nation towards liberation in the wake of British withdrawal from India in 1947. Ironically, after the occupation of Balochistan by Pakistan in 1948, Mir Sahib joined Muslim League, which was the party championing the cause of Pakistan and the ruling party of Pakistan after the partition of India.

When in 1955, *Ustaman Gal* was formed by Baloch nationalists, Mir Bizenjo left Pakistan Muslim League and joined the party. Ustaman Gal was later merged with other progressive and nationalist parties in Pakistan to form Pakistan National Party but ultimately PNP was also merged in a broad-based nationalist and leftist party 'National Awami Party' (NAP) in 1957. Mir Bizenjo played a pivotal role in political organization of Baloch students and was a source of inspiration for the involvement of the Baloch students in the national struggle. Mir Sahib was believed to be a secret member of the communist party of Pakistan although, he did not openly admit this. His joining of Pakistan Muslim League for a brief period after the occupation of Balochistan was believed to be on the instruction of his communist colleagues. Later, with the formation of National Awami Party, he emerged as one of the prominent leaders among the secular and democratic political elite of Pakistan.

Mir Sahib was believed to be a pragmatic leader among the Baloch leadership. While in detention in Hyderabad, being tried on treason charges; he developed political differences with his long term Baloch nationalist associates on future strategies of the Baloch national struggle. Mir Bizenjo was of the firm belief that the objective conditions were not favourable for the continuation of armed resistance. He emphasised that the Baloch cannot win independence without external support which was not readily available. He believed that the only feasible strategy for the Baloch was increased political mobilization and participation in the political process of Pakistan. His opinion was not acceptable to his long term colleagues Sardar Mengal and Nawab Mari. The youth segment of nationalist politics and the BSO saw his views on the national struggle as capitulation and betrayal of the Baloch cause. They therefore, dissociated themselves from the politics of Mir Sahib. When he formed Pakistan National Party (PNP) after his release from prison, no section of the BSO was ready to support his party. Once termed as *Baba e Ustaman* (father of the nation), Mir

Sahib and his party was defeated in the 1988 general elections and he failed to secure a parliamentary seat for himself.

He was diagnosed as suffering from cancer of pancreas in 1989 and died on August 11, 1990. His eldest son, Mir Bizen Bizenjo, was made the president of PNP after his death, but he was unable to keep the party together and many followers of Mir Sahib became dissatisfied with his leadership capabilities. A significant section of the party along with family members of Mir Sahib joined Sardar Mengal's Balochistan National Party in 1996. Mir Sahib's sons and family members left BNP when it was divided in 1998 and ultimately they joined the National Party in 2003.

BALOCH NATIONAL MOVEMENT AND ITS DIVISION

In 1989, the newly created youth movement, BNYM, was converted into a formal political party and renamed as the Baloch National Movement (BNM). It attracted the attention of a vast section of the Baloch society, especially the educated. Having the blessing of exiled leader-Sardar Ataullah Mengal and with a very active BSO as its student wing, it became the major political party of Baloch nationalists following the banning of the NAP. The BNM soon became the target of the state establishment. Many of the Baloch analysts believed that it was because of the active manipulation of powerful state agencies, which caused the immediate division of the movement, soon after its creation. Within two years it was divided and in 1990, it split into two groups; BNM-Mengal led by Sardar Akhtar Mengal and BNM-Hayee led by Dr. Abdul Hayee. At the time, activists belonging to BNM-Mengal accused the group headed by Dr. Abdul Hayee of hobnobbing with the establishment and betrayal of the nationalist cause. BNM-Mengal was merged into BNP in 1996 while BNM-Hayee suffered further divisions in 2003.

JAMHOORI WATAN PARTY

In 1990, Nawab Akbar Bugti, after the dismissal of his government and the dissolution of Balochistan National Alliance, formally launched his own political party and named it as Jamhoori Watan Party (JWP). The party pledged to struggle for the rights of the Baloch people. For various reasons, the party could not be organized in other parts of Balochistan, and it remained limited to Dera Bugti and its adjacent districts. Nevertheless, in early days of 21st century, it played a pivotal role in the political mobilization of the Baloch against Pakistani aggression on Baloch natural resources and coastline. JWP under the leadership of Nawab Akber Bugti raised the slogan of securing the Baloch coast and resources in order to mobilize masses in opposing the leasing out of Gwadar port to Chinese and exploitation of natural resources of the Baloch. In 2003, with the announcement of Pakistan to build new military cantonment in Balochistan and extensive land grabbing by establishment in Gwadar and other parts of Balochistan, JWP became part of a loose four party 'Baloch Alliance' to oppose these moves. With the martyrdom of Nawab Bugti in 2006, JWP split into various factions and ceased to be a potent player in nationalist politics of Balochistan when the political heir of Nawab Bugti, Mir Brahamdag Bugti decided to form Baloch Republican Party (BRP).

RETURN OF EXILE LEADERS AND PARTICIPATION IN THE POLITICAL PROCESS

During early years of 1990s, with the growing perception of an imminent collapse of the Afghan revolutionary government of Dr. Najibullah in Kabul, Baloch exiles in Afghanistan began to return to Pakistan including Nawab Khair Bakhsh Mari, Mir Hazar Khan Rahmakani Mari, Abdul Nabi Bungulzai and Wahid Kamber while Sher Muhammad Mari had already left for India. Severe differences of opinion developed between Nawab Mari and some of his staunch political, tribal and armed supporters while living in Afghanistan. Famous Guerrilla commanders of 1960s and 1970s and prominent leaders in the Baloch Peoples Liberation Front (BPLF), Mir Sher Muhammad Mari and Mir Hazar Khan Rehmakani parted ways with their long time tribal chief and leader Nawab Khair Bakhsh Mari. Sardar Ataullah Mengal ended his exile in 1996, and returned to Balochistan to play an active part in the political process. He was successful in the creation of a united nationalist party with the merger of PNP and BNM-Mengal. The party became the largest and most popular. It won the 1997 general elections and formed the third nationalist government in Balochistan in alliance with Nawab Bugti's Jamhoori Watan Party. Nawab Khair Bakhsh Mari after his return, became active in politics and formed a discussion group of its followers. This was named as *Haq Tawar* (the voice of truth). His sons-Mir Gangeez Mari, Mir Gazzain Mari and Mir Hairbyar Mari participated in provincial elections as independent candidates and became members of various nationalists and non-nationalist governments in Balochistan as ministers.

BALOCHISTAN NATIONAL PARTY AND THIRD NATIONALIST GOVERNMENT

When in 1996, Sardar Ataullah Mengal ended his long stay in the UK and returned to Balochistan, he managed to unite the Baloch nationalists on a single platform. The Balochistan National Party (BNP) was founded with the merger of PNP with BNM-Mengal. The party was also joined by many other nationalist groups and personalities and was considered to be the true image of NAP in Balochistan. After a prolonged period of near political anarchy among nationalist forces, the party became a beacon of hope for a united struggle after the banning of NAP and the collapse of 1970 movement. Right of self-determination for the Baloch was included in the party manifesto. The Party participated in the general elections held in Pakistan in 1997 and became the single largest party in the provincial assembly of Balochistan. An alliance of BNP, JWP of Nawab Bugti with the support of Nawab Mari, the third nationalist government in Balochistan was formed in 1997 and Sardar Akhtar Mengal became the Chief Minister of the province. For many Baloch nationalist activists, it was the reincarnation of the NAP government of 1972 as the whole Baloch national leadership was together for the first time in a political alliance since the traumatic events of 1970s. It was not only the true representative of the Baloch nationalists but joining of Nawab Akber Bugti, Sardar Ataullah Mengal, Nawab Khair Bakhsh Mari and the family of Mir Gous Bakhsh Bizenjo in the political process of the state was also a gesture from the Baloch nationalists that they were ready for a peaceful and honourable solution of the Baloch national question in Pakistan through political means.

However, the running the government was not smooth and relations between the governments in Quetta with that of Islamabad were not cordial. On many occasions, it became hard to retain even a semblance of a working relationship between the federation and Balochistan. Soon BNP leadership accused the state security agencies of intervention in the governance of the province. Severe differences developed with the central government on the ownership of the natural resources of Balochistan. The Baloch nationalist government was of the view that the federal government was keeping almost the whole share of the natural resources for itself, denying Balochistan its due share. The Balochistan government also viewed the decisions of the National Finance Commission (NFC is a constitution body responsible for the just division of national resources between the federating units of Pakistan) as detrimental to the interests of Balochistan. The BNP leadership was of the firm belief that the intelligence agencies were behind the differences which surfaced between BNP and JWP.

On May 28, 1998, the Pakistani government exploded several nuclear devices in the Chagai District of Balochistan. The Balochistan government protested that they had not been informed regarding the tests. The BNP and other nationalist parties declared May 28 as the Black Day, initiating a series of rallies and demonstration against nuclear tests on Baloch soil. This was more than the Pakistani military establishment could tolerate. With the active manipulations of state secret agencies, BNP was divided. Sardar Akhtar Mengal stepped down from the position of Chief Minister in 1998, on the pretext that he had not been kept in the loop on the nuclear tests carried out in Balochistan. However, it has been alleged that the division within his party forced him to resign from the government. With the end of the Baloch nationalist government, it appeared that the gesture on behalf of the Baloch leadership towards the state in their acceptance of participation in the political process of the state in order to seek a peaceful political solution to the Baloch national question, was altogether rejected by the state and a new showdown became inevitable between the Baloch and Pakistan.

The decades of 1980 and 1990 are important in the history of the Baloch national struggle in the sense that the Baloch nationalist politics underwent drastic and sometimes contradictory changes during this period. The armed resistance was suspended after the release of the Baloch leaders from prison in 1978. Deep divisions developed between the leadership and this trickled down to the rank and file of political workers. New political parties and groups were formed, alliances were made, and the Baloch Students Organization was united and then again divided into various factions. A campaign of dissociating the Baloch from the political process of the state was launched by Nawab Khair Bakhsh Mari and his followers. One of the significant developments was the assertion of educated Baloch youth in policy formation for national resistance. The BSO became a powerful political pressure group after the hanging of Hameed Baloch. The united BSO and subsequent youth movements encouraged a number of middle class activists to play a leadership role in the long absence of Sardar Ataullah Mengal and Nawab Khair Bakhsh Mari. Armed resistance became the popular slogan and the support of Mir Gous Bakhsh Bizenjo diminished among the youth as he was in favour of participating in the political process of Pakistan. However, soon, the nationalists who were very much against any participation of political process, became a part of it. They participated in the elections and made nationalist governments twice for short periods.

The decision of the Baloch leaders and some of the activists to go in exile and the migration of thousands of Mari tribesmen appeared not to be productive. Hopes of Sardar Ataullah Mengal and Nawab Khair Bakhsh Mari to gain international support for the Baloch national struggle in Pakistan did not materialize. The Western powers and their allies, seeing the Baloch resistance in a perspective of the Cold War, considered the Baloch struggle as leftist and an independent Balochistan controlled by leftist elements or a weak Pakistan would be to the advantage of Soviet Bloc. The Soviet Union either was not in a position to support the Baloch struggle, or it was also suspicious of the orientations of the Baloch national struggle in Pakistan. During their stay abroad, the Baloch leadership was also unable to make workable contacts with other national liberation struggles of Asia and Africa.

Sardar Ataullah Mengal and Nawab Khair Bakhsh Mari after failing to secure any international support for the Baloch struggle, were compelled to end their exile, returned and participated in the political process of Pakistan. The return of exiled leadership was also due to unexpected political developments in regional and international polity. With the sudden collapse of the Soviet Union, the position of the Afghan revolutionary government became untenable. An imminent takeover of Afghanistan by Mujahideen, forced Nawab Khair Bakhsh Mari and his follower to end their stay in Afghanistan. Sardar Ataullah Mengal became disappointed by any prospect of Western support for an independent Balochistan and had no option but to return. On the other hand, the Pakistani establishment was not ready to show any gesture of compromise in response to conciliatory gestures and actions of the Baloch leaders. Instead, the establishment was busy in creating rifts and divisions in the newly created Baloch nationalist parties. The two governments of the Baloch nationalists in 1988 and 1997 were only allowed to function for very short periods to rule in Balochistan. For many analysts, the decades of 1980s and 1990s were times of total confusion on the political and intellectual fronts.

CHAPTER 14

21ST CENTURY BALOCH NATIONAL STRUGGLE IN PAKISTAN

During last two decades of 20th century, the Baloch armed resistance was in a hibernating state and political activities were mainly focused on the formation of parties and alliances. After their return from exile, the Baloch leadership participated in the political process of the state and formed the third nationalist government in Balochistan in 1997. This was a reconciliatory gesture on the part of Baloch leadership; however, there was no positive response from the establishment of Pakistan. After the unceremonious fate of the last Baloch nationalist government and the role of the secret agencies in the division of the main Baloch nationalist parties-BNP and BNM, the Baloch nationalists became engaged in a seemingly endless political, intellectual and academic debate. This concerned the merit and demerit of boycotting all state institutions and adopting armed resistance as the only viable method to achieve the desired objective of national salvation. Announcements regarding the exploration of natural resources without taking into consideration reservations shown by the Baloch leadership, plans for colonizing the coastal regions of Balochistan with non-Baloch from Punjab and other areas of the country in order to bring about demographic changes, and preparations for the establishment of military cantonments in Balochistan were factors which prompted the Baloch nationalists to take immediate measures. Ultimately a series of events created the situation in which a bloody showdown became inevitable between Pakistan and the Baloch. In the contemporary conflict which practically began in 2002, the Baloch are suffering immense losses in men and material while Pakistan is continuing its policy of ruthlessly crushing the Baloch national aspirations using excessive force.

PAKISTANI ESTABLISHMENT GOT THE BLESSINGS OF CIVILIZED WORLD

At the dawn of 21st century Pakistan was under a new Martial Law regime. After the death of former military ruler General Zia ul Haque in 1988, the military establishment took a tactical retreat and ruled the country from behind a curtain for more than a decade. However, in 1999, the army came into open, ended the so-called democratic dispensation and all political activities were banned. Initially, there was a strong reaction from the West against the military takeover, and to pacify the Western criticism, the establishment declared military rule as the beginning of a new liberal polity in Pakistan. In practice, it was carrying the policy of Islamization initiated by General Zia ul Haque and the creation and strengthening of Islamic militant organizations. These became the foreign policy tools of the new military regime. Fortunately for the new military dictator, General Pervez Musharraf, its regime got a much needed boost from events of September 11, 2001 in the United States when terrorists attacked Twin Towers in New York. The United States and its allies blamed the Taliban government of Afghanistan and Osama bin Laden for the planning and execution of this attack and decided to invade Afghanistan after the Taliban government refused to deliver Osama bin Laden to the United States. For attacking Afghanistan and ousting the Taliban government in Kabul, the support of the Pakistani military establishment was thought necessary. The Pakistani military regime was granted international recognition, offered diplomatic support and handsome financial assistance. In return Pakistan became the frontline state in Afghan conflict of 21st century.

A FIGHT TO FINISH: THE PAKISTANI WAY OF RESOLVING THE BALOCH QUESTION

The Pakistani establishment found the unconditional and all out support of the civilized world in the wake of the September 11 attacks in New York, as an opportunity to complete its long term agenda of doing away with the Baloch national question once and for all. In this respect, a multi-pronged strategy was finalized by the establishment. To counter the designs of the Pakistani establishment, the Baloch nationalist parties began a process of political mobilization. As a result, the Baloch and Pakistan became involved in a head-on collision. A bloody and protracted resistance movement began in Balochistan with tales of much horror and brutalities.

After the dissolution of Hyderabad Tribunal which was trying the Baloch and other NAP leaders on treason charges, a section of the army establishment had been criticizing the decision of letting the Baloch leaders free. The security establishment was of the view that unless the power of three tribes-Mari, Mengal and Bugti-and their chiefs who had been prominent in the Baloch national resistance from 1960s, were not weakened, the Baloch would never accept the supremacy of Punjab. From early 2000, various think-tanks founded by the military establishment in order to formulate strategies on the Baloch national question, were of the view that both muscle power and political manipulations were imperative, in order to settle the issue in favour of the state. In December 2005, the Pakistani ruler General Pervez Musharraf told the media in Lahore that there were two or three tribal chiefs and feudal lords behind what was going on in Balochistan. He criticized past governments in Pakistan who showed leniency towards these chiefs by making deals with them and indulging them. He asserted that his government was determined to establish its writ in Balochistan and this time it would be a fight to the finish.

The state establishment adopted the strategy of not only weakening the hold of Nawab Mari, Sardar Mengal and Nawab Bugti on their respective tribes but in order to dilute and create confusion among the masses regarding the national struggle, a two pronged strategy was adopted. First, they successfully created a Baloch nationalist party of their own. In this context, many among the Baloch nationalists believed that National Party (NP) was formed with the active support of the establishment by uniting a section of BNM with the Balochistan National Democratic Party (BNDP) as its political front. BNDP was earlier formed by some activists of the BNP, who left the party in 1998 and was headed by the sons of Mir Gous Bakhsh Bizenjo. Second, the establishment openly patronized the religious elements in Balochistan. This was felt necessary in order to achieve the objective of weakening the nationalist support among the Baloch masses; as the whole philosophy of Baloch resistance was based on a struggle against the illegal occupation of Balochistan by the religious state of Pakistan. Rivals of Nawab Mari, Sardar Mengal and Nawab Bugti, in their respective tribes, were encouraged and brought into the fold of the anti-nationalist camp. A section of Mari tribe headed by Mir Hazar Khan Rahmakani began active collaboration with the military establishment. The Kalpar and Massoori clans of Bugti tribe were given assistance to oppose Nawab Akber Bugti and a family from Mengal tribe was openly groomed to counter Sardar Ataullah Mengal.

On the political and intellectual front, writers and political activists whose affiliations were with anti-nationalist forces from early 1960s were hired. This was in order to initiate a campaign of slander about the Baloch leadership and to spread doubts about the real intentions of people involved in the struggle. The old and time tested rhetoric of the Baloch struggle not being for the people of Balochistan, but for taking of favours for tribal leaders and their families was propagated through state controlled media. The National Party was portrayed by the state media, as the Baloch nationalist party and the true representative of the Baloch national aspirations. *Jamiat Ulema Pakistan*, *Jamaat e Islami* and several other religious groups were given financial and strategic support by the military government in Balochistan to enhance their credibility. The military regime made it certain that these religious parties under the umbrella of a united front *Muttahida Majlis e Amal* (MMA) secure a reasonable number of seats in the general elections held in 2002. Several religious militant organizations were also created by Pakistan's powerful and notorious Inter-Services Intelligence agency (ISI). These were used (as would became obvious later) against the Baloch nationalists in the coming years. The military regime encouraged the establishment of *madrasas* (religious schools) in every town and village of Balochistan. With political patronage and massive funding from multiple sources (religious elements were also being funded by Wahhabis of Saudi Arabia and other oil rich Persian Gulf countries), the social standing of the *Mullah* (clergy) was upgraded and the role of clergy was increased in such a way that was previously unheard of in a Baloch society of the liberal and secular mind-set. This Islamization project was to contest the secular element of the Baloch national resistance and officials from the security agencies boasted, on many occasions, that they have neutralized the 'infidel led' Baloch resistance with the 'force of Allah'. The regime also attempted to dilute the Baloch national question by launching a devolution plan. The plan was to bypass the provincial assembly by creating local governments entirely dependent on the central government for their functioning. The Baloch perceived the so-called devolution plan to be an imposition of a centralized form of government and a negation of provincial autonomy.

THE BALOCH POLITICAL MOBILIZATION

Tensions between the Baloch nationalists and the state increased as the state began implementing its long term agenda in Balochistan. Exploration of the natural resources of Balochistan, bringing about demographic changes in the guise of developing the coastal region of Balochistan together with the establishment of three more military cantonments in Balochistan, were the main elements of the new strategy of Pakistan to deal with the Baloch national question. The gold and uranium deposits of a huge area in Chagai District of Balochistan were already depleted by the Chinese. Negotiations were underway for the exploration of other natural resources with different Chinese companies and corporations. The Oil and Gas Development Corporation of Pakistan (OGDC) and the Pakistan Petroleum limited (PPL) were planning to begin a new phase of oil and gas exploration in the Mari, Bugti and Jhalawan regions. In the guise of developing the fishing port of Gwadar into a deep sea port, hundreds and thousands of acres of land were forcibly acquired from the local population and sold to overseas Punjabis settled in Europe and North America, serving and retired military personnel and Punjabi businessmen. In 2002, Mr. Shoukat Aziz, the finance minister of the military regime announced a plan to relocate 2.5 million people from outside Balochistan into the Gwadar area by 2025. This was a blatant move to bring about demographic changes in Balochistan. To counter any resistance from the Baloch, it was announced that three new army cantonments and a naval base would be established in Balochistan. This was considered an act of war by Baloch nationalists.

With the end of nationalist government led by Sardar Akhtar Mengal in 1998, there was a debate about how to counter the increasingly aggressive behaviour of Pakistani state among the Baloch intellectual and political circles. The role of the state establishment in the overthrow of a third nationalist government and its role in dividing the BNP in 1998 and the BNM in 2002, was perceived by nationalists that the Pakistani state was not demonstrating any gesture of a political settlement of the Baloch national question. Participation or non-participation in the political process of the state once again became the focus of the debate. Discussions began to take place among the nationalist circles whether to restart another round of armed struggle, in order to counter increased 'developmental' and military aggression in Balochistan.

A DIVIDED OPINION

Opinion was divided on the Baloch response against the aggressive measures of Pakistan. Some among the Baloch nationalists were of the opinion that the objective conditions for a new armed confrontation with Pakistan were not favourable for the Baloch as the whole Western world is behind the Pakistani military establishment. They believed that in the context of a unipolar world, the international community would not consider favourably the Baloch grievances against Pakistan, as it needed its support in order to defeat the Taliban insurgency in Afghanistan and the international terrorism threat from Al-Qaeda. They believed that without the support of United States or its allies, the Pakistani army would brutally crush any form of Baloch resistance. Human rights violations in Balochistan by Pakistani security agencies would go unnoticed by international community. They believed that for the time being, the Baloch should not show any sign of active resistance, no matter how great the provocation and aggression by the Pakistani authorities. According to them, the only feasible method of resistance at present, should be political agitation. Another segment of the Baloch nationalists, however, was of the opinion that it was a "now or never" situation with the Baloch. They believed that with the planned settlement of 2.5 million non-Baloch in the coastal region, and with the consolidation of the Pakistani strategic position with the establishment of three cantonments and a naval base, not only would the demographic balance in Balochistan shift against the Baloch, but if it became too late to respond, then the Baloch would never be able to confront the Pakistani army in a meaningful way. This view was espoused by Nawab Mari and his supporters and a section of the BSO and BNM. Even Sardar Ataullah Mengal who was considered to be the most pragmatic of contemporary Baloch leaders expressed his dismay over the behaviour of the state establishment. He observed that Baloch have tried their utmost to develop friendly relations with the Punjab-dominated establishment but in response, they had been pushed against the wall, and the idea of full autonomy for Balochistan would never be considered voluntarily by the state establishment. The former chief minister of Balochistan Sardar Akhtar Mengal, pointed out that after the debacle of 1970s, the Baloch felt that they could achieve their rights and goals in a democratic way; however, their experiences after 1988 and 1998 showed that this was not the case. He asserted that the Baloch now felt that all doors for a peaceful solution were closed and it was certain that they would need to resort to other methods to preserve the Baloch national identity and to save their natural resources. Nawab Khair Bakhsh Mari had already rejected any chance of a negotiated settlement of the Baloch national question taking into account the hegemonic mind-set of the ruling Punjabi nationality. Nawab Akber Bugti called for the safeguarding the Baloch coast and resources in whatever way possible. Although, the atmosphere in Balochistan was a generalized anger; nevertheless, the immediate response from the Baloch nationalists against state provocation was the beginning of a political agitation.

FOUR PARTY ALLIANCE AND PONM

The end of Baloch nationalist government in 1998 had already initiated a process of political mobilization in Balochistan. With increasingly aggressive measures of the state, the political response of the Baloch was to mobilize the masses under the banner of PONM and a four party Baloch nationalist alliance. Sardar Ataullah Mengal was instrumental in the formation of Pakistan Oppressed Nationalities Movement (PONM), with a manifesto of demanding a confederation of all nationalities comprising Pakistan. The PONM became the umbrella group of parties from minority national entities and was to struggle for the reconstitution of Pakistan on the basis of March 23, 1940 resolution passed by Muslim League, the proponent party of Pakistan as a blueprint of a constitutional arrangement for a future Pakistan. The resolution spelled out that various national entities should constitute Pakistan on an equal basis in a confederated state, where the centre should have jurisdiction over three main areas- defence, foreign affairs and currency-leaving all other matters to be decided by the constituent units of the state. PONM was to struggle for autonomy in a confederated Pakistan for smaller national entities, but it later became ineffective during the Martial Law regime of General Pervez Musharraf when Sardar Ataullah Mengal again went into exile and lived in the UK for many years.

In an unprecedented move, during 2001, the military authorities rampaged the house of Nawab Khair Bakhsh Mari in Quetta and arrested him on the murder charges of a high court judge. The way the most respected and veteran leader of the Baloch national struggle was arrested and implicated in a murder case was perceived by Baloch nationalists as the state policy of humiliating revered Baloch leaders and sending signals to the Baloch that the state was no more ready to treat them with honour and dignity. For many of the Baloch analysts, the arrest of Nawab Khair Bakhsh Mari in such a manner was the turning point of the Baloch resistance after a pause of two decades during which the Baloch kept a low profile regarding their grievances against the state and they tried to participate in the political process of the state. The army sent a clear message to the nationalists about how they would deal with them, should they try to assert themselves.

In 2003, a four party alliance of Baloch nationalists was formed to galvanize support among the masses to counter measures taken by the military government against Balochistan. It was composed of Jamhoori Watan Party (JWP) of Nawab Akbar Bugti, Balochistan National Party (BNP) of Sardar Ataullah Mengal, National Party (NP) of Dr Abdul Hayee and Baloch *Haq Tawar* of Nawab Khair Bakhsh Mari. Balochistan was engulfed in a new wave of political agitation with increased participation from all segments of society. In 2004, the alliance tried to formulate recommendations as the basis of a negotiated settlement on the issue, with the military regime. However, as the establishment had already opted for a violent confrontation, political moves were soon overtaken by aggressive behaviour and sabre-rattling by the army and its intelligence agencies and situation deteriorated. Agitation by PONM and the four party alliance manifested not only the increased alienation of the traditional Baloch nationalist leadership, but also the frustration of newly developed urban middle class of Balochistan who saw no economic or political space for themselves in the mind-set of the state establishment of Pakistan.

Perhaps to pacify internal critics from a section of the Punjabi ruling elite, the military-installed hapless civilian government headed by Shoukat Aziz, appointed a parliamentary committee on September 23, 2004 'to deal with the issue of Balochistan and inter-provincial harmony'. Its two subcommittees were to make appropriate recommendations on the situation in Balochistan and make recommendations 'to promote inter-provincial harmony and protect the rights of provinces, with a view to strengthen the federation.' The committee's recommendations were rejected by both parties in the conflict; the four party Baloch Alliance, and the military establishment. In July 2006, the four-party Baloch Alliance while rejecting the parliamentary committee's recommendations vowed to continue the struggle for the national rights of the Baloch people. The former chief minister and a leader of the four party alliance, Sardar Akhtar Mengal called for a joint meeting of the Pakistan Oppressed Nations Movement (PONM) and the Baloch Alliance to chalk out a joint strategy against what he called government's extra-constitutional measures. He accused the intelligence agencies of harassing and victimising families of those Baloch nationalist leaders, who had raised voices against the government's excesses in Balochistan. Again in 2006, the ruling Pakistan Muslim League agreed on a package of incentives for the Baloch that included a constitutional amendment giving greater autonomy to the provinces. However, the military establishment overruled the initiative and expressed its intention to crush the Baloch resistance with force.

Earlier, there was a move for the creation of a single Baloch nationalist party. Although, Nawab Bugti and Sardar Ataullah Mengal were hopeful of forming a single party of Baloch nationalists, for reasons still unknown, this move could not be finalized with a positive result. Indeed, with the murder of Nawab

Akber Bugti and Mir Balaach Mari, the four party Baloch alliance itself disintegrated as Nawab Mari was no longer interested in participating in the political process of the state and National Party came into open with its support to the establishment.

MURDER OF NAWAB AKBER BUGTI

At the time of growing tension between the Baloch and Pakistan, the veteran nationalist leaders and legendary figures of Baloch national struggle were getting on in years. Sardar Ataullah Mengal was not active because of health reasons and Nawab Khair Bakhsh Mari's activities have been confined within the four walls of his house in Karachi after his release from prison in 2002. Although, Nawab Akber Bugti had reached 80 years and faced some serious health problems; nevertheless, he took the responsibility of leading the mass mobilization efforts on his shoulders. This made Nawab Akber Bugti an irritant in the eyes of military establishment. There was another reason for the establishment to be angry with Nawab Akber Bugti. The latent tension between the Bugti tribe and the federal government over issues of employment, job security, and compensation came into open during 2002 as the fifty years land lease for Pakistan Petroleum Limited had to be renewed. Nawab Akber Bugti was not flexible in relaxing the Baloch demand for increased royalties from the gas fields, neither he was ready to grant any rights for new exploration in the area.

On the one hand, the civilian face of the military establishment, the ruling Pakistan Muslim League pretended to settle outstanding issues between the Baloch nationalists and the state through political means, whilst on the other hand, the army was mobilized in every district of Balochistan. The show of muscle power by the state, resulted in the crisis in Balochistan becoming worse and more serious. It was soon transformed from a political confrontation into an armed conflict. The state media was given the task by the military regime to portray the Baloch political mobilization against military cantonments, Gwadar project and issues of Gas royalty and exploration rights as anti-development activities by certain tribal chiefs. Quoting military and civilian intelligence agencies, the media and establishment affiliated political parties, were busy convincing the Pakistani public, that on a ubiquitous "foreign hand" which was responsible for all troubles in Balochistan. There began a vigorous propaganda that the international conspiracy was to dismantle the only 'Allah given country' on this planet Earth and that the Baloch nationalists were tools of foreign enemies of Pakistan.

Tension increased between the Bugti tribe and military forces in Dera Bugti and Sui and there was overall intensification of political activities from the Baloch nationalist parties on Gwadar and other related issues. In this situation of intense hostilities an event happened which became the ignition for a violent confrontation between the Baloch and the state. It was the rape of a Sindhi lady doctor working in Balochistan, to which the Baloch took as an affront to their traditional code of honour. Dr Shazia Khalid was working for Pakistan Petroleum Limited, which operated gas fields in Bugti area of Balochistan. The person accused for the rape was a major rank officer in the Pakistani army. The military ruler General Pervez Musharraf wasted no time, and publicly affirmed the officer's innocence. Dr. Shazia Khalid was later forced to flee Pakistan by the military authorities.

The Baloch sense of frustration and alienation was growing amid military provocations. General Pervez Musharraf and the military establishment were not prepared to concede to Baloch's genuine economic and political demands. Instead of addressing the Baloch grievances politically and through negotiations, the military government resorted to a greater use of force. General Musharraf added fuel to the fire when he publicly gave an ultimatum to the Baloch by saying that "Don't push us. This isn't the 1970s when you can hit and run and hide in the mountains. This time you won't even know what hit you." This statement further fuelled the already inflammable situation as the Baloch took it as an insult and a threat to their national honour by a ruler who originated from Indian immigrants (*Muhajir*) and was the son of a dancer girl, whom they did not consider as equal to a Baloch in social standings. With increased threatening postures and armed mobilization by the state, the Baloch were afraid that they would not only be humiliated into submission but would also be dispossessed of their land and resources and with forced demographic changes they would lose their distinct national identity.

When negotiations failed between Nawab Akber Bugti and the government regarding a new agreement for oil and gas exploration in Bugti area, the Pakistani army units were deployed and troops blockaded the town of Dera Bugti, alleging that the head of the Bugti tribe was protecting rebels who were sabotaging the infrastructure for the extraction of natural gas. With mounting tension between the Baloch and the armed forces, sporadic clashes were reported. The Pakistani security agencies blamed Bugti tribesmen for attacks on gas installation and security forces guarding those installations. Nawab Akber Bugti was accused of masterminding these attacks, which caused major disruption to the supply of gas to other parts of the country. This was the pretext when military action was taken by security agencies, resulting in widespread death and destruction in Bugti region.

In a bid to physically eliminate the most politically active of veteran nationalist leaders, on March 17, 2005, the paramilitary forces bombed and shelled the residence of Nawab Bugti and its surrounding areas for many hours. Nawab Akber Bugti was not hurt but 67 people died and more than a hundred were injured. Several houses and a Hindu temple was reduced to rubbles. In follow up operations in the area, thousands of Bugtis were forced to flee their homes. The Human Rights Commission of Pakistan (HRCP) reported accounts of summary executions of the Baloch by paramilitary forces. Various human rights organizations and the Baloch nationalist parties presented evidences of widespread instances of disappearance and inhuman torture of arrested persons by security agencies. Dera Bugti became a ghost town with frequent bombardment by security forces. The HRCP reported that up to 85 percent of the 22,000-26,000 inhabitants of Dera Bugti had fled their homes after artillery shells repeatedly hit the town. Similar reports of displacement were also published by HRCP for Kohlu region where thousands of Mari tribesmen were forced to vacate their abodes. There were alarming accounts of summary executions, allegedly carried out by paramilitary forces. The Pakistani media reported continued attacks by the Baloch on government targets, such as gas pipelines, railway lines and electricity networks. There were also reports of rocket attacks on government buildings and army bases. The army retaliated with indiscriminate bombardment of Baloch settlements and massive search operations of the surrounding areas. The army used heavy artillery and launched several air strikes against presumed insurgent bases.

In December 2005, the crisis took on an even more serious dimension after the military regime accused the Baloch militants of an attack on General Pervez Musharraf's public meeting in Kohlu. Reacting to this, the Pakistani military ruler promised to "fix" Baloch nationalist leaders. The army launched retaliatory operations against the Mari tribe in which many hundreds were killed and injured. In July 2006, General Pervez Musharraf reiterated his government's stance that his military regime was determined to re-establish its control on Balochistan and would protect national installations in Balochistan at all costs and ensure full security for the development activities and for Chinese investors there.

The constant rocket attacks and artillery bombardment on Dera Bugti town forced the 80 years old Nawab Akber Bugti to leave the township. He camped himself in the Chalgri area of Bhamboor hills of Dera Bugti district. On August 24, 2006, the Pakistan army launched a massive operation in the area involving air crafts, gunship helicopters and elite commando units. Nawab Bugti was killed, along with 37 of his companions on August 26, 2006. It was a well-planned murder of a respected veteran leader of the Baloch national resistance by the Pakistani military. Taking into account the open threats and a declaration of "fixing" the Baloch leaders by military authorities, Nawab Bugti was anticipating the worst. In the wake of increased armed activities and a massive crackdown on nationalist activists throughout

Balochistan, he had predicted his death at the hands of Pakistani armed forces. In April 2006, he observed that the army units have been given instructions that he and Mir Balaach Mari (Balaach was the son of Nawab Khair Bakhsh Mari, murdered a year after Nawab's martyrdom) — the two of us should be eliminated.

Nawab Shahbaaz Akber Bugti was born in 1927, became the chief of Bugti tribe at a very early age and remained one of the dominant personalities of the Baloch national resistance for nearly half a century along with Nawab Khair Bakhsh Mari, Sardar Ataullah Mengal and Mir Gous Bakhsh Bizenjo. A symbol of the traditional Balochi style of living, he remained adherent in practising the Balochi cultural and social code. During early years of Pakistan, Nawab Bugti remained active in Pakistani politics and was part of many federal governments, in the 1950s, as minister or deputy minister. He joined the ranks of the Baloch nationalists after 1958 and soon became one of the towering figures in the Baloch resistance. During the 1970s, he developed differences with other leaders and parted ways with the Baloch national resistance for many years. He again became part of the Baloch national struggle and played a pivotal role in the formation of Balochistan National Alliance (BNA) in 1988. The alliance won the elections held in 1988 and Nawab Bugti became chief minister of a second nationalist government in Balochistan. He was also instrumental in the formation of the Baloch nationalist government in 1997. After the promulgation of Martial Law in Pakistan in 1999, Nawab Bugti became an outspoken critic of state strategies in Balochistan expressing his determination to safeguard the Baloch coast and resources from the aggressive designs of the state establishment. He became active in the four party Baloch Alliance to mobilize the masses against the proposed construction of Gwadar port, the establishment of military cantonments in Balochistan and plans for the ruthless exploitation of the natural resources of Balochistan. He had a charismatic personality and politically was believed to be pragmatic. He was in favour of using all forms of struggle in the achievement of the Baloch goal of national sovereignty. During 2004, he was also active in uniting all nationalists into a single party; however, state-sponsored conspiracies and repeated attacks on his life slowed down the process of Baloch unity.

For many Baloch, Nawab Bugti lived honourably and embraced death gracefully maintaining the Baloch code of social ethics. The way he died elevated him to the pantheon of Baloch heroes and martyrs. His death will remain an inspiration for the Baloch for generations and will be among the sustaining factors of the Baloch national resistance. His death was followed by massive anti-government protests in Pakistan. The Baloch all over the world expressed their grief over his murder by taking out rallies and demonstration. There were widespread protest demonstrations and rioting in Balochistan. Quetta and many other townships in Balochistan remained under curfew and all train services to and from Balochistan were cancelled. The four party Baloch Alliance announced a 15-day mourning period and declared that protests would continue across the region. The alliance held a massive protest rally in Quetta, the capital city of Balochistan. On September 4, 2006, the Balochistan National Party announced the resignations of its members from the federal Parliament and the Balochistan Assembly in protest against the murder of Nawab Bugti. In October, 2006, the Baloch nationalists in a hurriedly arranged grand *Jirga* of tribal elite and political parties in Kalat, demanded that Pakistani army should vacate Balochistan and the status of Balochistan in Pakistan should be renegotiated between the representatives of the Baloch and the state. The *Jirga* tasked Mir Suleiman Daud, the grandson of the last Khan of the Baloch state, to plead the case for the independence of Balochistan in the International Court of Justice in The Hague.

A TALE OF BLOOD AND TEARS

The Baloch conflict with Pakistan in the 21st century is a tale of blood and tears. It brought much devastation for the Baloch in men and material. Compared to all other periods of active hostility between the Baloch and Pakistan, the highest numbers of casualties, disappearances and displacement of population occurred in the present conflict.

From the start of the new millennium, intensive mobilization of the army took place in Balochistan. It was on the pretext of protecting what the state establishment believed were the state interests. This took place in a milieu of an increased sense of frustration and alienation among the Baloch. As early as 2001, the army was ordered to take measures in order to create a conducive atmosphere for the construction of military cantonments and to have a firm security control over the Gwadar region for the construction of the proposed deep sea port. Reports of armed encounters began to appear in the media between the Baloch fighters and the army units in various parts of Balochistan, especially the in Mari and Bugti regions as early as 2002. After the arrest of Nawab Khair Bakhsh Mari, Quetta was already under frequent rocket attacks and the situation in the Bolan region became very tense with the increased activities of armed Baloch groups. In southern Balochistan, a Chinese delegation was attacked in August 2004 and there were many reported casualties. Air force and army helicopters attacked and bombed reported hideouts of nationalist militants between Turbat and Gwadar who were blamed as being behind the attack on the Chinese.

In 2004, the federal interior minister of Pakistan, Mr Faisal Saleh Hayat, warned the agitating Baloch nationalists, that the government was poised to launch a crash programme against subversive elements in the province. On Dec 8, 2005, the minister stated that only 4,000 people had been arrested in Balochistan. The security agencies clamped down on the Baloch nationalists and in early 2006, BNP sources claimed that at least 180 people have died in bombings, 122 children have been killed by paramilitary troops and thousands of people have been arrested since the beginning of the military campaign. The four-party Baloch Alliance and PONM, strongly condemned the spate of arrests of Baloch nationalists in Turbat, Gwadar, Kalat, Dera Bugti, Kohlu and Nushki, and accused Islamabad of having launched an unannounced military aggression in Balochistan.

The Human Rights Commission of Pakistan (HRCP) and Amnesty International in their reports mentioned massive human rights violations by security agencies during 2005 and 2006. They mentioned evidences of death and injuries among civilians during indiscriminate use of aerial and artillery bombardments on civilian targets. They reported several cases of torture, extrajudicial killings, disappearances and accused security forces of carrying out summary executions. The International Crisis Group (ICG) in 2006, appealed to the international community to pressurize the Pakistani government to end all practices that violate international human rights like torture, arbitrary arrests and extra-judicial killings.

After the murder of Nawab Bugti, a full scale political and armed conflict started between the Baloch and the state. Since then, the Baloch bore the brunt of the immense anti-Baloch measures taken by the Pakistani military establishment. In the brutal operation which has been going on for more than a decade, thousands have been killed, disappeared, and displaced. Indiscriminate arrests, unlawful custody and the use of inhuman torture of the Baloch political activists and mutilation of their bodies were the hallmark of the adopted strategies against the Baloch resistance. Thousands of political activists were rounded-up by security agencies under anti-terrorism law. Most affected were the workers of Nawab Bugti's Jamhoori Watan Party, the Baloch National Movement and the Balochistan National Party. Former Chief Minister of Balochistan, Sardar Akhtar Mengal, and leader of Balochistan National Party was arrested in November 2006, when he announced that he would lead a long march from Gwadar to Quetta. Tried in an anti-terrorism court, he was kept in a cage and humiliated in prison. In 2008, the Asian Human Rights Commission observed that Balochistan was the worst hit by the violence perpetrated by armed forces, including the Army and Air Force.

MURDER OF MIR BALAACH MARI

On November 21, 2007, Mir Balaach Mari, who was believed to be the commander of Balochistan Liberation Army (BLA), one of the armed resistance groups, died in mysterious circumstances. The majority of the Baloch believe that he was murdered by Pakistani secret agencies in Afghanistan where he had sought refuge following the crackdown in the Mari and Bugti areas in the wake of the murder of Nawab Akber Bugti in 2006. His death was a serious blow to the resistance struggle.

Mir Balaach Mari was one of six sons of Nawab Khair Bakhsh Mari and believed to be the political heir of the veteran Baloch leader. Popular among both the political and militant segments of the Baloch national resistance, he became a symbol of unity by keeping close ties with Bugti and Mengal tribes as well as with BNM, JWP and BNP. A believer in using all available resources in the national resistance, he remained a member of Balochistan Assembly until his murder. After his death, divisions appeared in ranks of the Baloch resistance and between his brothers which caused serious damage to the national struggle.

FORCED DISAPPEARANCES AND ILLEGAL DETENTIONS

In the ongoing conflict between the Baloch and Pakistan, forced disappearances and illegal detentions are being used by the state authorities as tools against the Baloch resistance. In 2007, the Human Rights Commission of Pakistan estimated the missing persons as 600. The Human Rights Watch found out that the government agencies most involved in enforced disappearances in Balochistan were Military Intelligence (MI), the Frontier Corps (FC), and the Directorate for Inter-Services Intelligence (ISI) and the Intelligence Bureau (IB). In 2008, according to the Asian Human Rights Commission and verified by the Interior Minister of Pakistan, Rehman Malik, at least 1,100 persons were included in the list of disappeared. A dossier by the BNP in 2009 claimed that 9000 people were being illegally detained in Balochistan. In September, 2010, Defence of Human Rights, an Islamabad based human rights group, put the number of missing person as 1700. However, in January 2011, the Balochistan Home Minister, Zafrullah Zehri, acknowledged that only 55 persons were missing.

In 2010, the Chief Minister of Balochistan, Nawab Aslam Raisani publicly accused the security forces of Pakistan of abductions and extrajudicial killings in the province. In July 2011, the Human Rights Watch in its report highlighted draconian tactics used by the military, the paramilitary Frontier Corps (FC) and intelligence services against Baloch political activists. The Human Rights Watch observed that an upsurge in the number of missing persons and the 'Kill and Dump' policy, in which the bodies of the Baloch activists are abandoned after extra-judicial killing, had brought brutality in the province to an unprecedented level. In 2015, the Interior Minister of Pakistan, Chaudhry Nisar Ali Khan disclosed that since June 2014, more than 10,000 intelligence-based operations had been carried out, mainly in Khyber Pashtunkhwa and Balochistan, in which some 36,000 persons accused of serious crimes, including terrorism and extremism, were arrested. On April 27, 2016, the interior minister in the government of Balochistan claimed that security forces arrested 12234 persons and killed 334 during last two years. On August 30, 2016, the Defence of Human Rights organization claimed that 549 people have been kidnapped by the security agencies between January and August. The majority of these persons were from Balochistan.

KILL AND DUMP POLICY: THE DEATH SQUADS

Abducting political activists, keeping them in illegal detention, inflicting inhuman torture and then dumping their mutilated bodies in remote and desolate areas in Balochistan has been another tool in the Pakistani war in Balochistan. In a planned way, the security agencies tried to physically wipe out the cream of the Baloch society. Anti-social and extremist religious elements organized by state security agencies in various parts of Balochistan were used in identifying, kidnapping and dumping bodies of the Baloch nationalist activists. They are popularly known in Balochistan as the army's 'death squads'.

According to lists provided by nationalist parties and Baloch human right organizations, during 2007, 938 Baloch political activists, intellectuals, writers, students, doctors, engineers and tribal elite were killed by the army in Balochistan. During 2008, 635 Baloch activists were killed either by security forces, intelligence agencies or their proxy militias and death squads. During 2009, 1104 people were killed which included well known political figures and intellectual personalities. On 22nd February, 2009, an assassination attempt was made on the life of a prominent scholar, writer and Chairman of the Balochi Academy, Mir Jan Muhammad Dashti, in which he luckily escaped death but he had to undergo several years of treatment in various UK hospitals. On June 1, 2011, Professor Saba Dashtyari, a literary person affiliated with the national resistance was assassinated by the security agencies. Several writers, singers and poets became victims of target killings by security agencies and their proxy death squads since the start of present conflict. According to the Human Rights Watch and Human Rights Commission of Pakistan, 143 bodies of missing persons were found during 2012. It was not only leaders and political activists but family members of the Baloch nationalists were also targeted by security agencies. The wife of Sardar Bakhtiar Domiki, who was also the sister of Republican Party leader Mir Brahamdag Bugti were killed by the Military Intelligence agency in 2012 along with her teenage daughter. Many family members of Dr Allah Nazar were also been murdered by security agencies in recent years.

Armed with the experience of dealing with Bengali nationalists in 1971 (the Pakistani army created *Al Shams* and *Al Badr* militias during the Bangladesh war of liberation which were blamed for the torture, murder and rape of thousands of Bengali nationalists), Pakistani security agencies created many militias to counter the nationalists in Balochistan. The Baloch nationalists are identifying several organizations run by security agencies to assist them in arresting their workers, torturing them and dumping their bodies. They organizations were successful in some areas in creating confusions and even disrupting the activities of resistance groups. Four main organizations are said to be operating in Balochistan today; although, they change names frequently. The *Baloch Musala*

Defaie Tanzen operates in Jhalawan area while *Sarawan Aman Force* has been active in Sarawan region. *Sepha Shuhda e Balochistan* and *Lashkar e Khurasan* are other militia outfits operating against the Baloch nationalists in southern Balochistan. In recent years, the Pakistani secret agencies are also using extremist religious outfits like *Lashkar e Janghwi* and *Tehrik e Taliban e Pakistan* in various operations against the Baloch political activists in recent years. The murderous activities of these squads had been reported by several regional and international human rights organizations. Many international organizations including the European parliament have called reports of the human rights situation alarming and stated that the main victims of the violence were the Baloch who were being systematically targeted by paramilitary groups, allegedly sponsored by the Pakistani authorities (Tarabella, 2015). The Human Rights Watch observed, on countless occasions, that the Pakistani government had not done enough to stop the violence, which include torture, enforced disappearances and extra-judicial killings. According to the BNM information secretary, during the month of August 2016 alone, 157 mutilated bodies of the Baloch activists were dumped by security forces (Daily Intekhab, 2 September, 2016)

MURDER OF GHULAM MUHAMMAD BALOCH

Ghulam Muhammad Baloch was born in the Kech District of Balochistan in 1959. From an earlier age, he became active in the student politics and later became the Chairman of a faction of the BSO affiliated with BNM (Hayee group). He joined the BNM and became one of the prominent leaders of the party. He began to oppose the move by BNM leadership of leaving the Baloch national struggle and of cooperating with state establishment. When BNM leaders merged BNM with BNDP to found National Party, Ghulam Muhammad parted ways with his colleagues and reorganized the BNM and was elected as the Chairman of the party. Ghulam Muhammad Baloch and Dr Allah Nazar were of the opinion that establishment using National Party, would try to replace genuine Baloch nationalist parties with so-called representatives of a Baloch nationalism that would become totally subservient to Islamabad.

After the murder of Nawab Akber Bugti, Ghulam Muhammad Baloch and his party were in the forefront of the agitation against the atrocities committed by the security agencies. The BNM under his leadership openly associated itself with the Baloch armed resistance. He and many other leaders and activists in his party were facing anti-state and terrorist charges in courts. On 9 April, 2009, Ghulam Muhammad Baloch, Lala Munir Baloch, and BRP Joint Secretary Sher Muhammad Baloch were picked up by the security agencies when they were conferring with their solicitor, after attending a court proceeding. They were shot dead and their bodies were supposedly thrown from helicopters. Their mutilated bodies were found 40 kilometres away from Turbat town.

PARTIES AND PERSONALITIES IN THE BALOCH RESISTANCE

The present conflict between the Baloch and Pakistan is being fought on political as well as on a military front. After the banning of the NAP in 1975 and the emergence of differences among the Baloch leadership, the political representation of the Baloch struggle has been carried out by various parties and groups. These groups, although, operating separately but have worked together on common issues. Calls for general strikes and demonstration by one group has always been supported by the others. The contemporary Baloch nationalist political parties include BRP, BNM and BNP. The sons of Nawab Khair Bakhsh Mari, Mir Hairbyar Mari and Mehran Mari; elder son of Sardar Ataullah Mengal, Mir Javed Mengal, Mir Noordin Mengal (grandson of Sardar Mengal) and Mir Suleman Daud, grandson of the last ruling Khan of the Baloch, have also been very prominent in organizing resistance in Balochistan and advocacy for the Baloch cause in international forums.

BALOCH REPUBLICAN PARTY (BRP)

After the murder of Nawab Akber Bugti, his political heir and grandson, Mir Brahamdag Bugti, left Balochistan and took refuge in Afghanistan for a while. In his absence and with considerable manipulation of the security agencies, the authorities in Balochistan were successful in dividing the Bugti family and the party of Nawab Bugti. Soon Jamhoori Watan Party split into various factions and became ineffective as a nationalist party. In 2008, Mir Brahamdag Bugti founded a new nationalist party-the Baloch Republican Party-(BRP) to unite followers of Nawab Bugti. The party which is being led by Mir Brahamdag Bugti from his base in Switzerland, stands for the sovereignty of the Baloch and Balochistan. BRP and its affiliated student organization, the Baloch Republican Students Organization (BRSO) have paid a high price for their stance and several of its leaders, activists and supporters were killed by the security agencies. Many of its supporters have been forced to flee and take refuge in other countries. In 2012, the party chief Mir Brahamdag Bugti suggested that the only way to resolve the crisis in Balochistan peacefully was to hold an internationally-supervised referendum under the auspices of the United Nations. Political observers believe that with the harsh measures taken by the establishment to curb the activities of those political parties, which openly affiliate themselves with Baloch armed resistance, markedly affected their functioning. BRP, like other Baloch political groups and parties currently lacks organisational strength inside Balochistan. Another factor responsible for the party not being proactive inside Balochistan, is that almost all the leadership of the party including its president Mir Brahamdag Bugti is in exile for the last ten years. However, in recent years, several party offices have been opened in different countries across the world and party workers and sympathizers are active in highlighting human rights violation in Balochistan in different international forums.

BALOCH NATIONAL MOVEMENT (BNM)

The Baloch National Movement (BNM) has been in the forefront of the national resistance since 2004, when the party emerged in its present form. As an offshoot of Balochistan National Youth Movement, there were two lines of thinking in the party from the start. One group of leaders which included Dr. Hayee Baloch, Dr. Malik Baloch, Moula Bakhsh Dashti and others were of the opinion that as the Baloch were not prepared to launch a successful struggle against Pakistan, it was better to end the confrontation with Pakistani establishment. On the other hand, Ghulam Muhammad Baloch and leader of a section of the BSO, Dr. Allah Nazar were against any collaboration with establishment. They were of the view that BNM must struggle for the restoration of Baloch national sovereignty at all costs. However, the majority of the party leadership decided to join the new party named as the National Party which was formed with the merger of BNDP with BNM. The National Party was blamed by various groups affiliated with national resistance, as having been created by the security establishment of Pakistan in order to politically counter the Baloch national struggle. As Senior Vice President of the party, Ghulam Muhammad Baloch and several others opposed the merger of BNM with BNDP, openly accused the party leadership of selling to the state and betraying the national cause. They organized their faction of BNM on new footings and started mobilizing the masses in a struggle aimed at the liberation of Balochistan.

The new manifesto of the BNM included clauses such as struggle in accordance with the United Nation's charter to regain the Baloch national freedom; struggle to reunite the Baloch territory according to historical, geographical, ethnic and cultural grounds; and struggle to develop a political alliance between the Baloch nationalist forces and those involved in the Baloch armed struggle. It was also declared by the party that it would not become part of the political, parliamentary, administrative and colonial set-ups of states occupying Balochistan. However, the most significant of the decisions which caused the blocking of party activities inside

Balochistan was the party's open pledge to work closely with forces involved in the armed resistance.

The reorganized BNM recieved the support of a section of the BSO under the leadership of Dr. Allah Nazar and soon it became the most vibrant political voice of the Baloch resistance. It is believed that during the present phase of the Baloch confrontation with Pakistan, BNM and its affiliated BSO (Azad) suffered tremendous losses. Party chairman Ghulam Muhammad Baloch was picked up and his body was dumped near Turbat by the security agencies on April 9 2009 along with another party leader Lala Munir and the BRP leader Sher Muhammad Baloch. Several other top leaders and activists of the party have been murdered by security agencies and many are still missing. It is believed that more than 300 of the BNM workers have been tortured to death by security agencies and their proxy death squads. Some of the prominent leaders of the party killed during the resistance struggle include Rasool Bakhsh Mengal, Central Joint secretary, killed on August 30, 2009; Abdul Samad Tagrani, Central Finance Secretary, killed on November 03, 2011; Haji Razak Sarbazi, Central Information Secretary, killed on August 21, 2013 and Dr. Mannan Baloch, Central Secretary General, killed on January 30, 2016. Presently led by Khalil Baloch, the party is carrying out its activities underground. Dr. Allah Nazar is believed to be the *de facto* leader of the party and the most influential person in the party regarding policy issues.

As a result of the declared association of BNM with armed resistance, the top leadership and cadre of the party were physically eliminated by security agencies and party structure has been significantly damaged. Some of the surviving activists, sympathizers and party activists managed to escape and are now living in different countries as refugees. With the heavy crackdown on the party by security agencies and the decision not to participate in the political process of the state, there appeared a huge disconnect between the party and the masses, weakening its once large popular support base. BNM activists under the leadership of party's international representative, Hammal Haider, have been active in highlighting the human rights situation in Balochistan recent years in several countries of the world in.

BALOCHISTAN NATIONAL PARTY (BNP)

Championing the cause of the Baloch right of self-determination, the Balochistan National Party, since its formation in 1996, has been in the forefront of the political mobilization in Balochistan. At the beginning of the present conflict, the BNP remained the main component of the four party Baloch Alliance formed to galvanize the masses in opposing the aggressive plans of the state against the Baloch. It has participated in every elections except the one held in 2008. In 2006, the BNP decided to quit the parliament in protest against the murder of Nawab Akber Bugti. In December 2006, Sardar Akhtar Mengal and many party leaders were arrested, while the party announced its plans for a 'Long March' against the murder of Nawab Bugti and military actions in Dera Bugti area. Sardar Akhtar Mengal was later brought into a Karachi court in an iron cage.

Although, the party has never openly endorsed armed struggle as the way forward for the Baloch national struggle; nevertheless, the BNP lost many of its prominent leaders in the present conflict. Prominent among its leaders killed either by security agencies or proxy death squads included Mir Aslam Gichki, Advocate Habib Jalib, Mir Noordin Mengal and many others. In 2015, party sources claimed that 76 party activists have been killed by security agencies since the beginning of the contemporary Baloch national resistance.

Rejecting the concept of provincial autonomy for Balochistan as envisaged in the 1973 constitution, the BNP claims that its struggle is in line with the United Nations Charter and is for the recognition of the "sovereign rights" of Balochistan and granting its people the "right to self-determination". In 2009, the party Secretary General, Habib Jalib emphasised his party's stance that granting the right of self-determination to the Baloch is the only viable option for the peaceful resolution of the Baloch national question (Dawn, 2009).

In 2012, the party Chief, Sardar Akhtar Mengal presented a 'six points agenda' for the peaceful resolution of Baloch conflict with Pakistan. His points included:

- Immediate suspension of all overt and covert military operations in Balochistan;
- production of all missing persons before a court of law;
- Disbanding of all proxy death squads operating under the supervision of the Inter-Services Intelligence (ISI) and Military Intelligence (MI);
- Allowing the Baloch political parties to function freely; and
- Rehabilitation of displaced persons as a confidence building measure.

On March 26, 2013, Sardar Akhtar Mengal, reiterated his party's demand for the right of self-determination for the people of Balochistan. "If the right of self-determination could be demanded for Kashmir, why not for Balochistan?" he said while talking to media at Karachi airport (UNPO, 2013).

With the absence of the leadership and the state crackdown on BRP and BNM activists, the BNP is the only nationalist party inside Balochistan carrying out open political activities, although, in a limited capacity. The party has taken a different line of action compared to the two other nationalist parties regarding the participation in the political process of the state. Although, it has been playing an important role in political mobilization and vigorously advocated its demand for the right of self-determination; nevertheless, it had faced severe criticism for its political stance from various nationalist groups and personalities.

BALOCH STUDENTS ORGANIZATION

The BSO has been an important and active part of the Baloch political and armed resistance struggle since its inception in 1967. It played a pivotal role in the political agitation and many of its activists participated in the armed struggle of 1970s. Mr. Khair Jan Baloch, Chairman of the organization at that period, led a group of fighters in Sarawan region of Balochistan. From 1979, the BSO underwent several changes. It divided, then united and again divided into several factions, which were the direct results of changing political stances by the Baloch leadership during that period. From being once the student wing of the NAP, it asserted its independence after the release of Baloch leadership from prison in 1978.

An attempt to unite various factions of the BSO failed in 2006 and it once again split into three factions. The BSO is currently divided into BSO (Pajjar), BSO (Mengal) and BSO (Azad). The BSO (Azad) is the offshoot of the organization originally founded by Dr. Allah Nazar in February 2002 when he broke away from his former colleagues in the BNM who were trying to merge their party with Balochistan National Democratic Party (BNDP) to form the pro-establishment National Party (NP). A section of the BNM under the leadership of Ghulam Muhammad and the BSO (Azad) under the chairmanship of Dr. Allah Nazar began openly advocating the armed struggle as the only way for liberating Balochistan.

Two factions of the BSO with significant followings among the Baloch students have been involved in the present Baloch national resistance, with varying degrees of involvement, are the BSO (Mengal) and the BSO (Azad) (an insignificant section of BSO known as the BSO (Pajjar), has been affiliated with National Party). The section of BSO known as the BSO (Mengal) affiliated with the BNP functions under the operative procedures adopted by the party. It claims to be working for the achievement of its goal for the right of self-determination for the Baloch and coordinating its campaigns with the BNP.

In the present conflict the most active politically and militantly has been BSO (Azad). In 2002, Dr Allah Nazar, then a student activist, succeeded in uniting at least two factions of the BSO into one. This united group in 2007 became known as the BSO (Azad) and openly associated itself with the Baloch armed resistance. The

BSO (Azad) has been the target of security agencies and their proxy militias and as a result lost many of its leaders. Some of its leaders including its Chairman, Mr. Zahid Kurd are still missing. It is believed that more than 700 of its members, sympathizers and affiliated persons were killed or disappeared during the conflict. Several of its activists were forced to flee and many are living as refugees in European and North American countries. Presently, the organization is being led by Ms Karima Baloch. The BSO (Azad) is also part of an alliance called Baloch National Front (BNF), which comprises different political parties and groups and is believed to be the political face of the Balochistan Liberation Front.

The Baloch nationalist parties and their affiliated student organizations have suffered from the brutal actions of the state security agencies in Balochistan. Although, the Balochistan National Party (BNP), the Baloch Republican Party (BRP), the Baloch National Movement (BNM) and the BSO consider themselves as the vanguard of the Baloch national struggle; it is becoming harder and harder for them to continue their political work in a safe and conducive atmosphere. In recent years, the issue of participation in the political process of the state has been contentious among the Baloch nationalist parties. The BNM and the BRP have openly expressed their disgust with any kind of participation in the political process of the state and their leaders believe that participation in state political processes is futile and a waste of energy while the BNP believes in the political participation at all levels. The policy of the BNP has also been criticized by a section of the nationalist leaders in exile. They argue that participation in the political process of the state would only be fruitful in a democratic country, and it needs a democratic Pakistan which should recognize the right of the Baloch people to self-determination. They find no hope of a Pakistan free from the clutches of the military directly or indirectly.

From early 2016, the pro-establishment parties and their leaders have jubilantly claimed that the political segment of the Baloch national resistance in Pakistan has been crushed or neutralized, and the Baloch nationalist political mobilization at present is limited to issuing press releases. However, in reality, parties claiming to be mobilizing people against subjugation are gaining ground. The hatred of Pakistan among the Baloch had never been as great as in today's Balochistan. Nevertheless, for many analysts of the Baloch national struggle, the survival and effectiveness of political parties associated with the Baloch cause is dependent firstly, upon the success of efforts and endeavours for uniting all nationalist political groups on a single platform and secondly, upon overcoming some significant policy differences between these parties and personal differences between their leadership.

ARMED RESISTANCE GROUPS

With the changing dynamics of nationalist politics in recent decades, the nature of the Baloch armed resistance is also changing. During 1960s and 1970s, the armed resistance activities were carried out by Mari, Mengal and Bugti tribes mainly under the umbrella of Baloch People's Liberation Front (BPLF). However, with the redundancy of BPLF during the exile years in Afghanistan, several new armed groups are claiming to be leading the Baloch armed resistance against Pakistan. A number of militant groups have actively engaged Pakistani security forces in Balochistan since the beginning of 21st century. These armed resistance groups have engaged in hit and run operations and sometime in pitched battles against army units. The majority of these groups are obscure as nothing is confirmed about their structure, leadership and political control mechanism. They usually claim responsibility for their actions against the security forces in the media through unknown persons. Nevertheless, it is widely believed that all militant groups operating against the Pakistani army are linked one way or the other with either political parties or tribal personalities affiliated with the Baloch national struggle.

Baloch Liberation Army (BLA)

After the ineffectiveness of BPLF during 1990s, armed supporters of Nawab Khair Bakhsh Mari were organized under the banner of a new organization-Balochistan Liberation Army. In the beginning, the four sons of Nawab Khair Bakhsh Mari-Mir Balaach Mari, Mir Hairbyar Mari, Mir Gazzain Mari and Mir Mehran Mari-were believed to be instrumental in the establishment of this group; however, neither Nawab Mari nor any of his sons claimed any link with BLA. The BLA was believed to be composed of experienced fighters and veterans of the 1970s armed resistance movement and started its militant activities in 2002. During the initial years of the present armed conflict, it provided logistic support and training facilities to all other armed resistance group. Although, Mir Hairbyar Mari has never confirmed any link with any militant organization; nevertheless, the Pakistani security agencies and a wider section of the people in Balochistan believe that he is leading the organization.

Mir Hairbyar Mari who is based in London for the last 10 years along with his colleague, Faiz Mari were arrested by the UK police on terrorism charges in 2008. At that time it was believed that the cases against Mir Hairbyar Mari and Faiz Mari were initiated as a result of pressure from the military government of General Pervez Musharraf. In 2009, the new government of President Zardari in Pakistan dropped allegations and Mir Hairbyar Mari and Faiz Mari were released on 11 February 2009. Mir Hairbyar and his followers among the Baloch Diaspora have been in the forefront of highlighting the human rights issues in Balochistan and the advocacy of the Baloch national question in various international forums. From 2016, Mir Hairbyar Mari's supporters are carrying out their activities under the banner of Baloch Freedom Movement.

UNITED BALOCH ARMY (UBA)

After the death of Mir Balaach Mari in 2007, differences surfaced between Mir Hairbyar Mari and his younger brother Mir Mehran Mari. These differences caused divisions in the rank and file of BLA. In 2012, the split of the BLA into two groups became inevitable and with the blessings of Nawab Khair Bakhsh Mari, a new resistance organization in the name of the United Baloch

Army (UBA) was announced. UBA is mostly composed of fighters from Mari tribe but there are also people in its ranks from other tribes in Sarawan and Bolan regions of Balochistan. A veteran of 1970s resistance and a devoted follower of Nawab Mari, Mir Abdul Nabi Bungulzai is believed to be coordinating the activities of UBA inside Balochistan. Mir Mehran Mari has frequently been accused by security agencies of Pakistan for leading the militant group but was strongly denied by him. Mir Mehran Mari who is based in London and the United Arab Emirate has been vocal in representing the Baloch case in the United Nations Human Rights meetings and conferences in Geneva.

BALOCHISTAN LIBERATION FRONT (BLF)

The Balochistan Liberation Front is a new phenomenon in the Baloch national struggle in the way that it is the only militant organization led by the middle class educated segment of the Baloch society (traditionally, the Baloch national struggle whether it was political or armed resistance, was led by tribal elite). Its volunteers are mostly educated and come from the activists of the BNM and the BSO (Azad). It is believed that BLF was formed in 2003 by young nationalist activists under the leadership of Ghulam Muhammad Baloch, Dr. Allah Nazar and Wahid Kamber. In the beginning, in its armed activities, it allied itself with the BLA and its volunteer's recieved militant training from BLA instructors. Politically, it is affiliated with BNM and its strength come mainly from the cadres of BNM and BSO (Azad). The BLF is the only resistance group in Balochistan which is overt and Dr. Allah Nazar is the declared leader of the organization. It is also believed to be the most organized of the resistance groups, engaging security forces and its affiliated militias and death squads in a wide area beginning in central Balochistan up to the coastal region. Its fighters have been engaged in many pitched battles with security forces in recent years and Dr. Allah Nazar himself was targeted by the Pakistan air force on many occasions.

BALOCH REPUBLICAN ARMY (BRA)

The Baloch Republican Army is considered to be one of the major resistance groups. BRA is mainly composed of Bugti tribesmen who were the followers of legendary Baloch leader Nawab Akber Bugti. In recent years it expanded its membership by recruiting volunteers in other parts of Balochistan especially in Kech and Gwadar districts, where its fighters operates in close coordination with BLF fighters. The group was successful in disrupting gas supplies from Sui to other parts of the country on countless occasions and is believed to be one of the most potent resistance group in the contemporary conflict. The Pakistani security agencies claim that BRA is the militant wing of BRP and Mir Brahamdag Bugti is running the militant group. This was vehemently and repeatedly denied by Mir Brahamdag Bugti and accused the intelligence agencies of finding excuses for the crackdown on the activities of Baloch Republican Party and BRSO inside Balochistan. The BRP has also denied any link with militancy and claimed to believe in a peaceful struggle for the liberation of Balochistan.

LASHKAR E BALOCHISTAN (LB)

Lashkar e Balochistan was formed in 2008 and operates mainly in the Jhalawan and Makuran regions. It is believed that it recruits fighting volunteers from the Mengal tribe and the BNP sympathizers, a charge BNP vehemently denied. The Balochistan National Party claims to have no role in the armed struggle and its declared objective is to achieve the right of self-determination for the Baloch in a peaceful struggle according to the United Nations Charter. Lashkar e Balochistan is said to be led by Mir Javed Mengal, elder brother of BNP chief Sardar Akhtar Mengal. Mir Javed Mengal lives in exile in London and the UAE. He denied any link with *Lashkar e Balochistan*. Mir Javed Mengal and his son Mir Noordin Mengal have been active in pleading the Baloch case and highlighting the human rights situation in Balochistan in different international forums. Mir Noordin Mengal has been active in UNPO and been instrumental in organizing some events in the United States on the Balochistan issue.

The Baloch fighters from different armed groups usually target government installations, gas and electricity facilities, outlying and isolated military positions, and troop convoys, informers of MI and ISI, the collaborators with the establishment and members of 'death squads'. In the beginning they established bases in inaccessible mountainous regions; however, as the use of the air force is making it very difficult for the militant groups to maintain camps and hideouts in the barren mountains of Balochistan, the majority of the fighters are now based in villages and townships. In the initial phases of the present conflict, the militant organizations used modern telecommunication technology very effectively in the planning and execution of their attacks on state security forces. The increased monitoring of communication systems by security agencies, resulted in sustained heavy losses because their whereabouts identified electronically, and were heavily bombed. At presently, most militant groups have reorganized their fighters into small mobile groups in order to make it difficult for the security agencies to locate them. The Pakistani government has accused India and Afghanistan for supporting Baloch militant organizations; however, all militant organizations have denied any foreign funding and claim that they are engaging the Pakistani army with material support of the Baloch masses.

DEATH OF NAWAB KHAIR BAKHSH MARI

Most respected of the Baloch nationalist leaders and a legendary personality of the Baloch national struggle in Pakistan, Nawab Khair Bakhsh Mari was born in Balochistan's Kohlu region in February 1928 and became the chief of his tribe in his youth. A Marxist in his political leanings, after joining the party, he emerged as a top leader of the NAP in 1960s. He became a member of Pakistan's national assembly in 1970. During his political career, he was arrested several times and spent many years in Pakistani prisons because of his staunch support for the Baloch national struggle. His last arrest occurred in 2002 by military authorities on a concocted murder charge. In 1973, he was arrested along with other NAP leaders and tried in Hyderabad Conspiracy Case. It is believed that major changes occurred in the political philosophy of Nawab Mari during his imprisonment in Hyderabad prison. He became disappointed with any participation in the political process of Pakistan and developed serious differences with his Baloch colleagues especially with Mir Gous Bakhsh Bizenjo on future strategies for the Baloch national struggle. After his release from jail in 1977, Nawab Mari flew to Europe for a brief stopover and then went into self-imposed exile in Afghanistan, along with his tribesmen. He returned to Pakistan when the Afghan revolutionary government led by Dr. Najibullah began to crumble and the occupation of Afghanistan by the Islamic Mujahedeen became eminent in 1991. Still in prison, he became the advocate of achieving independence through the bullet instead of the struggle for self-rule or provincial autonomy through the ballot box (However, after returning from exile, his sons became part of the political process by becoming ministers in a number of provincial governments during the 1990s).

Nawab Khair Bakhsh Mari remained a symbol of Baloch national resistance in Pakistan from 1960s until his death in 2014. His powerful Mari tribe spearheaded the Baloch armed resistance during 1970s in alliance with the Mengal tribe of Sardar Ataullah Mengal. He became a symbol of Baloch resistance against all odds. Age, political and personal losses, exile, and arrests in no way mellowed him. He continued to cherish the dream of liberating his nation till his last breath. Nawab Mari was arguably the father of the modern Baloch national resistance. No doubt, even after his death, he will not only inspire the Baloch youth for generations to come but also countless nationalist political workers among other national entities in Pakistan.

After his death, there occurred damaging divisions among his sons and tribal followers. A gathering of Mari tribesmen held on June 20, 2014 in Quetta 'elected' his eldest son Mir Gangeez

Mari as the new chief of the tribe. However, other brothers of Mir Gangeez Mari and elders of Mari tribe loyal to late Nawab Mari rejected his appointment as chief of their tribe. They alleged that Gangeez Mari had been appointed chief of the tribe with manipulation and at the behest of the state establishment. At a meeting of Mari tribal elders in Kahan in July 2014, it was observed that Nawab Khair Bakhsh Mari had nominated his younger son Mir Mehran Mari as his successor. In view of the will of Nawab Mari, the meeting decided to appoint Mir Mehran Mari as the new chief of the Mari tribe. Tribal elders from Mari tribe while expressing complete confidence in the leadership of Mir Mehran Mari as the new head of Mari tribe, also urged all Baloch tribes struggling for the rights of the Baloch to extend support to the newly elected chief of their tribe. Many Baloch analysts believe that failure organize his nationalist activities on a political platform was one of the weaknesses in Nawab Mari's long political career.

THE BALOCH NATIONAL QUESTION AND THE INTERNATIONAL COURT OF JUSTICE

At a grand *Jirga* of the Baloch tribal elders and political leaders held in Kalat after the martyrdom of Nawab Akber Bugti in 2006, it was decided that the Baloch case regarding the accession of the Baloch state with Pakistan in 1948 should be pleaded in the International Court of Justice in The Hague. Mir Suleman Daud, the grandson of the last ruling Khan of the Baloch, was nominated and given the task of preparing and presenting the Baloch case in the court. Mir Suleman Daud who is also the titular Khan of the Baloch has lived in the UK since 2008. Although, it had not been possible to submit the Baloch case in the court of justice in The Hague for various reasons; nonetheless, according to various legal experts on such issues, once presented, there are strong chances of a decision in favour of the Baloch regarding the illegal occupation of their land by Pakistan.

PAKISTANI RESPONSE TO BALOCH NATIONAL STRUGGLE

The Pakistani methods to counter the Baloch aspirations for national liberation have been multifaceted. It had persistently implemented a policy of divide and rule, terrorizing Baloch nationalist activists, adopted strategies for converting the Baloch into a minority and introduced religious fundamentalism into the Baloch society.

DIVIDE AND RULE

Pakistani establishment successfully created divisions not only among the cadre of the national struggle, but apparently even veteran leaders also became the victim of state manipulations. The division among the leadership began while they were in Hyderabad prison facing treason charges-the topic was dealt with detail in earlier chapters. In the context of the contemporary national resistance, many Baloch intellectuals are now openly blaming persons of dubious nature, who are surrounding the relatively young and inexperienced Baloch leaders, and are sowing seeds of mistrust, blowing out of all proportion some minor disagreements between the Baloch leadership, on the strategies and tactics of the struggle. In recent years, the secret agencies of Pakistan have proudly claimed their successes in creating divisions in nationalist parties like the BNP, JWP, BNM and other nationalist groups.

Pakistani security agencies are believed to have manufactured several "nationalist activists" and successfully planted them in various nationalist organizations and political fronts affiliated with the national resistance. Some hired writers have also been planted in the ranks of national struggle. With their help, the state, to some extent has been successful in forestalling the formation of a united front of all resistance organizations. Many of these state hired writers and intellectuals are busy portraying Brahui tribes as non-Baloch in order to seriously damage the unity of the Baloch. In recent years, the Baloch nationalist parties, groups and personalities are seen to be embattled on trivial issues and as a result efforts on bringing all nationalist forces under one platform were not successful.

Creating divisions along sectarian lines is another ploy of the state in Eastern Balochistan. The religious organizations affiliated with state security agencies are trying hard to foment sectarian strife among the Baloch by targeting *Zikris* as infidels. A significant number of the Baloch in southern Balochistan are followers of the *Zikri* sect. This sect deviates from the orthodox Islamic tenets on a number of issues. Historically, followers of the *Zikri* sect have been staunch supporters of the Baloch national resistance. For several decades, state secret services used their proxy militant Islamic organizations, to intimidate religious leaders and political activists from *this* sect. In recent years they have stepped up their activities and many of the *Zikri* religious activists have been physically eliminated. The state affiliated Islamic organizations claimed vociferously that the Baloch national struggle is un-Islamic as it has *Zikri* elements in its rank and file.

MAKING THE BALOCH PERFECT MUSLIMS

The essence of the Baloch national struggle is the assertion that the Baloch have their separate cultural, social and historical identity which is markedly different from the fundamentalist ideologies of the religious based states of Iran and Pakistan. Historically, the Baloch nationalist politics has always been based on secular and democratic principles. Socially, the Baloch identity regarding their religious beliefs is significantly different from their neighbouring nations with a clear attitude toward religious tolerance. They have an observable liberal and secular mind-set compare with the Persian, Afghan, and Pakistani fanatical religious mind-set. Religion was never politicized by the Baloch and it always remained in the personal sphere and tradition, without becoming a real socio-political imperative. However, in order to dilute the Baloch national resistance, in recent decades Pakistan adopted policies in order to introduce religion systematically as a political factor in Baloch society. The mission of extricating them from the 'darkness of ignorance' and saving their souls by making the Baloch become "perfect Muslims" is the crux of Pakistan's colonial doctrine. A web of mosques and religious schools was established throughout Balochistan from 1970s. With massive state funding, *mullahs* (priests) are becoming increasingly prominent in Baloch society, both socially and politically. Before the 1970s, a self-respecting Baloch would not have thought of becoming a professional *mullah* or priest. In contemporary Balochistan, one can observe that members of respectable Baloch families are taking up priesthood as a profession and becoming a *mullah* is no longer considered to be disrespectful or socially degrading.

It has been the declared policy of the Pakistani establishment to encourage the religious elements in order to weaken the hold of secular elements among the Baloch masses. For the last five decades, millions of dollars were invested on various religious parties and groups, and the establishment selected *mullahs* as members of the Balochistan assembly in many 'managed' general elections in order to create a political alternative for the Baloch nationalists. Various extremist religious groups were created not only to carry out subversive activities against Afghanistan or India, but also to be used in the target killing of Baloch nationalist activists. Religious terrorist outfits created and nourished by the security agencies are now becoming a real threat to the Baloch national resistance. Some of these outfits are known to be practically involved in kidnapping and dumping of bodies of the murdered nationalist activists. Another task which was given to these religious elements in Eastern Balochistan is to create division among the armed resistance groups on sectarian ground. The Baloch nationalists are convinced that success of such manoeuvres by the establishment would be a mortal blow to the Baloch national resistance in future.

INFILTRATING THE RESISTANCE

The armed resistance in Eastern Balochistan suffered some significant setbacks in recent years and it is believed that one of the reasons behind these setbacks is the joining of infiltrators into the ranks of armed resistance. Many resistance organizations blamed these infiltrators for massive casualties sustained by the Baloch during 2013-16. These were also responsible for some actions which caused much resentment from the Baloch masses, tarnishing the image of some resistance groups. One of the leaders of the Baloch national resistance while lamenting increased infiltrations by the state security agencies, believed that although, the phenomenon is disastrous for the national resistance, such happenings are inevitable when you are fighting against a state with considerable leverage.

Several targeted and precise attacks on the hideouts of Dr. Allah Nazar and Abdul Nabi Bungulzai and together with the success of security forces in locating underground leaders of the BNM and the BSO (Azad) are examples of deep penetration by the state agencies in resistance groups and parties.

TERRORIZE TO SUBDUE

The state security establishment of Pakistan, as a policy matter committed massacres and extra-judicial killings in Balochistan. Thousands of the Baloch have disappeared, thousands are being held illegally and the dead bodies of the Baloch social and political activists have been dumped by the security forces with visible marks of inhuman torture. Destruction and burning of the Baloch settlements and displacement of thousands are acts of terror perpetrated by the Pakistani state.

Military and civil intelligence agencies in Eastern Balochistan with the help of their auxiliary militias, death squads and religious outfits are involved in forced disappearances and illegal detentions of Baloch intellectuals, tribal elite, social personalities and political activists since 2002 (Rashid, 2014). According to reports of various human rights organizations and seconded by government functionaries on various occasions, thousands of people from Balochistan are still missing. They were picked up by security agencies and not seen again. In 2005, the then Interior Minister of

Pakistan Aftab Sherpao stated that an estimated 4000 people from Balochistan are in the custody of law enforcement authorities. Out of these only 200 were taken to court in 2009 and the rest were held incommunicado (Dwivedi, 2009). As Eastern Balochistan has been declared a no-go area for the international media and human rights organizations, nothing of these atrocities were reported in the international media. As observed by Rashid (2014), estimates of the number of disappeared in Balochistan were between hundreds and several thousand. The Baloch sources claimed more than 30 thousand missing since 2002. Dumping of disappeared person's mutilated bodies has been the daily occurrence in Balochistan for years. According to a Baloch human right organization working for the recovery of missing persons "Voice for Baloch Missing Persons" only in 2014 alone, 455 mutilated bodies have been found dumped in various places. In 2015, 463 people were reportedly picked up by security agencies and they are still missing. During the same year, 157 mutilated bodies were also found in desolate places. Worse still was the discovery of a mass grave site in Khuzdar district where the bodies of more than a hundred Baloch nationalists were found in 2013. According to the Human Rights Watch, which concurs on this point with the Human Rights Commission of Pakistan, there seems to be little doubt about the fact that most of these disappearances and dumping of bodies was perpetrated by Pakistan's intelligence agencies and the para-military Frontier Corps. They often act in conjunction with the local police. In most of the documented cases, the perpetrators acted openly in broad daylight, sometimes in busy public areas, with apparently little concern for the presence of numerous witnesses. In the process, it is estimated that thousands of people have disappeared or been arbitrarily detained (UNHCR, 2010).

As the religious state of Pakistan has only been relying on military repression in dealing with the Baloch national question, the increased deployment of security forces in Eastern Balochistan has always been a prime requirement. Since 2000, several new cantonments were established in various parts of Balochistan, making the number of cantonment to six, practically converting Balochistan into a war zone. Military roads and other infrastructure necessary for troop movements were developed on emergency footings.

PUNISHING THE WHOLE COMMUNITY

The draconian policy of collective punishment adopted by the Pakistani security agencies are being carried out with impunity in a 21st century world. With any resistance activity against the security forces, the nearby villages would be raided and mass punishment given to the civilian population. Frequent raids on villages, burning of houses and forcing the inhabitants to vacate their dwellings are examples of the collective and arbitrary measures in the protracted conflict. Pakistan is following the old colonial way of dealing with the dissent in Balochistan. Whole communities were regularly targeted by the security agencies after an attack on a security or government installation by the Baloch resistance fighters. In several districts of Eastern Balochistan, the Pakistani authorities, forced thousands of people to leave their homes. Worst affected are Kohlu, Dera Bugti, Awaran, and Kech districts where several settlements and villages are now ghost areas. According to Baloch nationalist sources, one of the objectives of this policy is to clear the area of the Baloch population from where the proposed 'China-Pakistan Economic Corridor' is established. The aim of such barbaric actions appear to be intimidating the Baloch population into docile submission. It is also seeking to break the morale of the masses who are whole heartedly behind the Baloch national resistance. This policy of collective punishment is in line with the thinking of the security establishment of Pakistan that collective suffering is bound to isolate and neutralize the militant elements in the community. Once isolated, it would be easy for security forces to deal with them. The measure being taken in the execution of their policy of collective punishment is aimed at destroying the sinews that link the Baloch masses with the national resistance, and national institutions affiliated with the national liberation struggle and its leadership.

TARGETING THE CREAM OF BALOCH SOCIETY

During the last 14 years, many of the Baloch political activists, intellectuals, doctors, engineers, artists, journalists and tribal elders have been taken away by the Pakistani intelligence agencies and the military. The International Crisis Group, Amnesty International, the International Committee of Red Cross, the Asian Human Rights Commission, the United Nation High Commission for Refugees, Human Rights Commission of Pakistan and various Baloch human rights groups in their various reports have graphically detailed numerous high profile cases where prominent personalities have been targeted. Pakistan is employing a state policy of inflicting terror on the leadership of the Baloch resistance. Arrest and humiliation of Nawab Khair Bakhsh Mari, the arrest of Sardar Akhtar Mengal and putting him into a cage, bombardment of the house of Bugti chief, the brutal assassination of 80 year old Nawab Akber Bugti, the murders of Mir Balaach Mari, Ghulam Muhammad Baloch, Dr. Din Muhammad, Habib Jalib, Dr. Mannan Baloch, Professor Saba Dashtyari, several Baloch writers, doctors, engineers, and artists, and assassination attempt on the life of the prominent Baloch scholar and writer Mir Jan Muhammad Dashti are just few examples of how the establishment has planned to harass, terrorize, and intimidate prominent personalities affiliated with the Baloch national resistance. In a horrible act of state terrorism, more than a hundred lawyers were killed and many were wounded in a suicide attack in Quetta in the month of July 2016. Many Baloch and Pashtun political figures openly blamed the Inter-Services Intelligence agency (ISI) of Pakistan as perpetrator of the act through one of its proxy religious organizations.

Many actions of Pakistani security forces and its auxiliary organizations clearly come into the category of war crimes according to the United Nation General Assembly resolutions. General Assembly Resolution 3103 (XXVIII) adopted on December 12, 1973, states that the armed conflicts involving the struggle of peoples against colonial and alien domination and racist regimes are to be regarded as international armed conflicts in the sense of the 1949 Geneva Conventions and the legal status envisaged to apply to the combatants in the 1949 Geneva Conventions and other international instruments should apply to the persons engaged in armed struggle against colonial and alien domination and racist regimes.

ASSIMILATING STRATEGIES

As part of the state policy of assimilating various national entities into the Pakistani state national identity, the education system was used. A school curriculum was introduced, which blatantly fabricated historical facts and human social values and rigidly followed the classical colonial approach which bore no relationship to historical and regional realities. The history and culture of the Baloch and other constituent nationalities were totally ignored. Since the objective was to create a non-existent Pakistani national consciousness out of nothing, the curriculum emphasized the negation of other languages and cultures, with Urdu imposed as the national language and portrayed as a divine language after Arabic. Notorious plunderers and savage rulers of the Middle East and Central Asia during the middle ages were portrayed as national heroes. Assimilation strategies adopted by the state include emphasis on the fallacious concept of Islamic nationhood which is the negation of all national identities. The imposition of Urdu as the national language and medium of instruction is also in line with strategies to dominate the languages of the Baloch and other nationalities. This policy has paved the way for the extinction of the thousand year old Balochi language. Imposition of north Indian social values over cherished Baloch socio-cultural traditions is one of the ugliest among the assimilation strategies.

THE SITUATION OF STALEMATE

The Pakistani authorities convey the impression to the international community that the situation in Balochistan is under control and that the armed resistance of the Baloch has been contained or crushed. However, for many observers, it is just to encourage the prospective investors in the country and allay the security fears of Chinese, in order to encourage them to begin their planned activities on the 'China Pakistan Economic Corridor'. The reality is that neither the armed resistance has been crushed nor the Baloch armed resistance been able to inflict a major blow on the Pakistani military in Balochistan. The present situation can be described as an impasse or a situation of stalemate.

After the murder of Nawab Akber Bugti, Balochistan came under the grip of a general uprising against Pakistan. Government installations and army positions were attacked by relatively inexperienced fighters without a firm command and control system. The initial years were very difficult period for the armed resistance. The Pakistani army had a vast experience of dealing with the Baloch armed uprisings, and reacted with the most extreme violence against the resistance groups and political organizations affiliated to the resistance. Lack of proper weapons, training and political control led to terrible losses and many avoidable deaths of some of the brilliant young activists among the Baloch. Lack of political training of armed fighters caused some unfortunate events involving resistance groups, which led to some distrust among the masses and credibility of the resistance movement was questioned. However, it appears that the Baloch resistance is now reconsidering their entire approach regarding political mobilization and armed activities and trying to evolve new strategies for the struggle. Grare (2013), observed that the Pakistani military has so far proven unable to eliminate militant organizations and the larger nationalist movement. This was despite conducting targeted assassination campaigns and kidnappings and making a variety of attempts to discredit the nationalist movement by associating it with organized crime or terrorist groups. Nearly all resistance groups are now seeing the Baloch conflict with Pakistan as a prolonged struggle and are devising methodology for a protracted struggle, involving both political mobilization and armed resistance.

After the end of the military regime of General Pervez Musharraf, the new civilian government of President Zardari attempted to resolve the crisis by announcing some reconciliatory measures. In early November 2009, the government promised to confer about more autonomy for the province and presented to parliament a 39-point plan for a more autonomous Balochistan, the so-called "Balochistan Package." Included in the plan were proposals such as the return of political exiles, freeing of jailed Baloch political activists, the withdrawal of the army from some key areas, a reform of the federal resources allocation mechanism, efforts to create jobs for the Baloch youth, and greater provincial control of Balochistan's resources by the provincial assembly. Although, the parliament adopted a resolution in this regard; nevertheless, it was rejected both by the powerful military establishment and the Baloch nationalists. The military was not ready to concede anything substantial to the Baloch and the Baloch nationalist parties expressed their concerns, fearing that the government's proposals were no more than a smokescreen behind which it would continue the systematic physical elimination of the Baloch activists and leaders. They insisted on the acceptance of their demand of the right of self-determination for the Baloch and negotiations under the auspices of UNO or the European Union. The Balochistan Package was never implemented. The military establishment also rejected a six point confidence building agenda presented by BNP chief Sardar Akhtar Mengal in 2013 in order to pave the way for a peaceful resolution of the issue. The military establishment is continuing with the implementation of its own 'fight to finish' policy and the army and the Baloch resistance became locked in a bloody, protracted and devastating confrontation with no side appearing as winner at present.

After a pause of 20 years during which the Baloch national resistance kept a low profile and the leadership showed conciliatory gestures towards the state establishment, the Baloch and Pakistan again engaged in a bloody conflict from the start of 21st century. While the Baloch believe that the resistance is to preserve the national identity and to regain their sovereign status, the Pakistani state is following a policy of fight in order to finish the issue once and for all. The Baloch are facing brutalities of immense proportions and the protracted conflict caused the murder of thousands and dislocation of millions of the Baloch. The state security agencies are targeting the cream of Baloch society and many prominent personalities, political activists, intellectuals, journalists, doctors, engineers and artists have been physically eliminated by security forces or their proxy death squads and auxiliary para-military units. The tale of blood and tears in Eastern Balochistan is continuing and Pakistan justifies its ruthless and brutal actions against the Baloch, as part of its efforts to maintain the writ of the state in Balochistan. For many of the Baloch analysts, the armed aggression by Pakistan is to settle the Baloch national question by force in order to perpetuate its occupation of Balochistan and exploitation of its natural resources for the benefit of ruling Punjabi nationality. The hallmark of ongoing conflict in Eastern Balochistan has been the excessive violations of human rights by the state security apparatus of Pakistan. With increased mobilization of the army, Balochistan has been transformed into a war zone.

CHAPTER 15

IRANIAN AND PAKISTANI STATE NATIONALISM AND BALOCH NATIONAL ASPIRATIONS

The religious states of Iran and Pakistan have their own historical contexts, but one thing is common to both, which is their artificial national identity. Iranian nationalism is based on a combination of ancient Persian glory and its faithfulness to the Shia sect of Islam which demands undiluted loyalty to the family members of the Prophet Muhammad and accepting them as leaders and rulers of Muslims for all time. Pakistan is a peculiar case in the political history of the world. This was the first state created on the basis of religious faith. From the very beginning, it has struggled to manufacture a nation out of nothing. With the occupation of their land by these neighbouring states, the Baloch national aspirations have faced the onslaught of the two artificially created state nationalisms of Iran and Pakistan.

THE FACE OF IRANIAN NATIONALISM

The pride of belonging to an ancient noble and imperial Persian nation with a blend of Shia Islamic identity is the essence of Iranian nationalism. Basking in the glory of once controlling most of the Middle East and Central Asia; the perception of having given the world artistic, scientific, and architectural treasures centuries before the Western domination, and having the blessings of Almighty Allah for the last 14 centuries, Iranian nationalism certainly held a racial overtone.

Iran has been a multi-national state; however, narrow Persian nationalism has always remained the base of the state power; creating a national perception of excluding non-Farsis from the corridors of state power. Zonis (1971), pointed out that Iranian nationalism is exclusive, and to a large extent xenophobic; it saw their national identity as unique, with no identifiable "cousin" nationality. He identified various reasons that Iranians tend to ascribe to their national uniqueness: the continuity of Iranian history; the greatness of the ancient rulers; and the uniqueness of being the only Shiite country in the world. Over a period of time, this false perception of Persian nationalism and national imagination took the selective approach for constructing an Iranian national consciousness which, because of its subjectivity, led to extreme self-recognition or Persian chauvinism. Although as a rhetoric, they identify themselves with Muslims in general, the scope of Iranian national identity remains that of the Persian-speaking Shiites within the borders of Iran. Kia (1998), observed that in the process, they ignored the multi-ethnic, multi-linguistic, multi-cultural, and multi-religious reality of the Iranian state. They overlooked the fundamental fact that ancient Iran was not Persia but rather it was a mosaic of diverse ethnic, linguistic and religious groups: each group possessing its own history, culture, language, religious values and traditions.

Discrimination towards non-Farsi national minorities in Iran is inherent in every aspect of Iranian national behaviour. This discriminatory behaviour manifested itself by adopting as the national policy, the complete assimilation of the non-Farsi minority national entities by subsequent Iranian dynasties and regimes. During the Pahlavi Dynasty, the identification of the Iranian state with Persian nationalism was fully expressed. Helfgott (1980), observed that Reza Shah Pahlavi tried to merge state, monarchy and Persian nationalism into an ideological unity. This explicitly rejected cultural pluralism as treason. The Persian language was imposed on the minority nationalities and in the same way, the economic policies were centered on Persian dominated regions. The policy of exclusivity adopted by Safavids, Qajar and Pahlavi dynasties, did not change during the reign of the Ayatollahs. Although, on the face of it, the Ayatollahs proclaimed that Islam should be perceived as the only source of legitimacy for the Iranian state, nevertheless, they could not minimize the expressions of Persian nationalism with its ethnic manifestation in the running of state affairs.

The present Iranian State is the continuation of the Persian Empire with the addition of a fanatical Shia Islamic ideology. Persian nationalism has always been focused on the perception of a glorious past and the hatred of 'others'. These others include neighbours and other constituent national entities in the Iranian state. The regime of Ayatollahs since 1979 has adopted a policy of historical continuity of Iranian national identity; the alliance between Shia Islam and Persian nationalism. There is no dichotomy in the expression of a Persian national identity. The emphasis on the Islamic Shia identity of Iran is a mere façade in order to isolate further other nationalities having different sectarian beliefs. In reality, the regime of the Ayatollahs with its emphasis on the religious identity of Iran, gave a new impetus to Persian nationalism and the inherent desire of the Persians to declare themselves' superior to others. Adopting the doctrine of *Vilayat e Faqih* (the governance of religious jurists) in itself is the manifestation of a hegemonic behaviour towards other nationalities. Declaring a Persian Shia *Mullah* as the "supreme" leader is in a way showing the divine approval of Allah of the superiority of Persian clergy over 'other *mullahs*'.

The Iranian state ideology seeks not only the complete elimination of other mythological and religious beliefs but also the elimination of any national or ethnic identity in the state. The state has constantly been downplaying factors which are distinctive of other national entities in Iran. In Iran, the term national denotes Persian-ness, which is a concept that excludes other national entities. The strategy of demarcation between Farsis (the pure Persians, speaking Farsi language) and non-Farsis has been an important element of Persian power elite which has created clear divisions and hatred between Farsis and other national entities of Iran. Helfgott (1980), emphasised that the Iranian state whether in the hands of a Persian or a non-Persian family, took on an increasingly Persianized character which tended to re-inforce the existing distinctions between Persian and non-Persian. By default, two different and diametrically opposed conceptions of political authority-the divine and popular-in the constitution of Islamic republic of Iran have become the cause of contest by various political and nationalist forces within Iran, which do not allow the expression of difference, whether it is national, ethnic or socio-economic. For the consolidation of power under such an artificial ideology of mixing the Persian glorious past and the divine approval of Shia supremacy, the use of force became imperative. Every regime used security services to ensure this purpose and there began the proliferation of various secret agencies within the military-security establishment to accomplish this end. In the process, Iran became a fascist style totalitarian state.

The historically baseless, and academically illogical perception and practice of Persian nationalism has led to the intensification of ethnic and religious sentiments and a hostile socio-political environment with resulting societal turbulence and insecurity where national minorities are involved in political and violent conflicts with the state. In contemporary Iran, two different types of ethno-nation mobilization can be observed in contemporary Iran. One is the mobilization of suppressed nations which have been marginalized and excluded from the power structures of the state on the basis of ethnic identity and the other is the mobilization on religious and sectarian grounds. The Baloch national struggle in 21st century Iran is composed of both the above mentioned ingredients (ethnic and sectarian).

PAKISTAN: THE ALLAH GIVEN COUNTRY

When with the grace of Almighty Allah, the British decided to create a country out of India in 1947, it came as a shock to the political analysts of the day. Whatever were the actual objectives of dividing India and creating Pakistan, on the face of it, the decision was justified by the colonial power on the grounds that as Hindus and Muslims practice two different mythological beliefs, they cannot live peacefully in one country and that religious faith alone is enough to define a particular people as a nation. It was the first and novel example in the political history of the World, that a state was created in the name of a particular religious faith.

The creation of Pakistan needed the 'two nation theory' (Two nation theory is based on the assumption that Hindus and Muslims in India are two nations) and the feasibility of dividing India on the basis of this theory. Work on the two nation theory commenced after the abortive attempt to overthrow the rule of East India Company in 1857. On instructions of the colonial administration, the history of India was made and written in such a way that the adventurers, plunderers and rulers of India who came from the Middle East and Central Asia were categorized as Muslim rulers. The history of India was modelled not on the national background of invaders but on their religious faith. A web of Islamic activists was created to propagate the Islamic nation theory (according to Islamic nation theory, the followers of Islamic faith constitute a nation) and Jamaluddin Afghani and Syed Ahmad Khan were put in charge of a project for the creation of a network of Islamic schools and political organizations. A pilot project to study the future division of India was implemented by dividing the province of Bengal in 1906, on administrative pretexts. The designs of a great imperial power became fulfilled in the final division of India and the creation of Pakistan in 1947. This brought untold misery and perpetual conflicts between various communities and national entities in the region for generations.

After the creation of Pakistan, in order to sustain the grip on different national entities, and to strengthen the hold of the ruling alliance over the state apparatus, strict imposition of "Islamic Ideology" became imperative. The alliance which was handed over the power by the British colonial administrators was composed of Punjabi landlord politicians, civil bureaucrats, army personnel belonging to the western part of a divided Punjab, religious elements and the refugees (*Muhajir*) from the north Indian provinces of Bihar, and the United Province. The only commonality between various components of the alliance was their unwavering allegiance with the colonial power and the bid to rule the 'Allah given and British created' country by hook and crook. Jalal (1994), noted that crucially, the *Muhajir/* Punjabi-dominated civil and military bureaucracy acquired almost unchallenged control over the levers of state power. Janmahmad (1989), observed that it was puzzling for social scientists of the time that an imported bureaucracy, imported military establishment, a cohort of imported politicians armed with an imported ideology of north Indian origin invented by a colonial power, and some thousand refugees became able to control a multi-national state to the extent that an alien language (Urdu) was also made the national language of an independent state. The cultural traditions of a refugee group were adopted as the national culture of a state where the population of Bengal, Sindh, Pashtunistan and Balochistan had languages and cultural traditions going back many thousands of years. Neglecting their languages and the imposition of an alien language was a part of the policy of destroying the national identity of minority nationalities and in line with efforts to manufacture an artificial national identity for Pakistan. In 1948, the first Governor General of Pakistan, Mr. Muhammad Ali Jinnah, declared that any one opposing the decision of declaring Urdu as the national language would be treated as the enemy of the state. Janmahmad (1989), observed that:

> *"Pakistan undoubtedly is a unique society. The philosophy behind adopting Urdu, Arabic, Persian or any other alien tongue as the national language or the medium of education and communication, cannot be comprehended by an ordinary*

> *intellect except those whose thinking has embraced a host of obnoxious ideas since the formation of this state (Janmahmad, 1989, p. 247)."*

Having superfluous and artificial ideological foundations and a ruling elite with no roots in the country, Pakistan became a laboratory for all kinds of hypocrisy, and social, economic and cultural corruption. With the passing of time, truthfulness, dignity, honour and sincerity became an anathema in Pakistani socio-political practices.

From the very beginning of the creation of Pakistan, confrontations arose between various national entities and the ruling alliance led by Punjab. Because of increasing tensions between component national entities, the state establishment had to adhere even more to its religious narrative and became dependent on the use of militant power to counter any attempt by other nationalities to either secede or destabilize the state. It became imperative for the ruling alliance in Pakistan to deny consistently the existence of different nations and national identities and Islam became the only binding force in the multi-national state. Janmahmad (1989), observed that:

> *"The Pakistani leaders emphasized the inviolability of 'two nation theory' in the preservation of the country's integrity and promptly dubbed 'un-Islamic' any advocacy of a socio-political system based on equality and justice; and branded those favouring progressive reforms as traitors disloyal to the cause of Pakistan and Islam (page, 76)."*

Faced with consequences of an artificial ideology and keeping control on the different nationalities amalgamated into the religious state against their free will, the Pakistani establishment created a ramified military organization with its affiliated political, and religious outfits to combat the national aspirations of the subjugated national entities (Cohen, 1984; Rizvi, 2000; Cohen, 2004). For the survival of the state it became imperative to concentrate all powers in the centre, thus denying due access into the power structure by minority nationalities. After the independence of Bangladesh in 1971, with a constant media propaganda, the Sindhis have been portrayed as inherently weak and docile, and the Baloch as ignorant and savages, not fully in line with strict Islamic tenets. This was in order to counter the voices raised from a section of Punjabi ruling nationality for the inclusion of these nations into the power structure of the state. Over a period of time, Pakistan became a security state and the military became the *de facto* ruler of the state, whether this was an overt takeover of the government or behind the scenes governance using puppet politicians as a facade.

Pakistani Islamic nationalism is a mix of Arab-Persian and Turko-Mongol socio-cultural traditions. In a bid to dissociate themselves from the Indian socio-religious and historical roots, in Pakistani historical narratives, the history of the sub-continent practically begins with the invasion of Bedouin Arabs on Sindh during 7th century. All adventurers, plunderers and invaders who came from the Middle East or Central Asia have been given the status of national heroes of Pakistan. The most notorious characters like Muhammad bin Qasim, Mahmud Ghaznavi, Ghuris, Suris, Mongols, Timurids and Abdali invaders of India are official national heroes of Pakistan. It is interesting to note that most of these invaders were responsible for the massacre and genocide of the Baloch, Sindhis and Punjabi people when they advanced on India for pillage. School textbooks not only teach a fictitious version of history, but Islam is also being portrayed in a way which supports the oppression of the minority nationalities in the name of Allah and Islamic solidarity. The education system is aimed at creating a population of fanatic adherent to a falsified religious doctrine based on hatred towards the followers of other faiths. The political history of the world in general and the region in particular has been distorted beyond recognition. Students graduating from state education institutions are armed with the non-existent past glories of a non-existent Islamic nation and with a firm belief of a guaranteed place in paradise for those who fought in the 'way of Allah'.

THE BALOCH NATIONAL ASPIRATIONS

A strong urge for independence has been the spirit of the Baloch nationalism from the very beginning of their entry into the history of Iranian plateau more than two thousand years ago. The contemporary Baloch national liberation struggle is the rejection of the negation of their historical process by the Persian and Pakistani states. It is for regaining their national pride, and overthrowing the Persian and Pakistani yokes. The Baloch national consciousness is the product of the perpetual conflicts of the Baloch with the dominating powers in the region. Their nationalism is the affirmation of the unity of the Baloch against the aggressions of the powerful. Although, during the 19th century, the Baloch land was divided; nevertheless, one of the characteristics of Baloch nationalism is that it never placed any significance on the divided frontiers of Balochistan. The Baloch speak of Balochistan as a single unit, despite it being divided into Iran, Pakistan or Afghanistan for the last two hundred years.

Having a proud sense of belonging to the Baloch national identity, the Baloch national struggle had been in direct confrontation with Persian national identity. A fierce and bloody struggle against the domination of Qajar Persia in Western Balochistan began the modern Baloch national resistance in Iran. This resistance gained momentum during the Pahlavi regime and is continuing against the Iran of the Ayatollahs. The Baloch have resisted the assimilation efforts of the Persians over a long period. Another factor of significant importance in the conflict between the Baloch and the Persian state is the religious or sectarian factor. The Persians are the followers of Shia sect, while the Baloch belong to Sunni sect of Islam, both sects are in constant confrontation with each other. Although, the secular mind-set of the Baloch has kept the religion peripheral to their social life, which was much related to their customs and cultural traditions; nevertheless, on many occasions it has been exploited politically in the long and tortuous history of relationship between the Baloch and Persians.

In Iran, as a matter of state policy, any debate on Baloch nationalism has been declared un-Islamic and treasonable. In official narratives, the Baloch are not recognized as a nation but as a tribal community of the greater Persian national entity. The Balochi language has not been recognized as the national language of the Baloch but as a dialect of the Farsi language. This is in line with the process of nation building which requires to construct a narrative of common language, shared origin and collective historical memory among Iranians. In order to justify the inhuman brutalities perpetrated by the Iranian state on minority nationalities, organized attempts are being made to convince the Iranian public that the Baloch and other national entities in Iran pose serious threats to the national security of the state. Perceiving the Baloch national resistance as a mortal danger to their fragile state, the eradication of the characteristics of a Baloch national identity became the prime objective of the Persian state. The state measures in this regard include:

- The banning education in Balochi,
- The banning of writing and publishing in Balochi,
- The banning of Balochi names for Baloch babies,
- Persianizing the names of Baloch townships,
- Officially belittling the Baloch cultural and social traditions,
- Creating official tribes in Balochistan.

In 1948, Pakistan occupied the Baloch state of Kalat which was the symbol of the Baloch national identity and sovereignty. In the beginning, it was hard for the Baloch leadership of the time to comprehend the real repercussions of the Pakistan phenomenon. As it came out of blue, it was hard for them to digest the fact that their 300 year old state had suddenly become part of a newly created religious state. It was hard for them to recognise Mr. Muhammad Ali Jinnah, as the 'Great Leader' (In Pakistan, Mr. Jinnah is being termed as *Quad e Azam*-the great leader). This man was the very lawyer, whom their Khan hired to plead the case of the leased areas of Balochistan with the withdrawing colonial administration. They believed he had betrayed them by not only mispleading their case with the British authorities but also invaded and occupied their state after being installed as the first Governor General of Pakistan.

Even after the collapse of the many resistance movements against Pakistan, the Baloch in their hearts, have never accepted the occupation and subjugation. However, during initial years of Pakistan, the Baloch leadership, which was mainly comprised of the banned KSNP leaders, some of the tribal elite and the family of the Khan of the Baloch, having no option, in a way, accepted as fait accompli the inevitability of becoming part of the new religious state. They focused their political struggle on demanding greater autonomy within a federated Pakistan. They joined the progressive and nationalist leaders from Sindh, Pashtunistan and Bengal in united fronts and single parties to ally their struggle with that of other nationalities. Although, they became part of the political process but were strongly opposed to any role of religion in the state affairs and wanted an appropriate state structure run on the basis of secularism, federalism and democratic principles. It is not because the Baloch are irreligious but as a national characteristic developed during their historical journey into present day Balochistan, they always kept their religious faith as a private not a state matter. The state establishment based its policies on religion and became intolerant to a degree that any talk of decency, secularism or autonomy for the constituent nationalities in Pakistan, which became equivalent to anti-Islam and anti-state activity and thus treasonous. This intolerant and violent attitude of the state provided the ground for the Baloch national resistance to become aggressive in reaction. With deep suspicion towards the newly created religious state and the subjugating measures taken immediately after occupying Balochistan, this soon resulted in open confrontation between the Baloch and Pakistan.

In Pakistan any objection, criticism or discussion on state ideology is not only anti-state or treasonous but also anti-Islamic. The use of state violence became necessary in Pakistan because the ruling alliance dominated by Punjab had nothing in common with the Baloch or other national entities in Pakistan except that of their religious beliefs. The futile efforts of the establishment to create a national consciousness for the state was based on self-imposed ignorance. The establishment failed to comprehend that the integration of various nationalities into the system of a newly created state required conceding to every national entity the right of national existence in an overall political arrangement within the state. However, recognition of the rights of constituent nationalities meant conceding a lot by the ruling alliance of Pakistan and for that reason, it has never given a thought on the subject. As observed by the veteran Baloch leader, Sardar Ataullah Mengal, it is now too late and a rather impossible task to correct the wrongs and to bring Pakistan's political and ideological footing into harmony with the socio-political realities of the world. Even in 21st century Pakistan, the ruling military establishment is persistent in its refusal to recognize the multi-national character of the state. For the ruling alliance, the integrity and solidarity of the country is based in its Islamic character and the perception of an overwhelming threat from infidel powers like India and the West.

Pakistani establishment has been very derisive of Balochi socio-cultural traditions from the very beginning. There began a planned strategy to falsify the history of the region in order to belittle the Baloch as a nationality. Sponsored writers portrayed the Baloch as barbaric and savage. In the text books, the Baloch were described as brigands and miscreants. With the occupation of Balochistan, came a set of alien laws and edicts which the Baloch considered repugnant to the spirit of Baloch traditions. It not only showed disrespect to Baloch social norms, but the state establishment invariably adopted a discourteous manners towards much loved Baloch leaders. Almost all of the significant personalities of the Baloch national struggle were tortured and subjected to inhuman conditions, while they were in detention. The second tier political activists suffered brutal treatment throughout and the attitude of the security agencies towards them had been of deep contempt and intolerance.

Concerted efforts were made to distort and mutilate the history of the region in the text books and publications in order to conceal the Baloch political and social existence in the region now comprising Pakistan. The language of the Indian immigrants was imposed as the national language of the Baloch and the medium of instruction in schools, colleges and universities. A media onslaught on the Baloch socio-cultural traditions has been the persistent policy of the state. The military personnel at their various check points in Balochistan had been tasked to insult any Baloch with long hair and wearing wide baggie trousers, perceiving them as showing the Baloch nationalistic outlook. The imposition of alien cultural and social traditions at the expense of the Baloch social values; the economic exploitation and violent curbing of any activity from the Baloch political and tribal elite for social, political, and economic rights resulted in a protracted national resistance against Pakistan. The Baloch national struggle in Pakistan has the expression of the Baloch will to overthrow the yoke of subjugation and exploitation by an artificial and fundamentalist religious state which had no historical, legal or moral justification for ruling the Baloch or occupying their land.

The economic exploitation is another enforcing element of contemporary Baloch national consciousness. The Baloch are among the poorest people of the world but their land is one of the richest. The gas fields in Balochistan have been pumping trillions of metric tonnes of natural gas into Pakistan in order to fulfil the commercial and domestic needs of the country. There remain unimaginable natural resources beneath the Baloch soil. Soon after occupation, Pakistan initiated a process of ruthless exploitation of natural and mineral resources in Balochistan. With Balochistan giving Pakistan billions of dollars in natural resources no development work was initiated in Balochistan. The perception gained firm ground among the Baloch that it is only the natural resources of their land, which Pakistan needed, not the people as there was no attempt to utilize the natural wealth of Balochistan to the benefit of Baloch people. Western Balochistan is rich in natural resources which include metal and mineral deposits such as chromite, copper, manganese, lead, zinc, tin, tungsten, as well as deposits of non-metallic elements. It is estimated that there are more than ten million tonnes of gold reserves in the Mir Javeh region only. The volume of gas reserves reportedly discovered in the coastal regions of Balochistan is equal to Iran's total gas and oil resources. Despite being rich in resources, Western Balochistan continues to occupy the lowest position in the development rankings in Iran. More than 70% of the population living in the province of Sistan wa Balochistan are living below the poverty line. This is indicative of the discriminatory economic policies of the state. The economic progress of Western Balochistan is held back for obvious security, political or even religious justification. The Islamic Republic News Agency (IRNA), states that the real rate of unemployment in this province is between 35-40%; however, according to Baloch sources, the unemployment rate among the Baloch is more than 50%. The literacy rate in Western Balochistan is the lowest in the country. In 2015, around 200,000 children and young people in the province were deprived of access to education. Those who manage somehow to graduate, face serious discrimination in securing employment.

Nationalism is the assertion of the uniqueness of a nation. The essence of Baloch nationalism is the strong urge for living a life in accordance with their own cultural values and social traditions; an overwhelming love for their land; and rejection of foreign domination. The Baloch national aspirations involve honouring their human rights, national identity and sovereignty. The objectives of their national struggle are for the control of their affairs- economic, political, social, and cultural. Throughout history, the Baloch national desires manifested themselves in violent confrontation with those powers who tried to dominate or subjugate them. The contemporary Baloch national struggle is the continuation of their resistance against the mighty Sassanid Empire and continued with Arab invaders, the Central Asian plunderers, Qajar and Pahlavi dynasties of Iran, and religious fundamentalist state of Pakistan. The phenomenon of modern Baloch nationalism began with the occupation of their state by the British in 1839.

Although, the resistance against the British was not successful; nevertheless, it sharpened the sense of subjugation among the Baloch and their desire to achieve the cherished goal of regaining their sovereign status once again. During 19th century, the division of their land provided another impetus for the development of the Baloch national consciousness to resist those who were responsible for the occupation and division of their country. The Baloch claim that the occupation of their land by Iran and Pakistan is illegal, they claim that they are not a willing part of these states, thus Iran and Pakistan are occupying powers. Events which occurred in Asia, Africa and Latin America during 20th century were of great importance in the evolution of the Baloch national liberation struggle. The revolutionary fervour of that period sparked the imaginations of the Baloch nationalist leadership and political activists. The fallacies and acts of repression and assimilation by Iran and Pakistan were other factors which gave impetus to the Baloch endeavours for national liberation. It can be observe that the main objectives of the Baloch national struggle throughout have concerned the central issues of culture and territorial sovereignty and reunification of their land.

Iran and Pakistan claim their legitimacy as states from Allah and are thus not answerable to anyone or bound to obey recognised international laws or norms of the civilized world with regard to the running of their state affairs. The Iranian state nationalism composed of two elements of Persian nationalism which is the perception of Persian superiority and Shiite fundamentalism, which seeks the complete elimination of other religious beliefs. It is exclusive, ignores the existence of several nationalities within Iran and is determined to the assimilation of other constituent national entities. The Pakistani state national identity is based on the superfluous ideology of Muslims being one nation and that the followers of a particular religious faith can form a nation. Its rulers, bureaucracy, political leadership, and national language together with cultural and social traditions were imported. For both countries, Islam became a shield cloaking their illegitimacy to rule over other national entities. Their nationalism is without a

253

nation. To develop their illusionary state nationalisms into realities, they resorted to repression on a large scale and in the process, both states became security states. It is not only the Baloch who are facing the state brutalities but also Sindhis, Pashtuns, Kurds, Azeris, Ahwazis, and Turcomens who are suffering. Iran is the face of narrow minded Shi'ism and a falsified Persian nationalism, denial of the existence of other nationalities is the fundamental element of this nationalism. Pakistan is not a nation-state; neither is it a voluntary multinational association. Rather, it constitutes a, post-World War II colonial order and is dedicated to the political and economic hegemony of the Punjabi nationality, sustaining itself on an ideology based on religious identity. The pillar on which the state nationalism of Iran and Pakistan are based is the brutal and inhuman use of state power in order to assimilate national minorities. The Baloch aspirations are for the unification and liberation of their divided country and for living a dignified life according to Baloch socio-cultural values and traditions. It appears that the Baloch desire for freedom and their secular mind-set is not compatible with hegemonic designs of Iranian and Pakistani states and their religious fundamentalist state ideologies. The long drawn conflict of the Baloch with Iran and Pakistan is the manifestation of the Baloch belief that their cause is just. They consider themselves as the master of their land and resources. They are not ready to abandon the dream of regaining their lost sovereignty and are hopeful for a bright future of liberation from alien subjugation.

CHAPTER 16

THE BALOCH NATIONAL QUESTION AND THE RIGHT OF SELF-DETERMINATION

One of the very significant changes occurred in world polity as a result of the two devastating wars in 20th century was the beginning of the end of colonialism. After World War I, issues of granting independence to many nations were resolved peacefully. This was made possible with the acknowledgement of the principle of the right of self-determination. However, seventy years after World War II, many nations in the world were occupied or merged into other states contrary to their will, and continue to struggle for national liberation. National liberation movements generally use the demand of right of self-determination as their political objective, in line with the United Nation Charter, which emphasized granting the right of self-determination for all people. The Baloch are among many other nations facing the curse of colonialism. Their land has been occupied by various countries and they are engaged in a protracted and bloody conflict with occupying states. The Baloch claim for self-determination has both legal and humanitarian aspects.

NATIONAL LIBERATION STRUGGLE IN CONTEXT

A national liberation struggle is the movement of a subjugated or colonized nation in the pursuit of freedom. It is the sum total of individual, organizational, and political expression, the goal of which is the realization of national aspirations. The African philosopher and writer, Cabral (1972) pointed out that the struggle of peoples for liberation and independence undoubtedly constitutes one of the essential characteristics of contemporary history. When the struggle against subjugation is supported by whole communities of an oppressed nation, it becomes the national liberation struggle of that nation. Taber (1965), asserted that these are struggles of rebellious nations against foreign invaders or ruling classes of their society, of the exploited against the exploiters, of the governed against the governors. Another characteristic of a national liberation struggle is that it is the movement of weak against the strong. National liberation struggles are fundamentally patriotic movements of a defensive nature as a reaction to occupation, economic, political oppression, and cultural genocide which is the attempt to wipe out their culture through forced assimilation.

National liberation struggles have always been accompanied by an ideological narrative. 20th century national liberation struggles expressed a tremendous range of ideological diversity. Many were left-wing with Marxist or socialist ideologies, appealing to the poor and to oppressed people. Some were right wing, while others claimed to be liberal or purely based on the idea of the past glory of a nation. However, despite the diversity of ideologies, national liberation movements were a combination of nationalism, socialism, and anti-imperialism. Contemporary national liberation movements are basically the result of the creation of artificial states after the collapse of colonialism in the aftermath of the Second World War.

PRINCIPLE OF SELF-DETERMINATION

The right of self-determination is the right for freely determining a peoples' political status and freely pursuing economic, social and cultural development agendas. Self-determination, as observed by Cassese (1995), started off as a political concept which was promoted by protagonists of the American Declaration of Independence and the French Revolution, by socialist leaders and by American president Woodrow Wilson during the First World War. The concept not only played a certain role in the post-World War 1 settlement of territorial arrangements within Central and Eastern Europe, but it became the principle of the decolonization process. Cassese (1995), pointed out that it has been one of the most important driving force in the new international community with an effect that changed the world community's game rules. The right of self-determination implies exclusively the right of independence in the political sense. It implies the right of free political separation from an oppressor state.

After the collapse of the League of Nations, the right of peoples to self-determination was enshrined in the charter of the United Nations Organization, and in the International Covenants on Human Rights. Article 1 of the United Nations Charter declares one of the purposes of the United Nations to 'develop friendly relations among nations based on respect for the principle of equal rights and self-determination of peoples'. The common article 1 of the International Covenant on Civil and Political Rights and the International Covenant on Economic, Social and Cultural Rights, which were both adopted by the UN General Assembly in 1966, appears to spell out this principle in unequivocal terms. 'All peoples', it says, 'have the right of self-determination. By virtue of that right they freely determine their political status and freely pursue their economic, social and cultural development'. The fact that the right to self-determination is the only right common to two human rights covenants of 1966, and the fact that it was placed in the first article of both, strongly suggest that the member states of the UN were recognizing its special importance.

The right of self-determination of the people also been resolved by the United Nations in various resolutions adopted by its General Assembly. These include:

- Declaration on the Granting of Independence to Colonial Countries and Peoples, adopted by the General Assembly on 14 December 1960;
- The Declaration on the Inadmissibility of Intervention in the Domestic Affairs of States and the Protection of Their Independence and Sovereignty;
- The declaration on the strengthening of International Security; Definition of Aggression;
- The Resolutions on Permanent sovereignty over natural resources;
- Resolutions on the International Development Decade and the establishment of a new international economic order;
- The Charter of Economic Rights and Duties of States; and
- The Declaration on Social Progress and Development.

In its land mark resolution 3382 (XXX) of 10 November 1975, the General Assembly reaffirmed the importance of the universal realization of the right of peoples to self-determination, national sovereignty and territorial integrity and of the speedy granting of independence to colonial countries and peoples as imperatives for the enjoyment of human rights, and it further reaffirmed the legitimacy of the people's struggle for independence, territorial integrity and liberation from colonial and foreign domination by all available means, including armed struggle (UNO, 1975).

Ambiguities in the interpretation of the principle of right of self-determination has been a matter of legal, political and academic discussions. Freeman (1999), emphasised that the literal interpretation of the right of self-determination is not possible because there is no agreed definition of 'peoples' in international law. However, the UN conception of the right to self-determination of peoples was closely associated with the world-wide movements against colonialism and racism. According to Frost (1996), international politics is driven primarily by self-interest and power; however, despite this, the principles, ideals and norms certainly constitute the discourse of international relations, and confused principles can have real, and serious outcomes. Heraclides (1997), emphasized that the principle of the territorial integrity of states, the restrictive interpretation of the right to self-determination, and the extreme caution in recognizing new self-determination claims were all normally justified by an appeal to the values of peace and the stability of the international order. The slow and cautious approach in recognizing the right to self-determination of federating units of the former Yugoslavia showed the confusion of the international community in their policy towards the self-determination principle. It became apparent in the case of Yugoslavia that the priority to territorial integrity over the self-determination of peoples left national minorities vulnerable and fearful. It encouraged 'ethnic cleansing' and generated massive refugee flows. It provoked violence and gross violations of human rights; threatening international peace and security.

THE RIGHT OF SELF-DETERMINATION AND INTERNATIONAL LAW

The right to self-determination of peoples is undoubtedly linked to the granting of independence to colonial countries', i.e., colonies were to be converted into nation-states. In its advisory opinion on Namibia, in 1971, the International Court of Justice (ICJ) confirmed that the right to self-determination had become applicable to non-self-governing territories such as Namibia, and that the very process of decolonization could be explained in terms of the application of the right to self-determination. The International Court of Justice in its Namibia case, expressed its affirmative support to the international legal norm of self-determination as enshrined in the UN General Assembly resolution1514 (XV). Sections 2 and 5 of the resolution state that:

> *(2) All peoples have the right to self-determination; by virtue of that right they freely determine their political status and freely pursue their economic, social and cultural development*

> *(5) Immediate steps shall be taken, in trust and Non-Self-Governing territories or other territories which have not yet attained independence, to transfer all powers to the people of those territories, without any condition or reservation, in accordance with their freely expressed will and desire, without any distinction as to race creed or colour, in order to enable them to enjoy complete impedances and freedom (Dietrich, 1997).*

The Court's words nonetheless displayed a conception of self-determination as a substantive right that accrues to peoples, or at least to non-self-governing territories, and that those peoples or territories might wish to see enforced (Klabbers, 2006). The declaration of the International Court of Justice on 22 July 2010, known as Advisory Opinion on Kosovo paved the road for the peaceful settlement of international disputes. With the decision of the Court, the position of Kosovars and their claim for independence were factually and politically strengthened.

According to schema developed by the UN resolution 1541 (XV) of General Assembly, there are three forms of exercising the right of self-determination:

1. The creation of an independent and sovereign state;
2. Free association with another state;
3. Integration into another state (UNO, 1960).

Decolonization in many instances was achieved by one of the above mentioned three methods (Rauschning et al. 1997).

Although, the concept of self-determination is enmeshed in academic controversy, mainly, whether it is a legal, political, or a politico-legal concept; observed Castellino (2014), while sovereign states view it as a threat to their sovereignty, the concept of self-determination with its attending promises of freedom from oppression, keeps raising its head in various differing contexts. If it is treated solely as a legal concept, then it may relate to the political and the constitutional rights of the people which form the foundation of the concept. In other words, an aspiration of self-determination is propelled by a sense of freedom, and political rights. In this perspective, the Baloch national struggle in Iran and Pakistan is based not only on morality but on law - the legal right of self-determination. The UN General Assembly declaration 2625 adopted in 1970 on the principles of international law concerning friendly relations and co-operation among states in accordance with the Charter of the United Nations clearly established that the forcible denial of self-determination - by imposing or maintaining by force colonial or alien domination - is illegitimate under the Charter. By all accounts, the Baloch demand for the right of self-determination is asserting an international right and Iran and Pakistan by denying that right, are in breach of international law.

BALOCH NATIONAL QUESTION AND PRINCIPLE OF INTERNATIONAL INTERVENTION

In the context of various UN resolutions, violation by a state of the right of people to self-determination is an international crime and constitutes a ground for international intervention. The breach by a state of an obligation deriving from the recognition by international law is an international crime, precisely characterized as such, which gives rise to an international responsibility governed by a specific regime (UNO, 1976). In this regard, it has been vehemently advocated by human right organizations and various working papers of the United Nations, that any criminal act committed by an individual, for the purpose of establishing or maintaining colonial rule should be a matter of international law. This prompted the trials of several military and civilian leaders of former Yugoslavia.

In 21st century world, conflicts between different national identities in artificially created multi-national countries are prime forces in both the promotion and destruction of peace, human dignity and social justice. The creation of artificial states and international borders by colonial administrators after Second World War are never completely just. The violation of the basic human rights of the Baloch by the Pakistani and Iranian states is among the major destabilization factors in south central Asia and the Middle East. The political and geographical division of the Baloch into many countries of the region, the growing armed resistance of the Baloch in Iran and Pakistan may be the cause of inter-state conflicts in the near future. With the displacement of thousands of refugees and violation of fundamental human rights by Pakistan and Iran, this regional conflict is bound to become international.

The Baloch struggle for the right of self-determination by implication has impacts on regional and global peace and the success of the Baloch national struggle would contribute to world peace and harmony. Balochistan is situated at the confluence of three zones which are now threatening not only the regional but also global security and peace. The Shia fundamentalism in the west, the Taliban terrorists in the north and the Pakistani religious fundamentalist state in the east with Balochistan imbedded by geography in the centre of what is now the most dangerous region on Planet Earth. Pakistan and Iran are without a doubt the epicentres of terrorism and religious fundamentalism. It is an open secret that Pakistan is exporting terrorism to India, Afghanistan, Chechnya, China and Europe. Iran also supports terrorist activities in the Middle East and is one of the factors in the continued turbulent situation in the region. A secular democratic Balochistan will be an oasis in the vast desert of fundamentalism and terrorism.

An independent Balochistan, as a result of exercising its right of self-determination, will bring about the geographical separation of Shia fundamentalism and Sunni fanaticism. It would also create a strong watching corridor against the rising Islamic fundamentalism in the Persian Gulf region. Allowing the Baloch to exercise their right of self-determination will lead to the achievement of this right by subjugated nationalities like Sindhis, Seraikis, Kurds, Azeris, and others in Pakistan and Iran. The emergence of democratic and secular sovereign states in the region will be a counter check for the religious fundamentalist states of Pakistan and Iran contributing to regional and world security. Uninterrupted access to energy resources is vital for the peace and prosperity of a future world. Balochistan stretching from Turkmenistan to the Indian Ocean is vital in securing energy transfer from Central Asia to other parts of the world. The international community should not look with favour at the prospect of the vast, strategically and economically important region of south central Asia being controlled by an amalgamation of religious fundamentalist states with a hegemonic mind-set and an agenda for international terrorism.

The extreme degree of injustice is imposing an alien rule on a nation. Facilitating the occupation of a nation or keeping a blind eye on the plight of a nation under alien rules is the certain injustice. Justice itself requires that the right to national self-determination is granted to the Baloch. Western nations and states have been at the forefront of facilitating by all means the independence of Central Asian states, the component states of Yugoslavia, East Timor, and South Sudan in recent decades. It is incomprehensible that the territorial integrity of rogue and failing states like Iran and Pakistan are so sacrosanct for the international community. The international community has not extended any support to the Baloch right of self-determination. This is illogical and against their much acclaimed protection of human values and democratic principles. Wellman (2005), observed that there is nothing conflicting or troublesome in valuing legitimate states on the one hand and, accepting their division on the other. There is also nothing strange about redrawing state boundaries, as they were drawn by colonial powers without the consent of local people; if it will save lives, and provide a better security, especially for those concerned and generally for the whole world.

Intervention by the international community and secession, are very relevant to the legal norm of self-determination. If there is a legitimate case of the right of self-determination, and the denial of this by the occupying state creates a situation where there is gross violation of basic human rights or there are threats to regional or international peace and security, then international intervention is legal. That principle was successfully applied in case of Kosovo when United Nation Mission in Kosovo (UNMIK) took over civil administrative responsibility as well as security of the province until 2008.

International intervention can be justified in order to undo repression when a distinct people or a minority national entity is systematically repressed within an existing state and denied an equal opportunity to participate in the political process or subjected to ongoing gross violations of human rights. In the Baloch conflict with Iran and Pakistan, the UN organs, such as the General Assembly, the UN Commission on Human Rights, and even the Trustee ship Council, may be in a position to act. According to Stromseth (1992), the question of a UN response to a struggle for self-determination and ultimately secession is part of the larger question of humanitarian intervention by the United Nations. The Baloch while asserting their right to self-determination are exercising an international right. Any member of the international community, in giving them aid in their struggle to assert that right, does not commit an act of intervention but will simply uphold the Charter of the United Nations and the fundamental principles of international law according to the Charter. The Persian and Pakistani states may try to invoke Article 2(7) of the UN Charter, claiming that such disputes are matters which are essentially within the domestic jurisdiction of a state; however, a majority of UN member states now agree that compliance with basic human rights standards, including protection of rights of national minorities, can no longer be regarded as a matter of domestic jurisdiction.

Iran and Pakistan have ignored repeated pleas from international humanitarian organizations to stop brutalities on the pretext of state sovereignty. The principle of State sovereignty is no longer a license to abuse the fundamental rights of a particular community or national entity. The principle of state sovereignty does not give licence to abuse the constitutional entitlements of a group and their legal rights, neither does it allow the state to resort to the unilateral threat or use of force in dealing with the political demand of a national entity. The United Nation General Assembly Resolution 2625(1970) para, 1 (3), demands that the States do not to oppress their citizens, as directed by the Article 1(3) of the Charter. This obligation is also included in para 5 and in the 1966 International Covenant on Civil and Political Rights Article 1 and in the compliance provisions of Articles 40 and 41.

The Baloch conflict with Iran and Pakistan has the potential of involving other states in the region, thus posing the sort of threat to international peace and security that warrants a Security Council involvement. In situations that endanger international peace, the Security Council can respond by taking enforcement action under Chapter VII of the UN Charter. Under Chapter VI, Article 34, it may investigate any dispute or any situation which might lead to international friction in order to determine whether international peace and security is likely to be endangered. It can then recommend appropriate procedures or methods of adjustment under Article 36. The international community by intervening in the dispute between the Baloch and Iran and Pakistan at this stage of the conflict, may be able to mobilize pressure on parties to exercise moderation and seek negotiated solutions. The international community can ask the United Nations to deploy peacekeeping forces as was the case in Bosnia-Hercegovina and Somalia. It can impose economic and diplomatic sanctions through Security Council.

The 1960 resolution of the General Assembly on decolonization stated that the subjection of peoples to alien subjugation, domination and exploitation constitutes a denial of fundamental human rights. It is contrary to the Charter of the United Nations and is an impediment to the promotion of world peace and co-operation. As enshrined in various covenants and resolutions of the United Nations Organization, the self-determination and the human right principles are inseparable and it might provide the international community with the best possible options to solve the most complex conflicts in the world in a peaceful way. In modern times, the independence of Bangladesh, South Sudan and East Timor were brought about with the application of the right of self-determination. In the 21st century, the incomplete agenda of ending colonialism is waiting completion. The drive for national liberation by many subjugated and occupied nations resulted in violent confrontation between the occupied and occupier. They have been source of tremendous suffering, misery and destruction. This is happening with the Baloch in a 21st century world. The only way to prevent another humanitarian tragedy which the world witnessed in case of former Yugoslavia is the granting of right of self-determination to the Baloch.

CHAPTER 17

INTERNATIONAL PERSPECTIVE ON THE BALOCH QUESTION

Historically, the Baloch national struggle has been analysed in the context of regional and superpower rivalry in south central Asia. The propagation of a perception of the Soviet and Afghan involvement in the Baloch struggle was a key foreign policy strategy of both Iran and Pakistan during the era of cold war and the Baloch national struggle was portrayed as supported by the Soviet Union. Although, unfounded, this was a deliberate attempt to fuel Western concerns over an imagined Soviet thrust towards the Indian Ocean through Balochistan. After the demise of Soviet Union, and with the development of Mujahedeen phenomenon in Afghanistan and the fall of Pahlavi regime in Iran, the dimensions of external involvement in the Baloch struggle have changed. Now Iran and Pakistan are expressing their concerns over foreign support to the Baloch and are targeting Western powers and their allies in this respect.

Balochistan is situated in one of the most politically volatile regions of the world. During the 19th century, it was the rivalry of Imperial Britain and Czarist Russia in Central Asia which engulfed Balochistan because of its geographical location. In the contemporary international political scenario, with its huge unexplored energy resources and its location at the mouth of the Persian Gulf, Balochistan is becoming increasingly important to many regional and global powers. This importance is because of the energy concerns of industrialized nations, their economic objectives and geo-political interests in south central Asia and in the Middle East. The governments of Iran and Pakistan believe that the Baloch resistance in their countries is being trained and funded by many countries and external forces. Iran has accused the US as supporting the Baloch militants through Arab countries. Pakistan has openly expressed concerns over Indian and Afghan support for the Baloch.

AFGHANISTAN: THE PLACE OF REFUGE

The present state of Afghanistan came into existence at a time when the Baloch state of Kalat was expanding its territories and influence in the region. Since the truce and treaty between the Afghan King Ahmad Shah Abdali and the Khan of the Baloch, Mir Naseer Khan 1, in 18th century, Afghanistan and Balochistan remained brotherly countries despite some ups and downs in their relationships. The British invasions of Afghanistan and subsequent occupation of Balochistan during 19th century changed the dynamics between these brotherly states to some extent, as the Baloch state was for a while under the sovereignty of Afghanistan when Shah Shujah was installed as Afghan king by the British. Both, Balochistan and Afghanistan were later divided by the drawing of Goldsmid, Durand and McMahon lines. However, with the creation of Pakistan, the Baloch and Pashtun national questions in Pakistan remained important foreign policy issues of various Afghan regimes.

Although, Afghanistan did not extend any support to Prince Abdul Karim in 1948, when he crossed the border into Afghanistan to organize an armed resistance against the occupation of Balochistan by Pakistan, it was the only country which opposed the admission of Pakistan into United Nations Organization. The Durand Line which was drawn during the 19th century to demarcate the border between British India and Afghanistan has never been accepted as legitimate by the Afghans and since the creation of Pakistan, the Durand Line had become a primary source of tension between Afghanistan and Pakistan. Afghanistan has claimed the North Western Frontier Province (NWFP) of Pakistan (now renamed Khyber-Pashtunkhwa province in 2010) and Pashtun majority areas of northern Balochistan as Afghan territories. Pakistan and Afghanistan both accused each other of supporting subversive activities across Durand Line. Afghanistan has always been sympathetic to the representative party of the Baloch and Pashtun nationalism, NAP, and openly supported the Baloch and Pashtun right of self-determination in Pakistan, in various international forums. Afghanistan had always been the place of refuge for Baloch political and militant activists whenever they were pressed hard by Pakistan. During the early phases of the Baloch armed resistance in 1970s, the Afghan government took a friendly stance towards the Baloch and provided every possible assistance to Baloch refugees entering Afghanistan. However, from 1975, because of increasing Pakistani pressure, the Afghan government of Sardar Muhammad Daud Khan became less sympathetic towards the Baloch resistance.

The revolutionary government in Afghanistan of 1978 was more sympathetic towards the Baloch national struggle in Iran and Pakistan. It began to advocate enthusiastically the cause of the Baloch and Pashtun right of self-determination internally and on various international forums. Officials of the revolutionary government began to talk openly about fraternal ties of the people of Afghanistan with Pashtuns and the Baloch across the border. The Baloch refugees were granted political asylum and close communication was established between the Baloch Peoples Liberation Front and the ruling communist Party of Afghanistan. A large number of Baloch students with Afghan passports were sent to various educational institutions in Soviet Union and Socialist countries of Eastern Europe. Following the takeover of Iran by the Ayatollahs in 1979, the Afghan government extended unconditional support to many resistance organizations from Western Balochistan and provided sanctuary to their political activists and resistance fighters. This policy was also prompted by the increased interference from Iran and Pakistan in the internal affairs of Afghanistan who were training, indoctrinating and sending Islamic Jihadists into Afghanistan for subversive activities.

A strong and integrated Pakistan is not compatible with the Afghan objective of securing peace, stability and economic prosperity. This is because since the 1970s, Pakistan has adopted a policy of making Afghanistan a subservient state-a policy known in Pakistan as the strategic depth policy against India. The hallmark of this policy is to install regimes of Pakistan's choice in Afghanistan. The Pakistani military establishment does not believe in a sovereign Afghanistan which might decide its friends and foes according to the need of its national interests. In recent years, Pakistan has tried its best to re-install a Taliban government in Kabul. It can be observed that the degree of Afghan support to the Baloch national struggle has not been consistent and varied according to changes in Afghanistan's own political situation. Its support for the Baloch has been a direct manifestation of its policy towards Pakistan and Iran: that is, with the lessening of tensions between them, Afghanistan has reduced its open support of the Baloch cause and with the strained relations between them, it has renewed its support for the Baloch right of self-determination.

For many analysts on Afghan affairs, the Afghan policy towards Balochistan would be based on its geo-political considerations. Although, there has not been any open support for an independent Balochistan, in the present context, openly supporting the Baloch national struggle in Pakistan might be important for Afghanistan on two counts. First, Pakistan is using Balochistan as a base for its destabilizing efforts in Afghanistan. Secondly, in any eventuality of the breakup of Pakistan, a friendly and allied Balochistan will not only bolster power and the international prestige of Afghanistan, but will also offer vast economic advantages with the easy access to the Indian Ocean.

INDIA: WAITING FOR WESTERN APPROVAL?

During the partition of India, the Indian leadership was not ready to interfere in the conflict between Pakistan and the

Baloch state despite various attempts by the Khan and Baloch political leadership to persuade the Congress leadership for the recognition of Independent Baloch state. Perhaps the Indian leadership was not in a position to interfere in British plans of making Pakistan a viable country. The British policy at that time was the merging of the Baloch state into the territories of the newly created religious state. Soon after its creation, Pakistan became the base for the destabilization of India by creating and supporting many terrorist organizations in the name of freedom of Kashmir. A part of Kashmir was occupied by Pakistan in 1948. But India was never able to take reciprocal measures or restrain Pakistan from its subversive activities because of the unconditional support of the West for Pakistan. Pakistan in total control of an alliance of country's powerful military establishment and *Mullahs* and *Muhajirs* rendered a harsh and inflexible stance towards India. From the outset, confrontation with India became the cornerstone of the state policy. Pakistan's policies will continue along these lines for as long as the military holds the same degree of power within the state. In near future there is no chance of relinquishing the power held by the military to a civilian dispensation.

Twenty first century India appears to be very different from the past. It has developed into a major regional power with an expanding economy, the fourth largest army in the world, and having a nuclear arsenal. After the fall of the Soviet Union, the newly established friendship with the West encouraged its ambitions of being recognized as the guardian of Indian Ocean. In order to sustain its role as a major power in the region, a sustained economic growth is imperative for India. With the Pakistani state policy of engineering frequent terrorist and subversive activities and fuelling religious disturbances in various parts of India; the economic ambitions may not be fulfilled as planned and the Indian establishment might be compelled to take reciprocal measures. One of the options for India is to help the Baloch and Sindhi national struggles in a meaningful way.

India is also worried about the Pakistani move of leasing out the Gwadar port in southern Balochistan to China which places its rival state in a very advantageous position in the strategically and economically important Persian Gulf. The leasing out of the port and its associated road and rail links have substantial strategic implications as it complicates the Indian navy's strategic planning and could be seen as a move by China in encircling India on its eastern, northern, and western borders. The Indians might see the Pakistani move to handover the strategic port of Gwadar to the Chinese as a move to counter their increasing economic and political influence in the Persian Gulf. Economically, Gwadar port and its associated pipeline networks could give an edge to Pakistan by materially strengthening its influence on Afghanistan and the Central Asian states.

The Pakistani authorities have blamed the Indians for aiding the Baloch resistance movement for many years. The Pakistani Prime Minister, Yusuf Reza Gilani, in 2009, in a meeting with his Indian counterpart, Man Mohan Singh, in Egypt, complained of Indian involvement in Balochistan. In 2015, the Pakistani government raised concern over Indian interference in Balochistan and FATA when Foreign Secretary Aitzaz Ahmad Chaudhry met his Indian counterpart Jaishankar in Islamabad. In March, 2016, the Pakistani authorities arrested an Indian citizen Mr. Yadev, in Balochistan accusing him of aiding the Baloch resistance movements on behalf of the Indian intelligence agency-Research and Analysis Wing (RAW). However, on the ground there is no visible evidence of any Indian involvement in the Baloch conflict with Pakistan. Diplomatically, however, once or twice, the Indian officials openly raised their voice concerning the human rights violation in Balochistan. During 2016, there were some references on human right situation in Balochistan by speeches of Indian leaders. On 11 and 15 August, 2016, the Indian Prime Minister spoke about the situation in Balochistan while addressing an all party conference and a rally marking the Indian Independence Day in Delhi. He said that it was time for Pakistan to answer the questions about the violation of human rights in Balochistan and Pakistani held Kashmir (BBC, 2016). In September, 2016, the Indian Foreign Minister Sushma Swaraj also mentioned the human rights violations in Balochistan in her UN General Assembly speech.

As the Baloch consider their national struggle in Iran and Pakistan as inseparable, Indian relations with Iran might be a problem in any policy move by India towards Balochistan. India has developed sustained and trustworthy relations with Iran. This relationship has not been affected by any regime change in Iran or in India. India is investing in various economic projects in Iran. It sees the Chahbar port in Western Balochistan as very important in its bid to access the Central Asian energy resources. In May, 2016, during the Indian Prime Minister's visit to Iran at least ten agreements were signed in Tehran, including the development of Chahbar port. Any prospective assistance to the Baloch national resistance from India might be conditional in excluding any action against the Persian state and could be Eastern Balochistan specific.

The ideological foundation of Pakistan, with the fanatical army establishment shaping every policy in the state in general and national security and foreign policies in particular, the prospect of any rapprochement with India is increasingly unlikely. The perception in India is growing that the use of Baloch card is imperative in order to force Pakistan to stop its various proxy wars against India. At present, the Indian shyness in openly or meaningfully supporting the Baloch struggle might be due to regional and international inhibiting factors. Regionally, any overt assistance by the Indians to the Baloch national struggle will certainly strain its relations with Iran endangering its vital economic interests. Internationally, the Indians are well aware that the West has not abandoned Pakistan and it is still a client state of the US and the UK. Without the tacit approval of the West, India perhaps is not in a position to take very bold steps regarding the Baloch.

Many analysts believe that at present there is no Indian policy regarding the Baloch national struggle. It is still adhoc and consists mainly of knee jerk reactions against Pakistani incursions in Kashmir and any subversive activity by the Pakistan sponsored terrorist groups in India. Some of the Baloch leaders also believe that meaningful Indian involvement in the Baloch conflict strongly depends on India's relationship with Pakistan. As there is no chance of any change in the policies of Pakistan regarding India, in near future, India has to decide a consistent policy regarding the Baloch question. India can use the Baloch card as leverage to force Pakistan to stop terrorist activities in Kashmir and other parts of India or taking any signal from the West, it might play a pro-active role in the creation of an independent Balochistan by supporting the Baloch resistance in a meaningful way. Some of the Indian think tanks and experts are also advocating a more careful and less aggressive policy regarding the Baloch question. They are stressing to the Indian government that it is better to keep the trouble in Balochistan going, by just giving minimal financial assistance to the Baloch resistance without formulating any formidable strategy for the creation of an independent Balochistan. Whatever strategy will be taken by India regarding the Baloch question will soon be known as the pace of events in the region is gaining momentum.

RUSSIA: THE INDIFFERENT POWER

Pakistan was a close ally of the West during the cold war era, and had constantly blamed the Soviet Union of assisting the nationalist politics of minority nationalities in Pakistan. As the representative party of the left was National Awami Party (NAP), which had an anti-establishment and anti-imperialist policy, the Soviet Union was regarded as sympathetic to the party. Despite the official narrative of the Pakistani establishment that Soviet Union was encouraging the secessionist movements of Sindhu Desh, Pashtunistan and Balochistan through National Awami Party, there was no visible support for the Baloch national struggle from the Russians. It appeared that Soviet leadership was not convinced about moving beyond the borders of Afghanistan, as they considered the ground beyond Durand Line was not firm enough for such a move. Another reason for the Soviet reluctance in venturing beyond Durand Line was that it might invite a direct confrontation with the West, as Pakistan was an active member of two Western military pacts, namely the Central

Treaty Organization (CENTO) and South East Asian Treaty Organization (SEATO) during the cold war era. The Soviets depended on sympathetic Afghan governments to deal with the Baloch and other national questions in Pakistan.

The policy of the Soviet Union regarding the Baloch was not in line with the declared commitment of the Communist Party of the Soviet Union to give support to national liberation struggles in the developing world. Many of the Soviet intellectuals were of the opinion that the Baloch national struggle was in its formative phase and should not be considered for official Soviet recognition. The leader of the Baloch national resistance Nawab Khair Bakhsh Mari on various occasions expressed his dismay concerning the question of Soviet help by saying that he is not aware of any Soviet support for the Baloch nationalists. Many times, he was quoted as saying that the Soviet Bloc gave us books, but it is not books and ideology but guns and weapons which played a more important role in a national struggle. The Soviets did not give the Baloch any guns, bombs or weapons. According to Selig Harrison, one of the factors for the removal of Hafizullah Amin as the ruler of Afghanistan in 1980s was his policy of forcefully playing the Pashtun-Baloch cards, as Moscow wanted to play down the Pashtun-Baloch issues until it had a secure foothold in Kabul (Harrison, 1981).

The post-Soviet Russia is still struggling with its own economic and political problems. For the moment, Russia is not interested in any South Asian issue. The Russian ambition of reaching the warm waters of the Indian Ocean appeared to be a thing of past. However, in recent years, Russia has tried to deepen its relations with Iran and develop a new relationship with Pakistan. The 21st century Russia is sending warm feelers towards Pakistan. In a milieu of growing tension between Russia and the West in Eastern Europe and in the Middle East, Moscow is apparently developing its ties with Iran and in recent years there have been some high profile reciprocal visits to Moscow and Islamabad from the civil and military leadership of Russia and Pakistan. Iran is among major consumers of Russian technology regarding its nuclear program and weapon system. With the growing tension between the West and Pakistan concerning the stability of Afghanistan and over Pakistan's nuclear weapons, there are observable initiatives to establish a strategic relationship between Pakistan and Russia. During 2011, after the exchange of some high profile visits by civil and military leaders of both countries, working groups were formed to build frameworks for mutual cooperation in the trade, energy, and military arenas. In September, 2016, for the first time, Russians and Pakistani military units conducted joint exercises. The Russian hope for winning greater influence in Teheran and Islamabad has deterred Moscow from considering the Baloch national resistance as a serious matter of interest. At least for the time being, the 'Baloch National Question' will not be an important issue with officials in the foreign ministry in Moscow. Perhaps if the situation became worse and the tension escalated between the Baloch and the occupying states, it is likely that Moscow would be on the sides of Islamabad and Teheran.

THE US AND THE WEST: DEALING WITH FRANKENSTEIN MONSTERS?

Iran and Pakistan have been regarded as client states of West under the leadership of the US and the UK for a long time. Iran has been a key Western ally in the Middle East during cold war until it was taken over by the Ayatollahs in 1979. After the collapse of Pahlavi dynasty, Iran and the West came into direct confrontation as the Ayatollahs became out of control and Iran slipped from Western orbit. Despite being financed and helped diplomatically by the British during early years of 20th century, the new generation of Ayatollahs unexpectedly took a strong anti-Western stance terming the United States as the 'Great Satan'. Its interference in the affairs of the Western allied Persian Gulf states; its ambitions to acquire nuclear technology and the open declaration of its leaders to wiping out Israel from the face of Earth have created a huge gap between Iran and the West. Pakistan was created by the UK and sustained by the West in order that it could be used to protect Western interests in the Middle East and Indian Ocean. However, after the collapse of the Soviet Union and the development of friendly relations between India and the West, Pakistan's involvement in the destabilization of Afghanistan, its involvement in terrorist activities in India and its nuclear ambitions made it a liability of the West. Now, there can be heard some feeble voices in Western capitals on the merit and demerit of sustaining the religious state of Pakistan. Historically, the Baloch national struggle for an independent state has been seen as anti-West and a move for the extension of Soviet influence in the Indian Ocean. However, some members of the US congress and the European Parliament in recent years, have condemned the gross human rights violations in Balochistan and some of them have demanded that assistance should be given to the Baloch national struggle.

For the regime of the Ayatollahs, the West is the declared enemy of the Islamic revolution. In response to the aggressive policies of Ayatollahs, the West worked at weakening the Islamic republic by taking various counter measures. The Ayatollah's frantic efforts in manufacturing nuclear weapons was most alarming and prompted stringent measures from the West. Years of trade sanctions forced Iran to concede and they signed an agreement with the West in 2015, curtailing their nuclear weapon program; however, the unpredictable Ayatollahs could revert to their previous position at any moment. It appears that the West is not interested in the truncation of the Persian state at present or it feels that any move towards the disintegration of Iran by providing active assistance to the Baloch and other ethnic minorities in Iran is not in the interest of the West; instead a regime change in Iran is considered to be the most favoured option in dealing with the Persian question in the 21st century.

Pakistan was a key partner of the West in the fight against socialism in the region and was a member of various defence pacts against the Soviet Union. Ensuring the stability of Pakistan has been a key aspect of Western strategy. From 1978, with the socialist revolution in Afghanistan, Pakistan has been viewed by the US and the West from Afghanistan's angle. Following the events of September 11, 2001, Pakistan became a frontline state in the Western war against terrorism and was declared a non-NATO ally in 2004; nevertheless, things have changed in recent years. The relationship between Islamabad and Washington are no longer cordial. Despite the grant of billions of dollars to Pakistan, there has been observable tensions over conflicting interests and challenges regarding Pakistan's destabilizing role in Afghanistan. In Washington, there is a growing realization that Pakistan's intelligence agency (ISI) has been extending support to Al-Qaeda leadership and maintaining active support to Taliban forces fighting in Afghanistan. WikiLeaks disclosures during 2010 only confirmed strong US suspicions that parts of Pakistan's military establishment have close links with Taliban insurgents in Afghanistan. Pakistan failed to comply with its commitment made in 2015 with the US and Afghan governments to force Taliban into a negotiated settlement with Kabul government of Ashraf Ghani.

In recent years, the Pakistani establishment, through its controlled media, expressed feelings of betrayal by the West particularly with regard to the Kashmir conflict or making Afghanistan as its strategical depth against India. The Pakistani establishment reacted very strongly against certain hearings in the American houses of congress. In February 2012, three Republican representatives Dana Rohrabacher, Louie Gohmert, and Steve King, introduced a resolution in the House of Representatives, advocating "self-determination" for Balochistan- the resolution was never voted on. Since then, there were more senate and congressional hearings on human rights situations on both Western and Eastern Balochistan, where congressmen and senators made sympathetic remarks towards the Baloch. However, no observable changes in the policy of the US government were manifested regarding the plight of the Baloch. Despite some developing tension, it would be very simplistic to hope for any drastic shift in the policy of Pakistan and the West and vice versa in near future. The United States and its European allies have counted on Pakistani cooperation throughout their military involvement in Afghanistan. Pakistan is heavily dependent on the US and the

Europe in the fields of diplomatic support against India, budgetary assistance, acquiring weapons and technological knowhow for its armed forces, and civil and military training. On 17 May 2016, the US State Department assured Pakistan that it did not support the demand for an independent Balochistan, as it respected the country's unity and territorial integrity. "The US government respects the unity and territorial integrity of Pakistan, and we do not support independence for Balochistan," a policy statement of the US State Department shared with Pakistani newspaper, Dawn. The statement followed two seminars which the Baloch nationalists in Washington held at the Carnegie Endowment and Capitol Hall, urging the US administration and lawmakers to support their struggle (Dawn, 2016). However, in future, the American point of view might undergo some changes as a result of mistrust, mostly over Pakistan's continued efforts to destabilize Afghanistan in its continued support to the Taliban and other Jihadist groups. Pakistan's nuclear prowess is increasingly being perceived in Western capitals as a threat to international security. Pakistan is becoming increasingly vulnerable with a takeover by extremist elements in the military establishment. A fanatical regime of a failing state having a nuclear arsenal is indeed a matter of grave concern for the Western World. This concern could be a factor in the reconsideration of its thinking in relations to Pakistan. Taking into account increasing divergence regarding the goals and interests of Pakistan and the US in the region, a sustained friendship between them could be difficult.

Although, South Asia has not been a major concern for European countries since a long time, the European Union in recent decades, has become increasingly alarmed about potential consequences that instability in Pakistan could cause their military and development efforts in Afghanistan. The policy planners at the EU headquarters in Brussels are genuinely worried that the internal developments in Pakistan could have broader regional and global implications. A report of Swedish Defence Research Agency (FOI) in 2011 expressed serious concern regarding the internal security of Pakistan. According to the report, the view among the EU countries was that a destabilized Pakistan would have far-reaching consequences for the political development of Afghanistan and the European countries' military forces there. Europe is also concerned about the likelihood of Pakistan failing as a state and how that would affect the country's ability to control its nuclear weapons (Atarodi, 2011).

From a practical standpoint, the role of Britain and the US are important in the Baloch conflict with Iran and Pakistan. Britain and the United States have played either the roles of creators, patrons and protectors of Iran and Pakistan from 20th century; regarding them as the first line of defence against a presumed Russian thrust towards the warm waters of the Indian Ocean. From a cold-war perspective, Pakistan's long-term stability was critical to the US interests in the region. The UK has been instrumental in maintaining friendly relations by the West with Pakistan despite Pakistan's overt actions against the Western interests in Afghanistan over many decades. Great Britain has always endeavoured to have good relations with Iran after the fall of Pahlavi regime. It was believed to have played a significant role in restraining the US from striking nuclear facilities in Iran or taking any other military measure at the peak of tensions between the regime of the Ayatollahs and the West. Ironically, Iran is still considered by the UK policy makers as a stabilizing factor in Iraq. Many observers on UK policy matters are not sure about any drastic change in its policy towards Pakistan in near future. The security agencies in the UK are increasingly dependent on intelligence sharing about terrorist organizations of Pakistani origin which threaten the internal security of the country. Many observers believe that politicians in the UK cannot afford to antagonize the decisive vote of the UK citizens of Pakistani origin by taking any realistic policy regarding Pakistan. For the time being, it appears that the British ruling elite is content with its appeasement policy towards Muslims of Pakistani origin. The Arabs, African and Pakistani Muslims have been given a free hand in establishing religious schools and institutions and recently a Pakistani origin Muslim who was accused of having alleged terrorist links by his opponents, was elected as Mayor of London-the second most influential position in the country.

Despite unlimited economic, strategic and political support from the US and its Western allies, the Pakistani establishment has given a detailed account of their view on the USA's inconsistent policy towards Pakistan. While hearings by US Congress subcommittee members on the issue of Balochistan was perceived as a moral victory for the Baloch cause, the Pakistani officials as well as the mainstream political parties including the opposition has seriously condemned such initiatives declaring it interference in the internal matters of Pakistan. Although, any US role as a super power or as third party mediator in the conflict may have legitimacy for the Baloch people and their national resistance; nevertheless, the endemic anti-American sentiments in Pakistan would not easily accept the US role for mediation in the Baloch conflict. Neither is there any indication that the US administration is thinking to exert pressure on the Pakistani military establishment to stop human rights abuses in Balochistan. Visiting Pakistan in January, 2006, the former Undersecretary of State, Nicholas Burns rejected out rightly the pleas by the Human Rights Commission of Pakistan for the US intervention to stop the gross human rights violations committed in Balochistan, by the military regime of the former President Pervez Musharraf. Rejecting the Commission's pleas, Burns said that the United States would not meddle in Pakistan's internal affairs.

Many, among the Baloch analysts believe that Iran and Pakistan's future relationship with the West will decide the Western policy towards the Baloch national struggle. There is another factor which might be responsible for an increase in interest by the West in the Baloch conflict with Iran and Pakistan and that concerns the energy resources. Being rich in energy reserves and the strategic location of Balochistan also makes it central to the energy policy of the US and the Europe regarding the region. The leasing out of the strategically important port city of Gwadar to China and the proposed road and rail links from Gwadar to Western China, have put the Chinese in a controlling position in the Persian Gulf. It might be a cause for alarm as it means the West will not be the only manipulator in the oil rich region.

Although, on the face of it, there is no meaningful change in the policy of the US and its Western allies regarding Balochistan or the Baloch national question in Iran and Pakistan; nevertheless, with the changing situation in the region where Pakistan and Iran are increasingly becoming destabilizing factors in Afghanistan, India and the Middle East, the Baloch question will ultimately be on the foreign policy agenda of Western nations in the near future. Chinese incursions through the 'China Pakistan Economic Corridor' in a region which was once believed to be the exclusive domain of the Western powers cannot go unnoticed for long.

CHINA: THE EMERGING IMPERIAL POWER

The Chinese interests in Balochistan should be seen in the context of the vast mineral resources in the region and its economic and strategic relations with Islamabad. China apart from its well-established military relationship with Pakistan, has major investments in various other sectors in the country, and became one of the biggest investors in Pakistan in recent decades. Pakistan is not only the consumer market for Chinese goods but also a place of unaccountable exploitation of natural resources. China has been involved in the ruthless exploitation of mineral resources in Balochistan; nearly exhausting the gold and copper reserves in Saindak. In 2015, China signed various agreements with Pakistan, investing 46 billion dollar to build road and rail links from Gwadar to Western China. Gwadar will be a Chinese naval outpost on the Indian Ocean designed to protect Beijing's oil supply lines from the Middle East thus coming face to face with Western presence in the region.

China has contributed materials, technologies and scientific expertise to Pakistan's nuclear weapon program and is the leading supplier of conventional arms to Pakistan. With wide spread stakes in the stability of Pakistan, China is very keen to see that any national struggle which could be a threat to its economic interests, financial investments and strategic ambition in the region is crushed. There are talks of Chinese insistence to finish by force any Baloch resistance before the start of China Pakistan Economic Corridor (CPEC). The Pakistani army has been ordered to clear the route of the proposed road and rail links from Gwadar to Western Chinese cities by either wholesale killing of the local population or by internally displacing them. China also has a close and cordial relationship with Iran. Iran has been the market for Chinese goods even before the Western sanctions were imposed on Iran. China is also contributing to the development of an Iranian nuclear program and has supplied military equipment to Iran. For China the Baloch national struggle is a destabilizing factor in a region where it has vital economic and strategic interests.

THE ARAB STATES: FACING THE DILEMMA

Historically, the Baloch and the Arabs of Persian Gulf have enjoyed contact, both economically and socially. The Gwadar and Chahbar regions of Balochistan were parts of Sultanate of Oman for more than a century and at present, the Baloch form a significant portion of the population in the Sultanate of Oman. But politically, the Baloch-Arab contacts were established in Iraq during the revolutionary governments of Ba'ath Party in Baghdad during the 1960s. Apart from the territorial dispute with Iran, the fluctuating Iraqi support to Baloch resistance in Western Balochistan was also in retaliation against the Iranian support for the Kurdish national resistance in Iraq. The support for the Baloch resistance in Iran suddenly ended in 1975 with the signing of the Algiers treaty between Iran and Iraq in which each side agreed to stop supporting the Baloch, Kurdish and other national resistances in their respective countries. After the fall of the Shah, Iraq again came into confrontation with Iran and there soon began a bloody and protracted war between Iraq and Iran. Iraq once again began giving propaganda support to the Baloch national liberation struggle in Iran and by extending financial assistance to various resistance groups engaged in militant activities against Iran in

Western Balochistan. However, this support terminated with the end of Iran-Iraq war in 1989.

With the demise of Soviet Union and collapse of the nationalist regimes in the Arab world, the Baloch question is seen by Arab countries in the context of the historical animosity between them and Iran, manifested by the ever present conflict of Shi'ism and Sunni Islam. The Arab-Persian rivalry for the supremacy in the Gulf may be a factor in increasing Arab interest towards the Baloch question in Iran. As observed by Hosseinbor (2000), the Arab countries are facing a dilemma regarding the Baloch national resistance. The support for the Baloch national struggle in Iran politically and strategically is in their national interest as a weak or bifurcated Iran would be less likely to challenge their economic and political ambitions. The Iranian government has blamed Saudi Arabia for actively supporting various Baloch religious groups like Jundallah and others, which have been involved in many attacks on Iranian military installations in Western Balochistan. However, the case for Pakistan is quite different. Historically speaking, one of the purposes for the creation of Pakistan by the British was to use Pakistan in protecting its client states in the Persian Gulf. For several decades, Pakistan has been obediently performing its given duty in the United Arab Emirates, Qatar, Bahrain and Saudi Arabia. There is a strong Pakistani military presence in these countries, the security establishment of Pakistan is deeply involved even in the internal security matters of these countries.

Any meaningful support for the Baloch national struggle in Iran and Pakistan by Arab countries depends on two factors: any change in the policy of the West regarding the 'Baloch Question' in Pakistan and Iran as these countries would always follow the policy guidelines from the West; or any drastic change in the political, social and economic situation within these countries. Presently, no Arab country seems willing to extend any support to the Baloch national resistance in Pakistan.

Pakistan and Iran have undoubtedly became irritants for not only their neighbours such as India, Afghanistan and Arab countries but also for the international community as a whole. The

Chinese presence at the mouth of Persian Gulf poses a grave threat to the vital energy supplies from the Gulf and the Indian ambitions of becoming the guardian of Indian Ocean. The internal security of Pakistan would also become a source of concern for the European countries in near future as likelihood of Pakistan failing as a state would affect the country's ability to control its nuclear weapons and the risk of proliferation of the nuclear materials. The Persian state under the Ayatollahs with the ambition of exporting its fundamentalist Shia revolution and its open threats to the security of Israel, alarm the international community.

The Baloch aspirations for a united and independent Balochistan raises the spectre of the breakup of Iran and Pakistan. The fear of the conversion of the region into many small unviable mini-states is perhaps one of the reasons for the cautious approach taken by the Western powers regarding the Baloch national question. Neither India nor the Western powers are in a hurry to jump in and announce their clear cut policies regarding the Baloch conflict with Iran and Pakistan. Nevertheless, Iran and Pakistan are intent on over-emphasising the international involvement and the threat of foreign manipulation out of all proportion. The Baloch nationalists believe that this is being used as an excuse to employ excessive force against the Baloch national struggle. The propaganda of foreign involvement in Balochistan is also serving the purpose of the intelligence agencies of Iran and Pakistan to criminalize any expression of national aspirations by the Baloch, whether the aspirations in question are from militant or from legal political parties working in the ambit of the constitutions of these states.

With increasing human rights violation by Pakistan and Iran, for the last two decades, the Baloch have been pleading for the intervention of the international community in Balochistan but getting no positive response, however, Balochistan's strategic location, and its great mineral wealth are bound to make the Baloch national question very important and central to the energy politics of the region and the World. Although, at present there appears to be no international help coming for the establishment of an independent Balochistan; however, one can observe some ground testing from different quarters of the states concerned. Many in the power structures of the West are now openly questioning the usefulness of Pakistan as the guardian of Western interests in South Asia and the Persian Gulf. A potential future stand-off in the relationship of the West with Iran is eminent. Pakistani state is becoming increasingly vulnerable to failure or internal breakdown. With these possible scenarios, there is an increased possibility of the Baloch national question becoming a major international policy matter and sympathetic attitudes towards an independent Balochistan might surface within the international community. Balochistan is believed to be a treasure trove of oil, gas, gold, uranium, titanium and many other minerals. Its geographical location makes it strategically important regarding access to the energy rich Central Asia and the Persian Gulf. The ports in Balochistan would provide the shortest access to the energy resources of Central Asia. A 1500 Kilometre Baloch coast line could play a pivotal role in controlling the Persian Gulf waterways. The strategic location of Balochistan and its mineral reserves could be the cause of policy changes in the relevant capitals. The Baloch question is bound to attract the attention of many forces having economic and strategic stakes in the region or other varied interests.

CHAPTER 18

THE BALOCH NATIONAL STRUGGLE: PROBLEMS AND PROSPECTS

The British writer Charles Caleb Colton once observed that liberty will not descend to a people, a people must raise themselves to liberty; it is a blessing that must be earned before it can be enjoyed. The success of any national liberation struggle can be analysed on the basis of internal strength of the movement, the strength of the occupying power and support from international community. Despite the bloody and protracted resistance against Iran and Pakistan, the hope of national salvation for the Baloch is still to be realized. The causes of the Baloch in-ability to achieve the desired goal of the struggle are several. Internally, their struggle has faced many problems. The Baloch are fighting a war against tremendous odds, their enemies are far more powerful and no external support has been extended to the Baloch cause. However, many developments in regional and international polity are increasing the prospect for the Baloch national struggle to achieve its objective.

THE PROBLEMS OF THE BALOCH NATIONAL STRUGGLE

The failure of the Baloch national struggle to achieve the desired goal of liberation reflects important deficiencies which the Baloch national resistance has faced in the past and is still facing in the 21st century. Major problems facing the struggle are emanating from elements which included the lack of a broad-based political organization, political control over the armed resistance, lack of resources, and lack of collaboration with other national liberation struggles.

PROBLEMS OF UNITY AND POLITICAL MOBILIZATION

A study of 20th century national liberation struggles clearly reveals that the prerequisite for a successful armed resistance is political mobilization- that is, the ability of a nationalist movement to generate sufficient support for its aims in order to be able not only to receive shelter and material support from the general population but, crucially, to sustain the recruitment of politically conscious volunteers for armed resistance activities. National liberation struggle is a political movement by definition. It requires political organization, skilled political leadership and resources to achieve its objectives. As emphasized by Taber, (1965) and Cabral, (1972), the archetypal organizational structure of a national liberation movement is composed of three basic ingredients:

- A nation who desires for liberation,
- A political organization or party to channelize the desire of the nation for liberation, and
- An armed resistance or guerrilla army which can confront the enemy forces on the ground.

In the past, the tribal set up of the Baloch society had provided most of the people with a workable mechanism of action on socio-political issues. It made up for the absence of political parties and groupings. However, with the breakdown of the tribal system, the need for political organization was felt and political groups emerged in Eastern Balochistan during first quarter of the 20th century. During the 1930s, the first political party, the Kalat State National Party was formed. As a quite new phenomenon, initially, it was not able to attract sufficient attention and participation of the Baloch masses. Nevertheless, in the following years it became the major voice of the Baloch people and played a vital role in the period of the short-lived independence and subsequent turbulent period following the occupation of Khanate of Kalat by Pakistan in 1948. However, the culture of political participation and organization could not prosper in Balochistan because the political parties with which the Baloch nationalists were affiliated after the collapse of the Baloch state were never given a free hand to function by the state establishment of Pakistan. They were either crushed, banned or disintegrated into a number of factions. With state manipulations, various factions of the Baloch nationalist parties were usually fighting more bitterly amongst themselves more bitterly than they fought the enemy of the Baloch national struggle. Even in 21st century, after sustaining serious losses, this phenomenon can still be observed among the nationalist groups whether they are functioning inside or outside Balochistan.

In Western Balochistan, historically, the Baloch national struggle was led by tribal chiefs and *hakoms* of various regions. The culture of the political organization only began with the formation of the Balochistan Liberation Front but it could not make organizational networks at grass root level as the leadership was based outside Balochistan and was more concerned with armed resistance rather than efforts at political mobilization. During 1980s, many political groups were formed mostly by political activists and the tribal elite of Western Balochistan living in exile. Divisions and infighting resulted in the creation of many small groups. These groups wasted their energy fighting over trivial issues. No attempts, so far, has been made to unite all groups into a single party or a united front. Earlier attempt at unification with the formation of the Baloch United Front in 2003, failed because of ongoing distrust between the middle class political activists and the tribal elite. Building trust for a workable alliance between the middle class activists and the tribal elite is essential for the progress of nationalist activities in Western Balochistan. Although, the influence of tribal chiefs and *hakoms* in Western Balochistan has been fading in recent decades; they remain, however, a force to be reckoned with and are able to instil enough national inspiration among the Baloch masses. They are still considered to be an invaluable assets in the Baloch national struggle as they can mobilize a large segment of Baloch society.

The history of the Baloch national liberation struggle in Pakistan has been tortuous. It has multiple aspects and its dynamics underwent many changes during the seventy years of occupation. Political agitation and armed resistance activities were simultaneously employed by the leadership of the struggle. In the early decades of Pakistan, the Baloch armed resistance activities were confined to tribal areas; controlled by tribal chiefs affiliated to the Baloch national resistance and mainly concentrated in the Jhalawan and Mari regions. In later decades, the armed resistance became a universal phenomenon in Balochistan and many among the middle class political leaders became involved in confrontational activities against the Pakistani forces. Despite countless restrictions imposed by the state establishment and security agencies, the Baloch nationalist parties in Eastern Balochistan, were able to expand their organizational activities during the past fifteen years. Although, divided, the parties involved in the Baloch national struggle have nevertheless, succeeded in setting up a host of institutions and grass-root organizations throughout Eastern Balochistan. These organizations have provided the infrastructure and local leadership during the ongoing conflict. These political networks and institutions are enabling the Baloch resistance to carry out its activities in a better organized way. However, the lack of unity among nationalist groups and personalities has been a major obstacle in the consolidation of gains in the national liberation struggle. In 2006, while lamenting the lack of unity among the Baloch nationalists, the veteran Baloch leader Nawab Khair Bakhsh Mari pointed out that unfortunately, they [the nationalists] were divided. He observed that although, such disunity happened everywhere in the world in national liberation movements, however, the better option would have been to have a single Baloch party. He emphasised that if this is not feasible, an alliance would do. At present, there is no positive development regarding the unity of Baloch nationalist forces in Eastern Balochistan.

National liberation struggles are the endeavours of the weak against the stronger and for their success it is imperative that they are fought on sound ideological footing under a well-organized party or united front of all nationalist forces. However, the situation of political unity and mass mobilization is far from being satisfactory for the Baloch struggle. The divisions within the nationalist movement is proving to have significant negative consequences. On the one hand, it has prevented the type of mass mobilization required to galvanize continued support for the national cause, and on the other hand, the longer it continues, the resultant outcome would create an unsurmountable disconnect between the masses and the national resistance. Personal, tribal and irrelevant ideological discord caused the Baloch national resistance to split into a number of competing groups, weakening the fighting spirit of resistance activists in recent years. For many analysts, the failure of the Baloch national struggle to develop a broad-based alliance of nationalist forces is detrimental to the aims of the resistance.

THE PROBLEM OF POLITICAL CONTROL OVER ARMED RESISTANCE

In order to achieve their cherished goal, national liberation struggles are bound to employ a wide variety of means and tactics. Although, beginning as peaceful resistance movements, diametrically opposing perceptions of the occupied and occupying nations are the triggers for national liberation struggles to become violent in many instances. Armed resistance has been the rallying cry of the Baloch national struggle throughout; nevertheless, its outcomes have never been more than marginal. Posen (1993), observed that the fear of ethnic extinction or domination motivate ethnic minorities to resort to armed resistance. Based on this threat perception, ethnic minorities arm themselves defensively. This mobilization inducing fear in the dominant nationality of the state, it results in the reciprocal arming and beginning of armed conflict. In this context, armed resistance has been one of the strategies adopted by national liberation struggles in their fight against colonizing and occupying powers. Taber (1965) pointed out that armed resistance is a defensive reaction as the struggle is for the survival of their nation, and the decision to fight and to sacrifice is a moral decision. It is for the people involved in the struggle to choose a particular form of struggle that is feasible, in the given situation of their society, taking into consideration the degree of maturity of their national liberation struggle and the prevailing political conditions in the occupying state. Violence against the Baloch was employed by the Persian and Pakistani states and the armed resistance by the Baloch in their national liberation struggle is a defensive mechanism.

Strict control of armed activities by political institutions of a national liberation struggle is considered to be of fundamental importance. The famous Vietnamese leader Vo Nguyen Giap was persistent in his views that political activities were more important than militant activities, and that armed resistance should be used to safeguard, consolidate, and develop political bases. The Chinese leader Mao se Tung did not conceive armed resistance as an independent form of a national liberation struggle but simply as one aspect of the struggle. The goal of national salvation can be achieved through a combination of different forms of struggle and armed resistance should be the extension of politics by means of armed conflict and not a means in itself. It is a form of political warfare guided by political rather than military considerations. The political education of volunteers involved in the struggle and political control of armed activities are fundamental. A national liberation struggle can only triumph when volunteers of armed resistance have great clarity about what they want and the reason for their involvement in the national resistance. In cases of general uprising many people who join an armed struggle come from different social origins, have less political consciousness and in a society like the Baloch, it is a daunting task for the leadership of the resistance to integrate people of diverse social origins and different levels of political maturity into a disciplined group. It can be observed that in every phase of Baloch resistance, some of the armed resistance groups were acting without a political control. Many analysts of the Baloch resistance movement against Pakistan identified as a major weakness of the struggle, the activities of those armed resistance units, who were without firm political guidance.

Guerrilla warfare is just one of the means, whereby a weak nation can inflict heavy losses on a more powerful enemy. There is a universal agreement among the analysts of national liberation struggle that to be successful, it is must that any resistance should follow the basic rules of a protracted warfare. Adventurism and seeking shortcuts have been identified by scholars on the resistance movements as the cause of major disasters in national liberation struggles. It was observed that in many instances, the resistance had forgotten the basic principle of a national liberation struggle which are to preserve oneself and to annihilate the enemy. Many actions of Baloch fighters, although heroic, resulted in grievous losses for the struggle. Thrill seeking and heroism has no part in a scientific national resistance struggle. In this context, the Baloch intellectuals and scholars have been urging the leadership and cadre of the resistance on the need to realize that there is no shortcut in wars of independence and any national liberation struggle involves protracted struggles against the enemy. They have been emphasising that the focus of a national resistance should not be based on achieving a short cut to victory.

Many among the cadre of the struggle and social analysts have identified another mistake committed by the resistance fighters, because of lack of political maturity. In some places in Balochistan, the armed resistance groups were responsible for antagonizing local power groups which resulted in the formation of rival hostile blocs. It is among the fundamentals of political behaviour in a national liberation struggle, that it should not try for too much and should not smash the existing social system but use it to its advantage. However, it appears that contemporary Baloch national resistance has not followed these basic norms with resultant mishaps. In order to defeat the aggression of a more powerful and a brutal occupying force, it is imperative for the Baloch resistance to understand dynamics of its own society. A prominent activist of the Baloch national resistance in Pakistan observed that this understanding only comes from political indoctrination and firm political control on activities of the armed resistance groups. He was emphasising that it becomes the duty of the political organizations and their affiliated workers to ideologically prepare volunteers for participation in a long and tortuous struggle for national salvation. He was of the opinion that the leadership should make very clear to them that they have to obey the basic principles of a national liberation struggle. Otherwise, he stressed that we [the leadership of the resistance] must realize the fact that without firm backing from the masses and without firm political control over the armed activities would provide the occupying state with the opportunity to portray the armed resistance fighters as bandits, terrorists or insurgents.

A national resistance against any occupation is composed of both- political and an armed struggle. The success of a national liberation struggle is heavily dependent on a proper or balanced combination of political and militant activities. On the one hand, the political struggle manifests itself with organizational structures, individuals, institutions, or groups who have set for themselves the objective of achieving the proclaimed goal of national salvation by adopting political strategies which serve their purpose. While on the other hand, the target of the armed struggle is to make the region ungovernable and to weaken the occupying state by draining its financial resources in a protracted resistance. A protracted struggle also makes the aggressive state morally bankrupt as it takes extreme and inhuman measures against the resisting nation. The lack of close collaboration between activities of both segments of the national struggle has been pointed out not only by the analysts but many among the resistance leaders in recent times as a major weakness of the Baloch national resistance.

THE PROBLEM OF RESOURCES

Finding enough financial resources for the national resistance has been a constant problem for the national liberation struggle in both parts of Balochistan. Balochistan was kept by occupying powers as one of the economically backward regions in the world. Basically, the Baloch economy is based on agriculture and animal husbandry. Unfortunately, with scanty rainfalls and a growing population, it became unsustainable in recent decades. Since the end of the 20th century, limited business activities have flourished in both Western and Eastern Balochistan. However, as the natural resources and financial leverages are in the control of the occupying states, the nascent Baloch business class found it hard to get established. As the financial sources of the Baloch resistance were donations from this class and from the pool of tribal resources, the resistance was never in the optimum position to carry out its activities as and when desired. The lack of resources is among the main reasons for resistance not being very effective.

THE PROBLEM OF RELIGIOUS ELEMENTS

The Pakistani and Iranian states have used political or extremist Islam as a retrogressive force in the achievement of their goals and objectives. Religion was also used as a political tool by these two countries in their assimilation endeavours. They have justified the subjugation of various national entities in the name of religion as they see Islam as the only unifying force for the state. Increased penetration of extremist Islam in a secular Baloch society and the mushroom growth of Islamic groups in both parts of Balochistan is a cause of worry for the Baloch national resistance.

In the case of Pakistan, Islam, from the very inception of the "Allah Given Country", has been an integral part of official dogma.

Primarily it was to justify the creation of Pakistan and later on, for the substitution of a common Muslim identity for Pakistan. As a political instrument, religion was considered important by the establishment in its efforts to sustain the artificially created state. From 1970s, Islamization in Balochistan was used as a weapon against the Baloch national struggle in a very planned and systematic manner. Islamic scholars were brought from other parts of the country, who helped the local religious elements in establishing *Madrasas* (religious schools) in every corner of Balochistan. The establishment also openly supported religious political parties in an attempt to dilute the overwhelming support for the NAP, which was the political face of the Baloch national struggle. The objective was to counter the Baloch nationalist sentiments with religious ones. Although, the State could not achieve its desired objective of Islamization in Balochistan, because of the fierce reaction from the Baloch nationalists; nevertheless, making the Baloch "perfect Muslims" remained an important component of a long-term state strategy. The military establishment during the last 15 years has encouraged the setting up of more *Madrasas* to achieve two objectives; firstly, to create and strengthen extremist groups in support of its counter-insurgency strategy and secondly, to recruit Jihadists for subversive activities in Afghanistan and India. As a consequence of these state policies, the role of the *Mullahs* in Baloch society has increased exponentially and in a secular and tolerant Baloch society there is growing danger of spreading religious fundamentalism. Signs of increasing sectarianism and radicalization can be observed in today's Balochistan. It is not surprising that the phenomenon of *Tablighi Jamaat* (the group is known for its jihadi preaching) is increasing in Balochistan over the last thirty to forty years. The military establishment facilitates the presence of extremist organizations such as the Taliban, al-Qaeda, *Lashkar-e-Janghvi, Sipah-e-Sahaba* Pakistan, Imamia Student Organization, and *Sipah-e-Muhammad, Harakat-ul-Mujadeen* and *Harakat Jihad-e-Islami* in the northern areas of Balochistan. Many death squads are run by these religious outfits in collaboration with state security agencies and openly used in the kill and dump policy of the state in Balochistan. These organizations are also used in fomenting sectarian clashes in Baloch society. In recent years, reports of attacks on *Zikri* community members are increasing in number. As emphasised by a leader of the resistance, the onslaught on the *Zikri* community is the part of a devious plan to stir up sectarian animosity among the Baloch and to divide the Baloch national resistance on sectarian grounds.

The Persian state is equally fanning the flames of religious sectarianism in Balochistan. There are reports of a concerted efforts by the regime of the Ayatollahs to convert the Baloch into Shi'ism in different areas of Western Balochistan. It has also been the part of regime's policy to facilitate the Baloch Sunni religious elements, in order to counter-balance the nationalist activities. The opening of *Madrasas* in the remotest areas of Western Balochistan is officially patronized. Although, Iran is in conflict with the Arab states for various political, economic and sectarian reasons, its otherwise very vigilant security agencies are keeping a blind eye in matters of funding for certain religious schools in Balochistan from Arab countries. The Persian state has also trained, equipped and facilitated the Shia Hazara community in Eastern Balochistan. This is believed to be the response of the Iranian state towards Pakistan's interference in Western Balochistan as the Iranian government believes that Pakistan is responsible for the militant activities of *Jundallah* and other Sunni organizations in Western Balochistan. With Pakistan, Iran and the Arab countries using sectarian and extremist Islam as political tools in the region, Balochistan is being used as a battle field for their proxy sectarian war which is very detrimental to the Baloch national struggle as these extremist religious groups are also being used to counter the Baloch national resistance.

Iran and Pakistan are militant religious countries poised towards proselytization. In recent years, the leadership of the resistance has been deliberating for adopting a feasible strategy to counter the state efforts of Islamization and radicalization in the Baloch society. They believe that devising such a strategy is imperative for the success of the Baloch national struggle. As a leader of the Baloch resistance from Western Balochistan expressed that now it became a priority for the leadership and organizations affiliated with the Baloch national resistance to oppose forcefully the lateral entry of religious extremism and sectarianism before it is able to inflict severe damage to the integrity of Baloch society and the struggle for national liberation.

SOLIDARITY WITH OTHER NATIONAL LIBERATION STRUGGLES

A struggle for national salvation cannot survive in isolation. The struggle for independence can benefit from the solidarity with other regional, and international nationalist movements, human rights organizations and other non-governmental organizations. One of the major problems facing the Baloch struggle is the lack of any meaningful collaboration with relevant organizations and national liberation movements in other parts of the World.

With the banning of the NAP which was an umbrella organization of various nationalist groups from different nationalities in Pakistan, the coordination between Sindhis, Seraikis and Pashtun was not re-established on a solid footing. The Confederation Front and PONM were good initiatives in this regard, but they could not be made into effective alliances for various reasons. One can observe some closeness between the nascent Sindhi national resistance and the Baloch national struggle in recent years. However, this closeness was not formalized. It is confined to personal contacts between the Baloch and Sindhi leadership inside Pakistan and cooperation between Sindhi and Baloch Diaspora in organizing demonstrations to highlight human right issues of Sindh and Balochistan.

In Iran, several national entities are struggling for their national rights. The Baloch leadership is convinced that an alliance with these national struggles could be in the advantage of the Baloch resistance in Iran; however, they have failed to devise a robust strategy for coordinating the activities of Kurds, Azeris and Turcomens. One of the vocal and active political figure of the

Baloch national resistance in Iran admitted that although, there has been some coordination between the Baloch, Kurds and other nationalist groups operating in Diaspora; nevertheless, a working alliance of national movements of various nationalities in Iran which could have provided much needed publicity and access to the Baloch national resistance internationally is missing.

THE PROBLEM OF EXTERNAL SUPPORT

Apart from factors of internal dynamics, the role of the international community is of vital importance in the triumph of a national liberation struggle. The prospect for gaining the right of self-determination, not only depends on adopting the strategies and tactics of a protracted national liberation struggle on behalf of a colonized nation, but also on the degree of international support. There is no example in the history of a national liberation where a powerful colonial power has been defeated without the help of another power. The Chinese leader Mao (1949), believed that it is a fallacy that victory over the occupying forces is possible without international help. For the moment, no external power has extended any material or diplomatic support for an independent Balochistan. The international community has kept a blind eye on the plight of the Baloch people, despite being well aware of the gross violations of human rights by Iran and Pakistan. The oppression and subjugation of the Baloch and other national entities in these states could not have lasted so long without the compliance of the major powers. To achieve some short term objectives, the civilized world has patronized and sustained states occupying Balochistan. The Persian and the Pakistani states are content that in the present circumstances, creation of a Baloch state is neither desired nor in the interest of any regional or international power. Some of the analysts believe that as the Baloch right of self-determination would certainly end up with the breakup of Iran and Pakistan; the international community has shown its anxiety concerning a possible breakup of these states and its consequences regionally and internationally. The principle of the sanctity of international borders is another inhibiting factor regarding international support for the Baloch national struggle.

THE PROSPECTS FOR THE SUCCESS OF THE BALOCH NATIONAL STRUGGLE

Several factors can enhance the prospects of the Baloch national struggle in the achievement of its desired aims. The Baloch will for living a dignified and independent life made them resilient to an unbelievable level. With the changing dynamics of Baloch resistance, the Baloch national struggle has gained new impetus. The states occupying Balochistan are becoming increasingly vulnerable because of internal social, economic and political tensions and their growing isolation in the international community.

THE BALOCH WILL FOR INDEPENDENCE

The desire to overthrow the yoke of foreign rule has been one of the defining characteristics of the Baloch. The Baloch retain a strong sense of national awareness. This had been very strong because of a long and tortuous history of facing oppression of many ways. Economic, cultural, political and physical oppression to the point of genocide has been instrumental in the development of the Baloch sense of belonging to a wider Baloch nation. Continued occupation and division of their land have sharpened their national feelings. These sentiments have been the prime force in the Baloch participation in their national resistance whether it was political mobilization or armed conflict. Throughout Baloch history, countless deeds of magnificent courage and determination to defend the Baloch land, dignity and sovereignty can be observed. The subjugating measures of the Pakistani and Persian states did not terrify the Baloch and instead of weakening the demand for national liberation, it has galvanised the situation in which the Baloch almost to a man are opposed to any form of compromise in their demand for independence. In contemporary Balochistan, there is not a single family unaffected by the long drawn conflict in one way or the other. This affliction of a universal nature among the Baloch appears to be the fundamental raw material which is being converted and utilized by various nationalist resistance groups to strengthen their organizational functionality and militant potential. It is the great success of the struggle that today in both parts of Balochistan, the majority of individual Baloch has become an actual or potential participant in the Baloch national resistance. From 2005 onwards, in terms of active resistance, young men, boys, and girls in towns and villages were involved in political mobilization or armed attacks against the Pakistani security forces and their sympathizers.

Both states failed in their endeavours to crush the Baloch national resistance. The Baloch resilience is extraordinary. The flame of overthrowing foreign domination has always burned brightly in their hearts. They have withstood the onslaught of two powerful states in the region with immense sacrifice in men and material. Taking into account, the historical context of the Baloch resistance, it appears that the Baloch will for living a dignified and independent life will haunt the occupying states for ever.

CHANGING DYNAMICS OF BALOCH RESISTANCE

It can be observed that in recent years, a wider debate has been initiated on the role of political mobilization and armed resistance. There has been observable realization among the leadership and cadre, that although armed struggle remains the highest stage of conflict with occupying states, it is not the only possible form of struggle. The understanding is gaining ground, that a successful militant campaign requires careful political mobilization of the masses, the building up of a well-structured political organization which must not only persuade the masses to support the armed resistance but also to control the militant activities.

With the changing dimensions of the Baloch resistance, the prospects for adopting feasible strategies in order to achieve the desired goal of the struggle are increasing. The Baloch society has undergone profound changes during the last fifty years. The traditional social and tribal structure has drastically altered. Nomadism had gone and with the development of numerous townships throughout Balochistan, a middle class has appeared on the Baloch socio-political horizon. With this change in society, the essence of leadership is also undergoing a change. It has altered from a movement being led by tribal chiefs to one where the middle class political activists and personalities are gaining ground. While during 19th and 20th century, the Baloch tribal chiefs and *hakoms* were in the forefront of resistance movements against the British, Iran and Pakistan, in the contemporary phase of the struggle, a large number of political cadre and some top leaders have emerged from the larger middle class segment of the population. Now the leadership of the national struggle is comprised of elements both from middle class and tribal elite. The Baloch nationalist circles and intelligentsia are hopeful that this combination of leadership will further strengthen the national resistance.

INTERNATIONAL ISOLATION OF PERSIAN AND PAKISTANI STATES

Increased isolation of the states occupying Balochistan is raising new hopes for the Baloch national struggle. Iran is heavily involved in various subversive activities in Iraq, Syria, Lebanon, Bahrain, Yemen and Afghanistan. Its efforts at imposing Shi'ism and exporting its brand of Islamic revolution to other countries has created socio-political disturbances in many Arab countries. Iran's nuclear ambitions and its desire to destroy Israel, are open challenges for the civilized world. It is actively involved in the civil war in Yemen. The Taliban insurgents in Afghanistan are reported to receive funding from Iran and some of them are given sanctuary in Eastern Iran. The ambition of the Ayatollahs is to dominate the region at all costs, thus causing the international isolation of this fanatical state.

Pakistan has adopted terrorism as a policy tool since its creation. Initially, this policy was aimed at India but from the

1970s, it became imperative for Pakistan to destabilize Afghanistan by creating and patronizing various religious terrorist groups. Taking advantage of efforts by the Western powers to dislodge Soviet Union from Afghanistan during the 1980s, the Pakistani establishment was successful in creating a web of extremist organizations capable of carrying out terrorist activities both regionally and internationally. Using these radical organizations, Pakistan has provoked religious turmoil in many parts of India, besides carrying out bloody attacks inside India on many occasions. It has been successful in destabilizing Afghanistan for many decades. It is now an open secret that Al-Qaeda, the Taliban, and sympathizers of Islamic State in Iraq and Syria (ISIS), together with countless other terrorist organizations are being supported by the state establishment of Pakistan. They are used as the first line of defence in their doctrine of the preservation of the integrity of Pakistan. In the context of international terrorism, Pakistan is now perceived to be part of the problem.

Iran and Pakistan are in possession of nuclear arsenals. Pakistan's nuclear program was supposed to be motivated as a deterrent against the conventional military prowess of India. However, with the export of nuclear know-how to Iran, Libya and North Korea, it soon became apparent that the Pakistani nuclear program was indeed a nuclear threat to World peace. It is the state policy of using the threat of its nuclear arsenal, as a bargaining chip in seeking economic and political concessions from the United States and the European Union as they are worried about the serious risk of nuclear weapons winding up in hands of terrorists. The case of Iran is not much different from that of Pakistan. The Ayatollahs pursuit for nuclear weapons has caused much alarm throughout the world. Although, the spectre of a military invasion to destroy nuclear facilities of Iran was postponed with the signing of an agreement with the international community in 2015. This allowed international observers to inspect its nuclear facilities; however, taking into consideration the Ayatollahs' mind set of dominating the region, Iran will never give up its nuclear ambitions. This will ultimately leads to Iran's further international isolation and it certainly invite a military response from the West and Israel.

The nuclear threat from Iran and Pakistan has another very dangerous dimension. Both religious fundamentalist states are constitutionally bound to impose Islam throughout the World. Both states are in the firm grip of a ruling establishment dominated by religious fanatics. Their national psyche has been moulded into a profound distrust of the civilized world. Dueck and Takeyh (2007), observed that the idea that Iran can be appeased or its ambitions curtailed, is an improbable one. The same conclusion holds regarding the Pakistani nuclear policy. There is now a growing realization in the West, that a strategy of pure accommodation with Pakistan and Iran could be positively dangerous. The fact is now increasingly being accepted by many policy makers in the West that as the socio-political systems in Iran and Pakistan are fanatical to the core, they are beyond redemption. It is now becoming more urgent for the international community to consider the real objectives of the nuclear program of these states. Neither Iran and nor Pakistan is in a position to withstand any real pressure or military attack from the international community and both states would crumble like a house of cards.

The Pakistani plan of leasing out the whole exploratory rights and coastal region of Balochistan to the Chinese, will affect the power balance in the Indian Ocean, giving China the ultimate control of the energy routes of Central Asia and Persian Gulf. This would not be acceptable to the US and the West. If the circumstances governing the geo-strategic situation of South-central Asia and Gulf region changed drastically against the interests of Western powers, then opportunities might arise that could see the Baloch case for independence being viewed more favourably by the Western powers.

Iran and Pakistan have implemented a persistent policy of destabilization in their neighbourhoods. There is an increased realization among the friends and foes of both countries that Iran and Pakistan are the epicentre of terrorism and a danger putting in jeopardy the stability of the region and the World peace and that their nuclear programs have become liabilities for the international community. There is also the realization that due to the inherent fallacies in the founding doctrines of these countries, there is no hope of any reform and the only way to secure peace and stability in the region is to dismantle these fanatical states. Sooner or later the international community will act. This will benefit the Baloch national struggle by default.

THE VULNERABILITY OF IRAN AND PAKISTAN

Weaknesses of a colonial power has always been the strength of a colonised people. The internal dynamics of Iran and Pakistan are changing and they are moving fast towards self-destruction. Both states occupying the Baloch land are facing severe social, political and economic crises. With flawed state ideologies, Iran and Pakistan have antagonized all constituent nationalities in their respective countries, creating insolvable internal conflicts. The masses in general, have been excluded from the political power structure by prolonged dictatorial regimes. With the security establishment taking the bulk of their gross domestic product in the guise of securing the national and territorial integrity of the state, both states are on the brink of economic collapse. Iran and Pakistan already fulfils many of the criteria that characterizes a failed state.

According to the list published by Foreign Policy in 2010, Pakistan is among the top ten of states defined as failed. Economically it is a known "basket case", surviving on the handouts of Western countries. Its superfluous Islamic nation ideology has manifested itself in a wide spread religious sectarian divide within its society. The Sindhis are organizing their national resistance and violent clashes have already started between armed Sindhi groups and security forces. The state establishment is reacting with great brutality, further alienating the second largest nation in Pakistan. With the denial of democratic rights, and the breakdown of political institutions, the state is solely dependent on its armed forces for its integrity. Pakistan has long been a security state and the welfare of its citizens has not been considered important by its military establishment. Sixty-percent of its 'Gross National Product' is being spent on its armed forces. The military establishment which facilitated the transformation of Pakistan into a security state is calling the shots in an atmosphere, where every national entity has been alienated; religious sectarianism and violence is at the highest level; and regional and international powers are being provoked to intervene in Pakistan. All rational individuals in Pakistan are losing faith in the future of this artificially created state. As observed by Shaikh (2009), the Pakistani state's dysfunctionality stems from causes ranging from its failure to withstand military dictatorship; uneven social and economic developments; its severe ethnic divisions; and the pursuit of a questionable foreign policy. The ruling alliance of military, *Muhajirs*, and *Mullahs* has successfully created deep fissures in the politics and social systems of the state. With unlimited corporate and political interests; a culture of rampant corruption in rank and file of the military is endemic, affecting the overall capability of the forces. With the moral bankruptcy of the *Mullahs* and the continuous fabrication and distortion of the history of the region by state sponsored *Muhajir* writers and intellectuals, the Pakistani people are forced to live in a fool's paradise. Every actor in the power structure of the state is busy building his own castle of sand. Construed on very false perceptions and for the achievement of the goal of dominating the various nationalities of Pakistan, the ruling alliance has witnessed observable cracks within in recent years. The *Muhajirs*, who were united into a political party by the military establishment in 1980s, are becoming out of control. The *Mullahs* have been transformed from a very insignificant social class into a dominant, power hungry force, and are threatening its own ally, the almighty military of Pakistan. Many socio-political analysts believe that the internal situation will transform into civil war as from the state patronized religious institutions which are spread all over the country, and especially in Punjab, nearly 350,000 religious fanatics are being produced annually, indoctrinated with militant sectarian dogma. The media, in the firm control of the army mostly through

Muhajir intellectuals, writers and journalists is working to spread hatred against the neighbours of Pakistan. Lies, hypocrisy and the rottenness of the state ideology is increasingly manifesting itself in the social, political and economic spheres. The infrastructure, on which a state's economy is run, increasingly in the process of complete disintegration. Tax collection is negligible, the economy is taking a downward path, the political processes and politico-social institutions are weakening rapidly, the standard of education has declined and the level of poverty has increased exponentially during last 30 years.

The Persian state has also struggled with its own internal social and political contradictions since the takeover of the Ayatollahs. The long term UN sanctions inflicted a high toll on the economy of the Islamic republic which is solely based on the oil resources. Fluctuations in the price of oil in recent years worsened the economic prospects of the state. Nearly all ethnic minorities have been totally alienated by the regime of the Ayatollahs. Within Persian society, the use of blatant and arbitrary coercive powers has created a definite schism. Iran's Islamization is no longer a banner for the new social order. Popular disaffection has increased because of the economic crash and social suffocation. Once attractive revolutionary/Islamic rhetoric sounds increasingly empty and outdated. The ruling clique of the Ayatollahs is clearly divided on how to handle the popular disaffection. With the worsening economic situation, the anger of the Iranian middle class is on the rise. Falling oil prices are preventing the state from carrying out its program of subsidizing basic goods, further alienating the lower classes in the population.

Among the factors which are important in the progress of a colonized nation's endeavours for salvation, the internal dynamics of the occupying state is of fundamental importance. Economic weaknesses and societal dissent within colonial powers have played vital roles in the post Second World War decolonization process. Pakistan and Iran are both vulnerable states and the process of degeneration in their religious fundamentalist and fanatical elite is observable. As will be discussed in the following pages, a combination of social, economic and political indicators shows the vulnerability of both the Pakistani and Persians states which are bound to be exploited by regional and international interest groups and states. With apparent social and economic collapse of the occupying states, the Baloch national struggle will be in a better position within the near future.

THE PROSPECT OF INTERNATIONAL INTERVENTION

The legitimacy of Iran and Pakistan as states can be questioned on many counts. Their use of terrorism as state policy, nuclear blackmailing and the brutalities and gross human rights violations of minority nationalities have exposed them to an increased prospect of physical international intervention.

Brilmayer (1989) observed that, the legitimacy of a state is assessed on the moral authority to govern. In contemporary international political milieu, generally, there are four criteria which indicate whether a country has credible and legitimate justification for achieving a status of being a sovereign state. These are:

1. When a state involves in any kind of genocidal act debasing all notions of human rights, individual liberties and human worth.
2. When a state harbors, promotes, finances or aids transnational criminal organizations, which includes terror organizations, drug cartels and human trafficking circles.
3. When the state violates the integrity of another nation which has legitimate claims to sovereignty.
4. When a state violates established norms dealing with nuclear weapons or illegitimate nuclear material.

Iran and Pakistan fulfil none of the criteria of a legal sovereign state. Iran and Pakistan have been actively involved in various acts of genocide. Iran has carried out mass murder of the Baloch, Kurds, Ahwazi Arabs, Azeri and other nationalities. The Iranian authorities have been involved in the physical elimination of the whole adult population of Baloch villages in recent years. Denying the Baloch and other national entities, the right of education in their mother languages, denial of the right of freely practicing their religious beliefs and denial of other basic human rights are acts of genocide. Iran is known to have harboured and nurtured various extremist organizations which have been involved in terrorist activities in Israel, Syria, Yemen, Bahrain, Afghanistan and several other areas in the Middle East. It has also facilitated human trafficking into Europe. Thousands of people from Pakistan and Afghanistan have entered Europe illegally through Iran. Iranian efforts to acquire nuclear weapons are serious threat to regional and international security.

The term genocide refers to violent crimes committed against a people with the intent to destroy its existence as a group. According to UNO, it is to commit following acts with the intent to destroy in whole or in part of, a national, ethnic, racial or religious group:

(a) Killing members of the group;
(b) Causing serious bodily or mental harm to members of the group;
(c) Deliberately inflicting on the group conditions of life calculated to bring about its physical destruction in whole or in part;
(d) Imposing measures intended to prevent births within the group;
(e) Forcibly transferring children of the group to another group (UNO, 1948).

Assimilation is the imposition of an alien language, culture, religious beliefs and national myths on a subjugated national entity by the dominant nation. In other words this is ethnocide which is the destruction of a people's culture. Iran and Pakistan have both signed various international covenants regarding human right issues including the International covenant on Civil and Political Rights (ICCPR), the International Covenant on Economic, Social and Cultural Rights (ICESR), the Convention on the Rights of the Child (CRC), and the International Convention for the Elimination of All Forms of Racial Discrimination (ICERD). Both countries had violated every one of these conventions regarding the Baloch. Both states have violated the UN resolutions throughout, with impunity.

The genocide actions of Pakistan in Balochistan and Sindh have been going on for many years. The violation of the rights of the religious minorities and the denial of the national rights of the Baloch, Sindhis, Seraikis and Pashtuns are genocide activities by the Pakistani religious state. The creation and nurturing of numerous terrorist and religious fundamentalist organizations by the state establishment of Pakistan is now an open secret. The Pakistani secret agency, Inter-Services Intelligence (ISI) is actively involved in destabilizing activities in Afghanistan through the Taliban and Al-Qaida. They are also involved in supporting the Islamic State in Iraq and Syria (ISIS). In order to sustain the insurgency in Afghanistan, Taliban and other fanatical groups are heavily dependent upon the military establishment for supplies, training and sanctuary. Carrying out terrorist activities in India is part of the Pakistani state policy of using terrorism for achieving foreign policy objectives. It is a known fact that the Pakistan army is carrying out its drug business in Balochistan and the Khyber Pashtunkhwa Provinces in collaboration with local and international drug dealers. Pakistan has not only illegally acquired nuclear weapons but it has exported nuclear technology to North Korea, Iran and Libya in violation of established international standards on nuclear proliferation.

Iran is not much different from Pakistan in killing its own citizens. Barbaric measures against political opponents, national entities and religious minorities, and an economy based on smuggling its oil products to neighbouring countries and the black market is the face of today's Iran. The Persian state has failed to meet national aspirations of its constituent national entities. It is not only the Baloch, but other national groups, who also strongly perceive their identities are threatened and targeted by state policies based on a concept of Iranian nationalism composed of

Persian chauvinism and Shiite sectarianism. This has led to societal insecurity, undermining the legitimacy of the state.

Iran and Pakistan are in clear violations of various UN resolutions and covenants. the UN declaration on the rights of persons belonging to national or ethnic, religious and linguistic minorities states that States shall protect the existence of national or ethnic, cultural, religious and linguistic identities of the minorities within their respective territories, and shall encourage conditions for the promotion of that identity. Both states are following a policy of assimilation of other national entities into their artificially created state national identities. Gross violations of human rights in both Western and Eastern Balochistan can be seen in the context of the Iranian and Pakistani attempts to quash the Baloch national struggle. During the long period of subjugation, any expression of nationalist sentiment by the Baloch has been an anathema to the authorities of these two states, and has provoked strong, ruthless and inhuman measures. These measures have not been limited to those who have been engaged in armed resistance, but has extended to any non-violent political, social or cultural activity. The Pakistani and Iranian security agencies, death squads, paramilitary forces and armed forces have committed individual or mass murders, inhuman torture, forced disappearance, fuelling religious and sectarian hatred, and kidnapping for ransom in both parts of Balochistan for many decades. Thousands of the Baloch in Pakistan have been internally displaced in recent years and thousands of others were forced to flee Iran and Pakistan to save their lives.

Iran and Pakistan are increasingly moving towards becoming failed states and their case needs urgent intervention by the international community. As pointed out by Miller (2011), the international community must be able to study the situation on the ground, and understand the type and degree of state failure, and formulate strategies accordingly. Buchanan (2003), emphasized that the legitimacy of states in the international legal system must be defined in some threshold approximation to full or perfect justice and basic human rights should serve as that threshold. Because of injustices and acts of genocide, illegitimate states cannot command the loyalty of their population. According to Rotberg (2003), failed states are tense, deeply conflicted, dangerous, and contested bitterly by warring factions; government troops battle armed revolts led by one or more rivals; the official authorities face two or more insurgencies; varieties of civil unrest; communal discontent, and a plethora of dissent directed at the state and at groups within the state. Convulsed by internal violence, economic and social turmoil, the Persian and Pakistani states are no longer in a position to deliver positive political, social and economic goods to their citizens. They are losing legitimacy in the eyes and hearts of their citizens. The Iranian and Pakistani state terrorism has also gone global, endangering the peace and tranquillity of faraway societies. Anarchic situations, dismal economic performance and increased sectarian divide together with tensions between various national entities have brought the fundamentalist religious state of Pakistan and Iran to the brink.

The persistent state of instability in a region which is vital for the energy supply of major industrial powers, can be another cause of international anxiety. The Baloch national resistance in both countries has been able to conduct fairly large-scale militant activities especially in Pakistani held Balochistan in recent years. In the context of continued bloodshed in both parts of Balochistan, causing destabilization in a strategically important region of the World, the international community, especially the West, will be forced to come to understand the reality of the Baloch national question, if they wish to safeguard their own national interests in the region or to secure peace and security in the region.

It is the reality of the interests of various regional and international powers in the region that could make an independent Balochistan a likely or unlikely outcome of the Baloch national struggle. It is clear that with the means of surveillance, modern weaponry and sources of control and violence available to states occupying the Baloch land, the Baloch national resistance could only effectively operate with international assistance. The reality is that the Baloch dream of regaining their sovereignty not only depends on the simultaneous collapse of Iran and Pakistan, but also on active support of the United States, its allies, Afghanistan and India, and the European Union. The Baloch resistance against Iran and Pakistan failed on many occasions to seize historic opportunities, when the Baloch could have gained meaningful assistance from the international community. However, many developments in the internal dynamics of Iran and Pakistan and some factors in regional and international polity might change the situation in favour of the Baloch national struggle. In the near future, the international community will be forced to take action against Iran and Pakistan for obvious reasons. Although, they may use the situation in their own national interests, by default, the Baloch resistance may receive support from unexpected quarters in the coming years.

THE BALOCH NATIONAL QUESTION IS WAITING FOR A JUST RESOLUTION

Following the devastations of Second World War, to maintain the physical hold on their colonial possessions in Asia and Africa became untenable for the colonial powers. Granting independence to many colonised people became imperative. However, to protect their long-standing economic and strategic interests, the withdrawing colonial powers created many artificial countries in Asia and Africa by drawing arbitrary state boundaries, dividing nations and incorporating several nations into multinational states against their will. This resulted in turmoil and protracted conflicts in many regions bringing untold miseries to the people. The Baloch conflict with Iran and Pakistan is one of the consequences of such policies of the colonial powers.

The Baloch national struggle evolved as a result of the illegal occupation of the Baloch land by Pakistan and Iran. It developed as a reaction to the imposition of alien cultural traditions, at the expense of the traditional Baloch socio-cultural and political value systems which were destroyed or corrupted in a systematic and organized way. The introduction of religious narrow-mindedness

313

and fundamentalism by occupying states was seen by the Baloch as an attempt to replace their secular and democratic identity. The Baloch consider that the exploitation of their natural resources and so-called developmental programs initiated by the occupying states are the ruthless plunder of their natural wealth. They see the state sponsored settlement of people from dominant nationalities of Iran and Pakistan in various regions of Balochistan, as an attempt to bring about demographic changes in order to achieve their aim of making them a minority in their homeland. The Baloch perceive these state endeavours a threat to the identity of the Baloch as a national entity. The past few decades have witnessed a massive acceleration in the rate at which the Baloch have been deprived of their lands and livelihoods by imposed development programs. Unchecked resource exploitation combined with what is perceived by the Baloch as 'developmental aggression' poses grave and irreversible threats to their economic existence.

The Baloch are a people that has had their country taken away and separated into many countries. The Persians and Pakistanis not only invaded and occupied their land, but also made intrusions in their socio-cultural way of life. Their history has been distorted, their language is at the brink of extinction and their secular beliefs are being over-shadowed by a fundamentalist Islamic social outlook. They want to live in freedom and dignity in their own land according to their own socio-cultural traditions. The Baloch claim to independence is based on an interpretation of specific rights in international law or convention and the more general right of all nations to self-determination. Blood and tears should no longer be the destiny of the Baloch. The Baloch desire dignity, liberty and prosperity in a peaceful way. They are not fond of war and neither have they wanted to create conflict. They have never cherished the idea of dying or killing in their conflicts with superior powers. However, the powers which occupy Balochistan have left no other way for the Baloch but to take arms and fight in order to regain their national sovereignty.

The Persian and Pakistani state repression against the Baloch is counter-productive. The momentum for a Baloch state will increase rather than to recede. The popular support for the resistance is growing and both states are unable to prevent this phenomenon. The Baloch national question in Iran and Pakistan will not only be a constant source of destabilization for these repressive states, but the Baloch struggle for the right of self-determination, by implication impacts on regional and global peace. The growing armed resistance of the Baloch in Iran and Pakistan may also cause of inter-state conflicts in near future, causing regional and global insecurity.

The Baloch, with their immense sacrifices have proved that they are committed to freedom and human values in a part of world which is engulfed with extremism, terrorism, fundamentalism and fanaticism of all kinds. Resolving the Baloch national question is in the interest of the international community. The Baloch national question could be a key factor in the seemingly unending war against terrorism. While the international community is busy dealing with other disturbances in the Middle East, it has neglected or over-looked the protracted and bloody conflict of the Baloch with Iran and Pakistan. The powerful stake holders in the war against international terrorism, emanating from Islamic fundamentalism, have ignored the importance of the Baloch national question as an important fulcrum for changing the balance of power between Islamic fanaticism and the democratic-secular forces in the region. The Baloch with their secular mind set and with their geographic location in the centre of the region, surrounded by the intolerant religious and fanatical mind-sets of the Arabs, Persians and Pakistanis, can play a vital role in bringing peace and stability in this volatile region. The emergence of democratic and secular sovereign states in the region as a result of granting the right of self-determination to the Baloch and other oppressed nations, will counter the religious fundamentalist states of Pakistan and Iran and will contribute to regional and world security.

The Baloch conflict with Iran and Pakistan is a tale of oppression, subjugation and ruthlessness on the part of powers occupying the Baloch land. The Baloch are trapped in the vice grip of two religious fundamentalist states of Iran and Pakistan which are determined to subjugate them. This has led to human suffering on a genocidal scale. The conflict between the Baloch and Iranian and Pakistani states is among the bloodiest and protracted national liberation struggles in contemporary history. However, it appears that the tale of blood and tears will continue in Balochistan, because neither of the states occupying it will listen to the voice of reason, by stopping their policies of repression and assimilation nor the Baloch will give up their struggle for a dignified existence in a sovereign Balochistan.

The silence of international community on the plight of millions of the Baloch, is a black stain on the conscience of the humanity. The International community must act before it is too late for the Baloch. The Baloch conflict with Iran and Pakistan needs resolution and the intervention of the international community is imperative in this respect. The resolution of the protracted conflict of the Baloch with Iran and Pakistan lies in creating a polity that recognises the legitimate national rights of the Baloch to a sovereign state. The only peaceful solution of the Baloch conflict with Iran and Pakistan is ascertaining the free will of the Baloch people by holding a referendum under the auspices of the UN, after putting the entire Baloch land under the mandate of the UN for a limited period.

REFERENCES:

Abbas, Hassan (2005) <u>Pakistan's Drift into Extremism: Allah, the Army, and America's War on Terror</u>. Arbor: Pluto Press.

Adontz, N (1970) <u>Armenia in the Period of Justinian</u>. Translated by N. G. Garsoïan. Lisbon: Calouste Gulbenkian Foundation

Ahmad, K (2006) "Pakistan: Vision and Reality, Past and Future," <u>The Muslim World</u>, April, 96.2, pp. 363-379.

Ahmad, K.S (1964) <u>A Geography of Pakistan</u>. Karachi: National Textbook Board.

Ahmad, S. I (1992) <u>Balochistan: it's strategic Importance</u>. Karachi: Royal Book Company

Ahmadzai, M.N.K (1995) <u>Tarikh e Baloch o Balochistan</u> (in Urdu). Quetta: United Printers.

Aitchison, C.U (1929) <u>A collection of treaties, engagements and sanads relating to India and neighbouring countries</u>. Calcutta: Government of India Central Publication Branch

Akhtar, A. S (2007) "Balochistan versus Pakistan". <u>Economic and Political Weekly</u>, Vol. 42, No. 45/46 (Nov. 10 - 23, 2007), pp. 73-79

Amnesty International (2007) <u>Iran: Human Rights Abuses Against the Baluchi Minority</u>. London: Amnesty International Secretariat

Amnesty International (2016) Iran 2015-2016. <u>https://www. amnesty.org/en/countries/middle-east-and-north.../iran/report-iran/</u> accessed on 14th July 2016

Amnesty International (2012) <u>We are ordered to crush you: expanding repression of dissent in Iran</u>. London: Amnesty International Limited

Arrian, L.F. X (1958). <u>The Campaigns of Alexander</u>. Translated by Aubrey de Sélincourt. London: Penguin Classics

Atarodi, A (2011) <u>Insurgency in Balochistan and why it is of strategic importance</u>. Stockholm: Swedish Defence Research Agency

Awan, A.B (1985) <u>Baluchistan: historical and political processes</u>. Lahore: The Century Publishers

Axenov, S (2006) <u>The Balochi language of Turkmenistan: A corpus-based grammatical desposition</u>. Stockholm: Uppsala University

Axmann, M (2009) <u>Back to the Future, the Khanate of Kalat and the Genesis of Baloch Nationalism 1915-1955</u>. Oxford: Oxford University Press.

Azad, A (1988) <u>India wins freedom</u>. Michigan: University of Michigan Press

Baladhuri, Ahmad ibn Jabir (1924) <u>The Origins of the Islamic State</u> (Kitab Futuh Al-buldan) Translated by Francis Clark Murgotten. New York: Francis Clark Mugotten

Baloch, I (1987) The Problem of Greater Baluchistan: a study of Baluch nationalism. Stuttgart: Steiner Verlag Wiesbaden GmbH

Baloch, M.A.Y.K (1975) Inside Balochistan. Karachi: Royal Book Company

Baloch, M.S.K (1958) The History of Baloch Race and Balochistan. Karachi: Royal Book Company

Baxter, C (1998) Bangladesh: From A Nation To A State. New York: Perseus

Beck, L (1990) 'Tribes and the State in Nineteenth and Twentieth Century Iran'. In Philip S. Khoury and Joseph Kostiner edited, Tribes and State Formation in the Middle East. Oxford: University of California Press

Bizenjo, G.B (2009) In Search of Solutions: The Autobiography Of Mir Ghaus Buksh Bizenjo. Edited by B.M. Kutty. Karachi: Pakistan Labour Trust and University of Karachi's (KU) Pakistan Study Centre

Bosworth, C.E (1963) The Ghaznavids: their empire in Afghanistan and Eastern Iran. Edinburgh: U.P

Bosworth, C.E (1968) Sistan under the Arabs: from the Islamic conquest to the rise of Saffarids. Rome: ISMEO

Bosworth, C.E (1977) 'The Kufichis or Qufs in Persian History'. In Bosworth, C edited, The medieval history of Iran, Afghanistan and Central Asia. London: Variorum, Pp.9-17

Brilmayer, L (1989) "Consent, Contract, and Territory," Minnesota Law Review 74, no. 1 (1989): 1-35

British Broadcasting Corporation (2016). <u>Pakistan must answer about the excesses</u> http://www.bbc.com/urdu/regional Accessed on 15 August 2016

Buchanan, A (2003) <u>Justice, Legitimacy, and Self-Determination: Moral Foundations of International Law</u>. Oxford: Oxford University Press.

Cabral, A (1972) "Identity and Dignity in the National Liberation Struggle". <u>Africa Today</u>, Vol. 19, No. 4, (Autumn, 1972), pp. 39-47

Cardi, B. De (1966) "<u>Excavation at Bampur: A third Milleneum Settlement in Persian Balochistan</u>", Volume 51: Part 3, Anthropological papers of the American Museum of Natural History, New York

Cassese, A (1995) <u>Self-determination of people-a legal appraisal</u>. New York: CUP

Castellino, J (2014) 'International Law and Self-determination', in Christian Walter, A. V Ungern- Sternberg, and K. Abushov edited, <u>Self- Determination and Seccession in International Law</u>. Oxford: Osford University Press

Chaliand, G (1980) 'Introduction', in <u>People Without a country: the Kurds and Kurdistan</u>. Edited by Gerard Chaliand. London: Zed Press

Cohen, S. P (1984) <u>The Pakistan Army</u>. Berkeley: University of California Press.

Cohen, S. P (2004) The <u>Idea of Pakistan</u>. Washington: Brookings Institution Press

Curzon, G (1966) <u>Persia and the Persian Question</u>. London: Frank-Cass & Co

Dames, M.L (1904) <u>The Baluch Race: a historical and ethnological sketch</u>. London: Royal Asiatic Society

Dashti, N (2010) <u>The Cultural Context of Health</u>. Quetta: Balochi Academy

Dashti, N (2012) The Baloch and Balochistan: a historical account from the beginning to the fall of Baloch state. Bloomington: Trafford Publishing

Dawn (2009) April 14, 2009 accessed on 23 July, 2016 from <u>http://www.dawn.com/news/976691/karachi-bnp-demands-balochistan-s-right-to-self-determination</u>

Dehwar, M.S (1994). <u>Contemporary History of Balochistan</u>. Quetta: Third World Publications

Dueck, C and Takeyh, R (2007) "Iran's Nuclear Challenge". <u>Political Science Quarterly</u>, Vol. 122, No. 2, pp. 189-205

Dickson, W.E.R (1924) <u>East Persia: a backwater of the Great War</u>. London: Edward Arnold & Co.

Dietrich, A (1997) <u>Key Resolutions of the UNGA 1956-1996</u>.New York: CUP

Dixit, N. J (2002) India – Pakistan, in War & Peace. London: Routledge

Dreyfuss, R with Lemarc, T (1981) <u>Hostage to Khomeini</u>. New York: New Benjamin Franklin House Publishing Company

Dwivedi, M (2009) <u>South Asian Security</u>. Delhi: Gyan Publishing House. pp. 103–4.

Dyre, R (1921) <u>Raiders of Sarhad</u>. London: Witherly

European Union (2009) Pakistan-European Community, Country Strategy Paper. Retrieved on 11 June 2016 from http://www.eeas. europa.eu/pakistan/csp/07_13_en.pdf

European Union Institute for Security Studies (2009) European Union Aid to Pakistan: Steadily on the Rise, ISS Analysis. Retrieved on 11 June 2016 from http://www.iss.europa.eu/uploads/ media/EU_aid_to_Pakistan.pdf

Fairservis, W.A (1961) "Balochistan Finds: Ruins of a 4000 years old culture still exists in West Pakistan". Natural History 70 (6) 23-28

Farzanfar, R (1992) Ethnic Groups and the State. Azaris, Kurds and Baluch of Iran. Ph.D Thesis. Massachusetts Institute of Technology

Firdausi, A (1915) The Shahnama. Translation by Warner and Warner. London: Kegan Paul, PP. 241-243

Freeman, M (1999). "The Right to Self-Determination in International Politics: Six Theories in Search of a Policy". Review of International Studies, Vol. 25, No. 3 (Jul., 1999), pp. 355-370

Frost, M (1996) Ethics in International Relations: A Constitutive Theory. Cambridge: Cambridge University Press

Frye, R (1963) The Heritage of Persia. London: Weidenfeld and Nicolson

Gankovsky, Y.V (1971) The Peoples of Pakistan. Moscow: Nauka

Gershevitch, I (1962) A locust's leg, studies in honour of S. H. Tagezadeh. London: Percy Lund, Humphries & Co

Gershevitch, I (1962) Philologia Iranica. Berlin: L. Reichert

Ghirshman, R (1954) <u>Iran from the Earliest Times to the Islamic Conquest</u>. Harmondsworth

Gold, M (1976) <u>Tarikh e Sistan</u>. (Translation). Roma: Instituto Italiano Per Il Medio Ed Estremo Oriente

Goldsmid, F (1873) <u>Central Asia and its Question</u>. London: Edward Standford

Grare, F (2013) <u>Balochistan: the State Versus the nation</u>. Washington, D.C: Carnegie Endowment for International Peace Publications Department.

Gulati, M.F (2013) "Balochistan: the regional tinderbox". <u>Eurasia Review: News and Analysis</u>, November 13, 2013

Hurts, .H (1996) <u>Autonomy, Sovereignty and Self-determination</u>. Pennsylvania: University of Pennsylvania Press Philadelphia.

Haqqani, H (2005) <u>Pakistan: Between Mosque and Military</u>. Washington, D.C.: Carnegie Endowment for International Peace.

Harrison, S. S (1981) <u>In Afghanistan's Shadow: Baloch Nationalism and Soviet Temptations</u>. New York: Carnegie Endowment for International Peace

Helfgott, L. M (1980) 'The Structural Foundations of the National Minority Problem in Revolutionary Iran. <u>Iranian Studies</u>, Vol. 13, No. ¼.

Heraclides, A (1997) "Ethnicity, Secessionist Conflict and the International Society: Towards Normative Paradigm Shift". <u>Nations and Nationalism</u>, 3 (1997), pp. 493-520.)

Herodotus (1996) <u>Histories</u>. (Translated with notes by George Rawlinson). Hertfordshire: Wordsworth Classic of the World Literature.

Herzfeld, E (1968) The Persian Empire. Studies in Geography and Ethnography of the Ancient Near East. Wiesbaden: Franz Steiner Verlag

Hoshang, N (2015) "Sunni Militants in Iran: Activities, Ideological Sources and Political Strategies". International Research Journal of Social Sciences Vol. 4(3), 79-87

Hosseinbor, M.H (2000) Iran and its nationalities: The Case of Baloch Nationalism. Karachi: The Royal Book Co.

Human Rights Council (2011) 'Report of the UN secretary General on the situation of Iran at the Human Rights Council in Geneva', Document: A/HRC/16/75. March 28, 2011

Human Rights Watch (2015) World Report 2015. https://www.hrw.org/world-report/2015/country-chapters/iran

Istakhri, Ibrahim bin Muhammad (1800) The oriental Geography of Ebn Haukal (translation by Sir William Ouseley). London: T. Cadell and W. Davies

Istakhri, Ibrahim bin Muhammad (1961) Masalik al-mamalik (Persian). Tehran: Bungah-i Tarjumah va Nashr-i Kitab

Jahanbani, Amanullah (1929) Amaliath Qushun Dar Balochistan in Persian. Second edition. Tehran: Chapkhana e Majlis

Jahani, C (1996) 'Poetry and Politics: Nationalism and Language Standardization in Balochi'. In Titus, Paul edited, Marginality and Modernity: Ethnicity and Change in Post-colonial Balochistan. Karachi: Oxford University Press

Jahani, C (2003) 'The Case System in Iranian Balochi in a Contact Linguistic Perspective'. In Carina Jahani and Agnes Korn edited, The Baloch and their Neighbors: Ethics and Linguistic Contact in

Balochistan in Historical and Modern Times. Stockholm: Reichert Verlag Wiesbaden

Jalal, Ayesha (1994) 'The State and Political Privilege in Pakistan' in Ali Banuazizi and Myron Weiner edited, The Politics of Social Transformation in Afghanistan, Iran and Pakistan. New York: Syracuse University Press

Janmahmad (1982) The Baloch Cultural Heritage. Karachi: Royal Book Company

Janmahmad (1989) Essays on Baloch National Struggle in Pakistan: Emergence, dimensions, repercussions. Quetta: Gosha e Adab

Keddie, R. N (1972) Sayyid Jamal ad-Din "al-Afghani": A Political Biography. Berkeley: University of California Press

Kendal (1980) 'Kurdistan in Turkey' in People Without a country: the Kurds and Kurdistan. London: Zed Press

Khimjee, H (2013) Pakistan: A legacy of the Indian Khilafat Movement. Bloomington: LLC

Kia, M (1996) "Pan-Islamism in Late Nineteenth-Century Iran." Middle Eastern Studies, Vol. 32, No. 1, (1996): 30-52.

Kia, M (1998) "Persian nationalism and the campaign for language purification". Middle Eastern Studies, 34:2, 9-36

Kiddie, N (1968) An Islamic Response to Imperialism. Berkeley: University of California Press

Klabbers, J (2006) "The Right to Be Taken Seriously: Self-Determination in International Law". Human Rights Quarterly, Vol. 28, No. 1 (Feb., 2006), pp. 186-206)

Korn, A (2003) 'Balochi and the Concept of North-Western Iranian'. In Carina Jahani and Agnes Korn edited, The Baloch and their Neighbours. Ethnic and Linguistic Contact in Balochistan in Historical and Modern Times. Wiesbaden, pp. 49-60

Kuzmina E. E (2007) Origin of the Indo-Iranians. Brill: Leiden and Boston

Landau, J. M (1990) The Politics of Pan-Islamism: Ideology and Organization. Oxford: Clarendon Press

Lange, C.R (2011) The Seljuqs: politics, society and culture. Edinburgh: Edinburgh University Press.

Lapidus, I.M (1988) A history of Islamic Societies. New York: Cambridge University Press, 1988.

Lenczowski, G (1949) Russia and the West in Iran, 1918-1948: a study in big-power rivalry. New York: Cornell University Press

Lifschultz, L (1983) "Independent Baluchistan? Ataullah Mengal's 'Declaration of Independence'". Economic and Political Weekly, Vol. 18. No. 19/20 (May, 1983), pp 735-752

Lockhart, L (1938) Nader Shah Afshar. London: Luzac & Co.

MacKenzie, D.N (1961) The Origins of Kurdish. Transactions of the Philological Society, 1961, pp. 68-86.

MacKenzie, D.N (1998) 'Eran, Eransahr', in Encyclopaedia Iranica. Online Edition, Originally Published on December 15, 1998. Available at http://www.iranicaonline.org/articles/eran-eransah

Malik, M. A (2001) The Making of the Pakistan Resolution. Delhi: Oxford University Press

Mao Tse-tung (1949) <u>On People's Democracy</u>. Moscow: Novesty Press

Maqaddesi, A (1906) <u>Ahsan at-taqasim</u>. Translated by M.J.de George. Leiden: Damas

Mari, K. B (1974) <u>Search Lights on Baloches and Balochistan</u>. Karachi: Royal Book Company

Matthew, W. W (1999) "The Earliest Persians in Southwestern Iran: the Textual Evidence". <u>Iranian Studies,</u> 32, 1999, pp. 99-107.

Meskawiah, Abu 'Ali Ahmad b. Moḥammad (1915) <u>Ebn Meskawayh's Tajareb al-omam</u>, vol. II, Cairo

Miller, P (2011) "The Case for Nation-building: Why and How to fix failed states." <u>Prism</u>, Volume 3 No. 1 December 2011 p. 63-74.

Minorsky, V (1937) <u>Ḥudud al-Alam, "The Regions of the World": A Persian Geography 372 AH–982 AD</u>. London: Gibb Memorial Series, N.S. XI

Minorsky, V (1958) <u>A History of Sharvan and Darband in the 10<u>th</u>-11<u>th</u> Centuries'</u>. Cambridge: Cambridge University Press

Mojtahed-Zadeh, P (1995) <u>The Amirs of Borderlands and Eastern Iranian Borders</u>. London: Urosevic Foundation

Mojtahed-Zadeh, P (2004) <u>Small Players of Great Game: settlement of Iran's eastern borderlands and the creation of Afghanistan</u>. London: RoutledgeCurzon

Moon, P (1964) <u>Divide and Quit</u>. London: Chatto & Windus

Morgan, D (1988) <u>Medieval Persia: 1040-1797</u>. London and New York: Longman

Morris, C (1888) The Aryan Race: its origin and its achievements. Chicago: S.C. Griggs and Company

Muir, W (1924) The Caliphate: its rise, decline, and fall, from original sources. Edinburgh: J. Grant

Naseer, M.G.K (1979) Tarikh e Balochistan (Urdu). Quetta: Kalat Publishers

Nizam ul Mulk (1960) Siyasat Nama: The Book of Government or rules for Kings. Translated by H. Darke. London

.Posen, B.R (1993) "The security dilemma and ethnic conflict" Survival, 35 (1993), pp.27-313

Ram, H (1985) Tarikh e Balochistan.(in Urdu): first published in 1904. Lahore: Sangemeel Publications

Rashid, A (2014) Balochistan: the untold story of Pakistan's other war. BBC News, 22 February 2014. Retrieved 22 June 2015.

Rashid. A (2000) Taliban, Islam, Oil and the New Great Game in Central Asia. London: I. B. Tauris

Rashiduzzaman, M. (1970). "The National Awami Party; Leftist Politics in Crisis". Pacific Affairs, (Colombo), Vol.43, No.3 (1970), pp.394-409

Rauschning, Weisbrocl and Lailach (1997) Key Resolutions of the UN Assembly 1946-1996. New York: CUP

Rotberg, I. R (2003) When States Fail: Causes and Consequences. New York: Princeton University Press

Saldanha, J (1905) Precis of Mekran Affairs. Calcutta: Government Printing Press.

Salzman, P.C (1971) "Continuity and Change in Baluchi Tribal Leadership". International Journal of Middle East Study, 4:428-439

Sarila, N.S (2006) The Shadow of the Great Game: untold story of India's Partition. London: Constable

Schmitt, R (1991) The Bisitun Inscriptions of Darius the Great. Old Persian Text, Corp. Inscr. Iran., Part I, Vol. I, Texts 1. London: The British Museum

Schmitt, R (2000) The Old Persian Inscriptions of Naqsh-I Rustam and Persepolis, Corp. Inscr. Iran. Part I, Vol. I, Texts III. London: The British Museum

Scholz, F (2002) Nomadism and Colonialism: A Hundred Years of Baluchistan (1872-1972) London: Oxford University Press

Shaikh, F (2009) Making Sense of Pakistan. London: Hurst & Company

Shustheri, M. A (1925) Iran Nama ya Kaarnamagan e Iranian dar asr e Ashkanian (Farsi). Tehran: Chapkhan e Farus

Spooner, B (1983) 'Who are the Baloch'. In Bosworth, E and Hillenbrand, C edited, Qajar Iran: Political, Social and Cultural Change 1800-1925. Edinburgh: Edinburgh University Press

Spooner, B. (1988) 'Baluchistan: Geography, History, and Ethnography. In Ehsan Yarshater edited, Encyclopedia Iranica, Volume 3, London: Routledge and Kegan Paul. pp.93-110

Strabo (2009) The Geography of Strabo with an English translation by Horace Leonard Jones. BiblioLife LLc

Stromseth, J.E (1992) 'Self-Determination, Secession and Humanitarian Intervention by the United Nations'. Proceedings of the Annual Meeting. American Society of International Law, Vol. 86 (APRIL 1-4, 1992), pp. 370-374

Sykes, P.M (1902) A history of Afghanistan. London: Macmillan & Co

Tabari, Abu- Jaffer Muhammad (2007) The History of al-Tabari. Edited by Ehsan Yar-Shater. New York: University of New York press

Taber, R (1965) War of the Flea: The Classic Study of Guerrilla Warfare. New York: Brassey

Tapper, R (1983) The Conflict of Tribe and State in Iran and Afghanistan. London: St. Martin's Press

Tarabella, M (2015) "EU cannot ignore dire human rights situation in Balochistan". The Parliament Magazine.

Tedesco, P (1921) "Dialektologie der westiranischen Turfantexte". Monde Oriental 15, 1921, pp. 184-258.

Thomas de Marga (1893) The Book of Governors. Translated by E. A. W. Budge. London: Gilbert and Rivington

Thornton, T (1985) "Sir Robert Saneman and the Indian Frontier Policy". Asiatic Quarterly Review. July-October, 1985

UNHCR (2010) REDRESSING A HISTORY OF NEGLECT: Discrimination of Ethnic Groups and Indigenous People of Pakistan. United Nation High Commission for Human Rights. Accessed from the website of the UNHCR

United Nations Organization (1948) Text of the Convention on the Prevention and Punishment of the Crime of Genocide, accessed from the website of the UNHCR. https://treaties.un.org/doc/ Publication/ 1021-English.pdf

United Nations Organization (1963) <u>United Nations Declaration on the Elimination of All Forms of Racial Discrimination. Resolution adopted by the General Assembly 1904</u> (XVIII). Accessed from, <u>http://www.un-documents.net/</u>

UNO (1960) <u>Official Records of the General Assembly</u>. Available at www.un.org/en/ga

UNO (1975) <u>Official Records of the General Assembly, Thirtieth Session, Annexes, agenda item 77, document A110309</u>

UNO (1976) <u>Yearbook of the International Law Commission, 1976</u>, vol. 11, part one: United Nations publication

UNPO (2013) <u>http://unpo.org/article/</u>

US Department of State (2014) <u>Iran 2014 Human Rights Report-US Department of State</u>. Accessed from http://www.state.gov/documents/organization/236810.pdf

Von Voigtlander, E. N (1978) <u>The Bisitun Inscription of Darius the Great Babylonian Version</u>, CII, Part I, Vol. II, Texts 1. London: The British Museum

Watson, R.G (1866) <u>A history of Persia</u>. London: Smith, Elder & Co

Wellman, C. H (2005) <u>A theory of secession: the case for political self-determination</u>. London: Cambridge University Press

Windfuhr, G (1975) "Isoglosses: A Sketch on Persians and Parthians, Kurds and Medes". <u>Monumentum</u> H.S. Nyberg II (Acta Iranica-5), Leiden: 457-471

Wynn, A (2003) <u>Persia in the Great Game: Sir Percy Sykes; explorer, consul, soldier, spy</u>. London: John Murray

Zamani, Fakhteh Luna (2014) 'Iran: The Importance of Receiving Education in One's Mother Tongue', available at: http://bit.ly/mtnged

Zonis, M (1971) The Political Elite of Iran. Princeton: Princeton University Press

INDEX

333